Richard P. Thiel

The Timber Wolf in Wisconsin

The Death and Life of a Majestic Predator

With a Foreword by
L. David Mech

The University of Wisconsin Press

The University of Wisconsin Press
114 North Murray Street
Madison, Wisconsin 53715

3 Henrietta Street
London WC2E 8LU, England

Library of Congress Cataloging-in-Publication Data
Thiel, Richard P.
    The timber wolf in Wisconsin : the death and life of a majestic
predator / Richard P. Thiel.
    278 p.   cm.
    Includes bibliographical references and index.
    ISBN 0-299-13940-9   ISBN 0-299-13944-1
    1. Wolves—Wisconsin—History. 2. Wolves—Michigan—
Upper Peninsula—History. 3. Wolves—Control—Wisconsin—
History.   4. Wolves—Control—Michigan—Upper Peninsula—
History. I. Title.
QL737.C22T475   1993
333.95'4—dc20   93-3577

To my daughters,
Allison and Cassandra,

and to their generation and succeeding generations of
Wisconsinites in the hope that our society may secure
a time when timber wolves are tolerated, and once
again roam wild and free.

Contents

Illustrations

Figures and Maps

Figures

Maps

Tables

Foreword

The return of the wolf to Wisconsin is a great success story. Gone from the state since 1959, this charismatic animal made its way back as a direct result of the Endangered Species Act of 1973. That act protected the wolf in adjoining Minnesota starting in August 1974, and within a few years dispersing animals from Minnesota began the long and difficult process of recolonizing northern Wisconsin.

Nobody knows this story better than Dick Thiel, originally a solitary volunteer with a mission to monitor wolf recovery in the state. Thiel took it upon himself to try to locate every Wisconsin wolf when this recovery began. For many years, Thiel's lonely howl was probably the only wolf call heard in most areas of Wisconsin. But his persistence paid off, and he began to get replies—one here and another there. Despite these results, state authorities may not have been convinced. Nevertheless, the wolves came, and Thiel was the first to find them.

Now, almost on the verge of formally defined "wolf recovery," Wisconsin's wolves have gone so far as to colonize northern Michigan. The population in the two states combined, even when Michigan's Isle Royale in northern Lake Superior is excluded, has reached 65 as of this writing (1993). When the population in the two states reaches 100 for five consecutive years, the wolf population in the Lake Superior area (Minnesota, Wisconsin, Michigan) will have formally recovered. The animal will then be an official success story of the Endangered Species Act, and will be declassified, or removed from the list. Thiel's vision of the early 1900s will finally have been realized.

Before that happens, it will be wise for everyone interested in the Lake Superior wolves to decide the best way to manage the population. Although it would be wonderful if habitat and land-use patterns were still appropriate to allow wolves to live anywhere they please, that is clearly not the case now. There are only certain places in Wisconsin, Michigan, and Minnesota that are still suitable for wolves. Suitable means supporting enough large prey (deer, moose, beaver, etc.), and also being wild enough, away from people and their pets and livestock. Otherwise, errant wolves caught in a time warp not of their making will end up intruding on human interests and will be persecuted for it.

Wolves that do start colonizing agricultural areas will have to be managed, which translates to killing them where they do not belong. This will help prevent their increasing in those areas and spreading the problem. Wolf control can be carried out by government agencies or through allowing hunters to hold wolf numbers down just like is done for deer, bear, and other wildlife. Because the wolf is on the endangered species list and has such a strong and passionate public constituency, it may be difficult for the public to accept wolf control. This means that strong efforts at public education are necessary.

Thiel has also recognized the need for public education and has long been a leader in educating the Wisconsin public about wolves. His early efforts went into helping found the Timber Wolf Alliance. Since then he also started the Timber Wolf Information Network (TWIN) to help educate Wisconsin school children.

Thiel's initial work was as a volunteer, and he later was hired under contract by the Wisconsin Department of Natural Resources to study and monitor the increasing Wisconsin wolf population. There he applied the latest technology of aerial radio tracking. Although he no longer is in charge of that program, Thiel continues his efforts on behalf of the Wisconsin wolf through TWIN.

In addition, Thiel has now summarized for us the historical literature about wolves in Wisconsin in this present book. Like pioneers in other states, Wisconsin settlers thought of the wolf as evil incarnate. However, it is a tribute to Wisconsin's remaining wilderness that Wisconsin's wolves survived, unlike in many other areas, into the late 1950s. Details of their eventual demise pervade Thiel's book and make clear the historical attitude toward the wolf.

Thiel has done us all a service by assembling and synthesizing the available historical information about wolves and about the human interactions with them in Wisconsin. At the same time, we must read these old accounts with a certain amount of skepticism. No doubt they are, in general, accurate, but the standards of scholarly writing were not necessarily adhered to by pioneers. Thus, we can expect a certain amount of exaggeration, misinterpretation, or even fabrication in at least a few of the accounts. Nevertheless, overall the historical writings Thiel has pulled together here express the attitudes, ideas, and general perceptions of the day about the wolf. They demonstrate that originally the wolf lived throughout Wisconsin, as it did throughout the rest of North America, and they document the wolf's demise.

Fortunately the story ends happily. Just as the public attitudes apparent in these historical writings led to the wolf's demise, so too the attitudes of new generations of the public have restored the wolf to Wisconsin. Dick

Thiel was part of the vanguard and remains totally committed to the wolf's recovery in Wisconsin. This synthesis of historical accounts is the latest in a number of significant contributions Thiel has made. It deserves close reading by anyone interested in the history of wolves in Wisconsin.

U.S. Fish and Wildlife Service   L. DAVID MECH
March 30, 1993

Preface

In the spring of 1945 the *Lake Mills Leader* ran an editorial entitled "Passing of the Wolf": "One of these years the last doleful song of the native wolf will be carried through the night air of Wisconsin and its passing will sever another cord that ties back to this state's former forest greatness. . . . There are difficulties in the way of protecting the timber wolf, but without him Wisconsin will be just that much less of the original commonwealth."[1] Sadly, within 15 years that prophesy was fulfilled.

My childhood, spent in suburban Milwaukee, was far removed from the final retreat of Wisconsin's wolves. I had heard the usual—Little Red Riding Hood, the Three Little Pigs, Peter and the Wolf, and of course my favorite, The Boy Who Cried Wolf (I wonder why I heard that story so often). Like most of us I believed wolves ate people.

Having been born in the very decade when our native wolves met their demise (1950s), I became a member of the first generation of Wisconsinites unable to "experience" wolves. As I grew older and more focused in my inquisitiveness, I learned that the state of Wisconsin was responsible for managing the state's wildlife—which, from my naive way of thinking, included wolves. In 1966, at 13 years of age, I sent a letter to the Wisconsin Conservation Department (the ancestral version of the Wisconsin Department of Natural Resources), inquiring about the status of rare wildlife. I found their response on timber wolves especially disturbing. Our wildlife officials weren't sure whether any remained in the state.

Further inquiries led to more questions about the wolf's fate in Wisconsin, but little was known about Wisconsin's wolf population in its twilight years. Although no one really knew how the wolves had become extirpated, many proffered that their ruin was related to the notion that this creature needed "wilderness."

Unsatisfied, I continued probing peoples' minds to learn what had happened. This book's beginnings extend back to that time and a boy's meddlesome curiousity. It grew from a sense that the wolf was, somehow, not deserving of the fate that had been meted out to it by humans. Why did generations of Wisconsinites condone this creature's annihilation? And, just how was its obliteration accomplished? I wanted to know, but explanations were lacking.

Between 1968 and 1982 I carried on correspondence with over 60 individuals who had first-hand experience with and knowledge about Wisconsin wolves. Some were early-day biologists who worked for the state. Some were U.S. Forest Service employees. Others were the old-timers who had bountied wolves. Many of these individuals became friends.

I also visited the deep, dark passages of the State Historical Society of Wisconsin's archives, searching through hundreds of unmarked file boxes containing old Wisconsin Conservation Department records. Microfilm files of old newspapers were also consulted.

In 1981 the laborious process of writing began. I even promised Debbie, pregnant at the time, that I would complete the project before she delivered. Our daughter Allison is already 11 years old and her sister, Cassie, is 8.

This book provides a critical historical account of the wolf and what we humans did to cause its extinction in Wisconsin. It was written with the hope that future generations of Wisconsinites may learn of the shortcomings of our ancestors while they struggled to bring order to the natural world.

The wolves living in Wisconsin and Upper Michigan were actually one biological population separated only by an imaginary political boundary (the same cannot be said of Minnesota's wolves, because they existed northeast of Duluth, above Lake Superior). In putting the pieces together I felt it was necessary to include some information on the wolves that existed in Upper Michigan, especially regarding the bounties that fueled the process of annihilation, and the regions in the two states where the last family groups of wolves were found.

This book presents historical material dealing with a complex resource management issue from the perspective of a person trained in the science of wildlife biology. I have attempted to keep science to a minimum, relegating most of that data to a series of appendices at the back of the book. Because it is a historical treatise, the usual exhaustive documentation is provided in the reference section, also at the back of the book.

For novices in wolf biology, chapter 1 provides an overview of the species' life history. It is not intended to be comprehensive. Readers desiring further information are encouraged to consult the many good works found in the reference section.

Chapters 2 and 3 deal with the history of humans and wolves in Wisconsin and Upper Michigan. These chapters review the changes that occurred while settlement progressed and how humans and wolves interacted with each other. Chapter 4 is devoted to anecdotal accounts of wolves from the people who probably knew them better than others—the trappers who brought about their downfall.

Chapters 5 and 6 discuss the politics that have revolved around wolves and our curious shaping of official dealings with the species. These chapters discuss the bounty programs that stoked the annihilation campaigns, and the unsophisticated condition of state wildlife agencies during their struggles to deal with the gulf between public and political perceptions and the evolving ecological philosophy that it was unwise to eliminate predators.

Chapters 7 and 8 reveal aspects of Wisconsin's "secret wolf study," and describe the wolf population's decline into extinction in the forested region south of Lake Superior. Chapter 9 enlightens the reader with an update of recent developments of the wolf's modest return to northern Wisconsin and the Upper Peninsula of Michigan, which began in the 1970s.

The historical research for this book provided answers about what happened to our state's wolves and how and why it happened. In the several decades it took to prepare the book I have become a firm believer in the old adage that history may, indeed, be destined to repeat itself. Dates, locations, and names are not what matters in history; it is the actions, the values, and the attending rationale of the people that are important. These manifestations of humanity are destined to be repeated *unless and until* a concerned society takes the time to analyze, interpret, and alter its attitudes and practices.

The timber wolf is a part of Wisconsin's past, its present, and potentially its future. I, for one, cannot imagine a Wisconsin without its magnificent wild wolves.

Acknowledgments

Many people have helped make this book possible. Some have provided encouragement, while others have contributed information, critiques, and most of all, their friendship. As the saying goes, it is impossible to mention all by name, but each has my appreciation.

To Sharon Wisnaski of Tomah, who double-handedly typed the entire first draft, I owe a debt of gratitude. The same goes for Michael Schoop, who entered the first chapters of the second draft into those modern contrivances—word-processing computers. It sure was exciting to see those chapters take form, one by one.

Ruth Hine, Dan Thompson, Bernie Bradle (deceased), and Walter Scott (deceased) reviewed earlier drafts for historical accuracy and redundancies. Similarly, my friends Bernie Bradle and Dan Thompson shared with me many of their personal files and experiences with wolves while working over 40 years ago on a little-known wolf project. Professor George Becker (University of Wisconsin–Stevens Point emeritus) shared his files with me on correspondences he had with government officials in the 1940s. The premier Wisconsin wildlife historian, Walter Scott, also allowed me to use materials from his extensive personal files.

Nancy Kaufer, former archivist at the State Historical Society of Wisconsin, arranged my visitations to the "vaults" containing all the Wisconsin Conservation Department's records, as yet unprocessed, in search of wolf-related material.

Thanks go to my brother Scott Thiel for assistance in retrieving old newspaper articles, sharing with me innumerable hours of straining blurry eyes and holding back urges to upchuck while cruising through the Historical Society's microfilm newspaper files. My other brother, Bill, provided insightful material from the legislative archives regarding the old Wisconsin bounty laws. Thanks, Boodie! My father, Ray, proofread the entire draft, searching for typographical and other less mentionable errors.

I must thank Bill Creed, retired Wisconsin Department of Natural Resources research biologist, who allowed me to borrow a box of "old field notes" stashed away in some dismal corner closet in the attic of the old Rhinelander ranger station. They proved to contain the majority of notes recovered from Bill Feeney's super secret timber wolf study. My search for that one dusty box extended over a seven-year period, and I could hardly believe it when I discovered the pot of gold contained within. I also thank the staff at the University of Wisconsin's Department of Wildlife Ecology at Madison for allowing me access to the Aldo Leopold archival materials.

To Shirley Swendson (deceased) and Walter King, two high school teachers who inspired me to pursue my interest in wolves in Wisconsin, thanks. If Shirley could have seen this book, she would have had to concede that I would never need to write another paragraph in my life.

My old college buddy Bob Welch shared with me the same ideology about the contribution that wildlife history should (but rarely does) play in forming present-day wildlife policy. He accompanied me on several whirlwind interview tours, inspired by an appreciation of history and a love of wildlife, the land, and our home state of Wisconsin.

Last, and certainly best of all, I owe one heck of a lot to Deborah and our daughters, Allison and Cassandra. Deb tolerated countless nights of putting the kids to bed while I hammered away at "the book," persevered through sharply worded reprisals of her ever-wise critiques of the book, assisted in archival and library searches, and joins me in thanking our lucky stars that the book is finally finished.

The Timber Wolf in Wisconsin

1

The Wolf: A Biological Review

Wolf Taxonomy and Distribution

In 1944 Stanley P. Young and Edward A. Goldman, pre-eminent biologists with the U.S. Bureau of Sport Fisheries and Wildlife, published a book on the wolves of North America. The gray wolf (*Canis lupus*),* they said, had the greatest distribution of any land mammal in recent geologic history, "and this wolf may, therefore, be regarded as the most highly developed living representative of an extraordinarily successful mammalian family," the Canidae, or dog family.[1]

Indeed, the range of the wolf has been impressive. They have roamed most of the Eurasian continent from Saudi Arabia and central India to the Arctic Ocean, and from the Japanese isles to the Rock of Gibraltar. They have also been found on Greenland and most of North America from central Mexico to the Arctic Ocean.

The wolves' success has been due in part to their ability to adapt to any landscape and climate outside the tropics. Biologists consider wolves to be *habitat generalists*, capable of surviving anywhere they can find food and water. Their widespread distribution, ranging from frozen tundra to temperate forest regions, reflects an amazing adaptability. They have been a dominant feature of predator-prey systems, at least in North America, for tens of thousands of years—that is, until recently.

Their distribution has changed dramatically over the past 200 years. Today the wolf is found in significant numbers in most Canadian provinces, Alaska, and from eastern Europe to Siberia. Wolf population sizes in the Middle East, the Indian subcontinent, China, and Mongolia are unknown but suspected to be declining. In western Europe isolated populations survive in the mountains of Italy, Greece, Spain, Portugal, and Finland, with just a few individuals reported from Norway and Sweden.[2] In North America wolves probably became extinct in the isolated Mexican plateau country around 1980. South of Canada the only significant population exists in north-

---

*In the upper Great Lakes region of Ontario, Michigan, Minnesota, and Wisconsin, people call it the timber wolf.

ern Minnesota, where an estimated 1,600 wolves remain. Northern Michigan, Montana, Idaho, Washington, and Wisconsin together support an additional 100 or so individuals.

Eradication programs were so effective in many areas of the eastern and southern United States that wolf populations were annihilated before zoologists could describe their physical features and compile essential elements of their life history. By the time science caught up with the wolf in the early 1940s, the species was found only sparingly in the upper Great Lakes forests and some of the more remote mountain ranges in the northern Rockies and the Cascades.[3] By 1960, the gray wolf had been eliminated from all but Minnesota and neighboring Isle Royale National Park.

Around the turn of the century federal predator control officers like Vernon Bailey, Stanley Young, and J. Stokley Ligon began crating and shipping the hides and skulls of wolves, bears, cats, and lions to the Natural History Museum collections in Washington, D.C., and other institutions. In some cases these specimens represented the last of their kind from areas the size of individual western states.[4]

Biologist Edward Goldman painstakingly sorted through the skins and skulls of hundreds of museum specimens, looking for subtle features among molars, skull shapes, and pelage patterns that might reflect regional differences among wolves. In 1944 he published an authoritative account describing 24 *distinct* subspecies of wolf in North America.

One subspecies he described was the eastern timber wolf, *Canis lupus lycaon*. On the basis of an examination of 77 specimens, Goldman concluded that *lycaon*-type wolves extended from the northeastern United States through Quebec and Ontario to Hudson Bay south through Minnesota, Wisconsin, Ohio, and southeast to Florida.[5] (See appendix A.)

The eastern timber wolf comes in one basic color, grayish brown with rufous undertones and a salt and pepper pattern on its mane. Black or white wolves have rarely been recorded.[6] Wolves whiten with age, which may explain an observation made along the Sugar River flats of Green County, Wisconsin, in 1844: "One day old John Armstrong shrieked to us. We ran up on a high bank and he showed us a very large white wolf. It was a monster in size, so much so that we thought it was an Indian pony."[7]

According to Goldman the eastern timber wolf is a small subspecies. Unlike their northern Canadian and Alaskan counterparts, this race seldom exceeds 100 pounds in weight. Goldman noted, though, that the Great Lakes specimens tend to be larger than elsewhere within the range of the subspecies.

Since the 1930s Michigan, Minnesota, and Wisconsin biologists have recorded weights of hundreds of timber wolves. Wolves in this region usually weigh between 50 and 100 pounds and average around 70 pounds.[8]

Variations in weight normally reflect age, sex, and seasonal differences in individuals. Adult males are usually heavier than females, and all wolves regardless of sex weigh more in winter than in summer.

Old newspaper accounts on bountied wolves in Wisconsin indicate that male wolves weighed around 80 pounds and females 65 pounds. Eight Wisconsin wolves averaged 76 inches in length from nose tip to tail tip and averaged 34 inches in height at the shoulder.

Diet and Effects on Prey

Key elements in understanding the dynamics of wild animal populations are determining what individuals need to survive (the *arrangement* of food, water, and cover) and to reproduce (replace those that die). Sufficient space is needed to compete effectively for food, water, and shelter requirements. Reproduction, in turn, is affected by sex ratios, age, and survival rates. Individual survival needs and reproductive performance determine the relative growth and vigor of wild animal populations. This type of information used to be difficult to obtain, but, since the advent of radio telemetry, retrieval and interpretation of this information have become fairly sophisticated.

The wolf's predatory nature won it disfavor and disdain amongst people of Eurasisan descent. Popular accounts of their food habits glamorize wolves as mouse eaters (e.g., Farley Mowat's *Never Cry Wolf*), destroyers of game,[9] or accomplished consumers of human flesh (Little Red Riding Hood fame).*

In reality the wolf's energy system is fueled mostly by large-hoofed animals.[11] Ungulates (animals like bison, elk, moose, muskoxen, caribou, deer, mountain sheep, antelope, and, unfortunately, sometimes domesticated livestock) constitute a major portion of the wolf's diet. In fact wolf distribution is determined by the presence or absence of these large, hoofed mammals.

Wild wolves' diets are determined in a variety of ways. In the past, biologists examined stomach contents of control-killed wolves to obtain information on food items. Wolf droppings and prey kill-sites have typically been used in more modern studies of wolves. And, most recently, radio telemetry studies where *both* the wolves and their prey are radio collared provide insights into the relationships between predator and prey.[12]

These techniques have revealed that wolves rely primarily on ungulates and beaver. Extensive studies have revealed wolves' tendancy to select

*Since the advent of scientific inquiry into North American wolves' diets in the early 1900s there is no evidence that people have been attacked, killed, and eaten by wolves.[10] However, it is fairly likely that in the distant past wolves probably did prey on humans at least occasionally.

vulnerable cohorts, such as the young, old, and infirm individuals within prey populations. In Isle Royale National Park (Michigan) and in portions of Minnesota, northern Ontario, Quebec, Alaska, and Sweden, moose are the chosen prey. In arctic and tundra regions caribou, muskoxen, and other large prey constitute a major part of the wolf's diet.[13]

In southern Ontario, northern Michigan, Wisconsin, and Minnesota the wolf's primary prey is white-tailed deer.[14] In the forested region surrounding Lake Superior, deer are sedentary; that is, they have discrete home ranges and move only locally. During the summer months does raise their fawns in secluded, individual ranges. Bucks roam in small bachelor bands. At this time of year deer are fairly widely distributed. Wolves usually hunt alone or in pairs, radiating out from the pup homesites in a shotgun pattern, which increases their chance of capturing deer on a regular basis.

During the fall rut, bucks breed the mature does. Shortly thereafter the does take their fawns to local "yards" where large numbers of deer congregate for protection against severe winter weather and wolf predation. The bucks follow the does, but are usually in poor condition because they seldom eat during the rutting period, which can last up to 30 days.

Wolves' hunting strategy changes abruptly in autumn. Throughout winter, wolves move from deer yard to deer yard, searching for deer. They hunt together as a pack. More bucks are taken than does, and fawns and older-aged deer compose the major portion taken by wolves.[15]

Most wolf packs situate their territories so that more than one deer yard exists within their range. But because competition is so stiff between wolf packs and the balance between wolf and deer populations so interdependent, deer yards tend to exist on wolf pack boundaries. Wolves' visits to an individual deer yard tend to be brief because they do not desire an encounter with neighboring packs which may share the yard. This, of course, offsets impacts on the deer herd and reduces the chance that any one deer in the yard will be killed by wolves.[16] It is by these mechanisms that wolves and their prey have managed to survive together through the millennia.

Much controversy exists over whether wolves adversely impact ungulate populations. This concerns big game hunters who fear that, in the presence of severe winter weather and other environmental factors, high wolf densities drive down populations of deer, moose, and caribou, making game less available.

In some cases wolves have influenced prey populations. However, wolves' greatest impacts were felt *after* the prey populations had declined. In these instances wolves suppressed recovery of deer and moose populations, because they exerted considerable predatory pressure on the young (fawns and calves), the very building blocks upon which population regrowth depends. The actual "crashes" in these deer and moose populations were caused by a combination of severe winter weather, excessive harvests by humans, and predatory pressure from bears and wolves.[17]

A recent, very thorough study of deer and wolf dynamics in an area with a declining deer herd was conducted in north-central Minnesota by biologist Todd Fuller. Both wolves and deer were radio-collared and the results were interesting. The greatest source of mortality to deer was caused by humans (legal harvest and poaching, combined) and severe winter weather, followed by wolves and dog predation.[18]

Wolf and prey populations exert influences on each other. The Isle Royale wolf-moose studies suggest that wolves may not affect their prey numbers as much as the moose affect the number of wolves. On that island ecosystem, scientists have been observing predator-prey rituals for over 30 years. Moose seem to be more influenced by vegetative changes and severe winter weather than by wolves, although the wolves do exert changes on age structures within the moose population that propel changes in its reproductive performance and future vulnerability to wolves.

Prey such as deer, moose, and beaver affects the distribution of wolves, because as food sources they supply needed energy. Individual survival of wolves is considerably enhanced in regions with a constant food supply. Individuals whose energy and shelter needs are met are able to reproduce. Reproduction offsets a major deficit among all animal populations—the inevitability that individuals die.

Reproduction

Another important aspect in comprehending wolf population dynamics is their reproductive performance. How often do they reproduce, at what age, how many young do they have, and what influences their reproductive ability? Early-day biologists in northern Michigan, Wisconsin, and Minnesota knew fairly well the breeding season, denning behaviors, and litter sizes of wolves. This had been common knowledge amongst bounty trappers and hunters for over a century.

In Wisconsin, Michigan, and Minnesota females come into heat from late January to mid-February. Biologists watched for signs of this condition by searching for evidence of blood in the scent-posts made by resident packs in the snow. Stanley Young and Adolf Murie verified that wolves, like dogs, have a gestation period of about two months. Breeding activity in the upper Great Lakes occurs in February, and whelping usually occurs in late April.[19]

In 1907 biologist Vern Bailey of the U.S. Bureau of Biological Survey reported that bounty hunters in Upper Michigan removed five pups from a hollow log in Marquette County and nine pups from two other dens located in Dickinson County. In 1923 or 1924, woodsman Perry Petts and his brothers discovered a timber wolf den along the north branch of the Pine River in Wisconsin's Forest County. They removed six pups from an old hollow pine log. Michigan biologist Adolf Stebler reported a raid on a den in Chippewa County in 1941. Eight pups were taken from a hollow log.[20]*

Like elsewhere within the wolf's continental range, observed litter sizes in Upper Michigan and northern Wisconsin averaged between five and six pups. In neighboring Minnesota, biologist Milt Stenlund reported an average litter size of six pups during the early 1950s.[21]

In the wild, wolves first display sexual maturity at 22 months. Until recently the longevity of wild wolves was not known. U.S. Fish and Wildlife Service biologist Dave Mech radio-tracked one individual wolf in northeastern Minnesota over a period of 12 years. Several other wolves were known to live between 9 and 12 years, and among these he noted reproductive activity up to about 11 years of age.[22]

On the basis of the age of maturity and maximum longevity, it is thought that the wolf's reproductive capacity may last about nine years. When mortality and survival rates are taken into account, however, the number of reproductive years is much lower for most wolves. Yearling wolves die at much higher rates than adults and pups. And it is a rare adult that lives to 12 years in the wild.

Sex ratios provide clues to reproductive performance by displaying the relative availability of males to females. Michigan's Adolf Stebler obtained a sex ratio of one male to one female from 478 wolves bountied between 1935 and 1949. He reported the same sex ratio from two wolf litters. In more recent times sex ratios have been determined from samples of wolves captured for marking or radio-tagging studies. An even sex ratio was reported from a stable wolf population studied in northeastern Minnesota in the early 1970s; and a ratio slightly favoring females was reported from an expanding population in northwestern Minnesota in the mid- to late 1970s.[23]

The social nature of wolves also affects reproduction. Wolves are highly social creatures. The basic social unit is the pack—the reproductive unit of wolf populations. Packs normally consist of a breeding pair and their offspring. Because wolves bear litters annually, and offspring take almost two years to reach maturity, members of two or more litters may live together in a pack.

Social dynamics within the pack are complex. In the upper Great Lakes region a typical pack consists of two adults (sometimes more), yearlings, and pups. The male and female of the breeding pair are typically the domi-

---

*The hollow log phenomenon was a temporary situation brought about by a profusion of culled white pine logs left behind in the woods in the wake of the great logging era.

nant, or *alpha*, wolves. The alphas control the behavior of the other wolves, patrol the pack's territory, and conduct most of the hunting.

Wolves can establish close ties with one another. Stories from old bounty trappers attest to the intensity of bonds that can develop between wolves. Stanley Young related the activities of an Arizona wolf following the capture and death of its mate: "From the evidence of its tracks, this female, following the capture of the male, showed much bewilderment and gave every indication of being on the hunt for its lost mate. She never missed a night in covering this part of the[ir] runway. Sixteen days later, she was trapped within 20 yards of the set that took her mate."[24]

Similar stories were told by Wisconsin trappers. Walt Rosenlaf was once trailed closely for quite a distance by a Willow pack wolf when Walt carried the carcass of another wolf through the woods to his car. In 1951 Bernie Ernest caught a wolf in a staked coyote trap in southern Ashland County, and the wolf spent a considerable amount of time in the trap before it managed to free itself. Upon checking the trap three days later, Ernest discovered that another wolf had brought several rabbits to the trapped wolf to eat.[25]

Although these stories suggest that wolves are monogamous this is not necessarily always true. Studies indicate that the consistent year-to-year breeding of two individuals within a pack may result from forces other than mutual choice. Sometimes, if no other adults are present, mate selection is not an option. On occasions when more than two adults exist in the pack, the dominant individual's aggressive behavior towards others of its sex essentially eliminates choice on the part of its partner. The aggressor thus usurps mating rights. This results in a situation termed *forced monogamy.*[26]

Spacing Mechanisms

Territoriality, or the defense of space against others of the same species, is another very important dimension of the wolf's social order. It affects survival and hence reproduction amongst wolf populations. As top predators, the individual pack's survival as a reproductive unit depends on its ability to maintain a discrete space. Resident packs must defend the territory against the trespasses of nonpack wolves that could otherwise pilfer the resources (principally food) found in that territory. This task is the responsibility of the pack's alphas.

The alpha wolves maintain the integrity of the pack's space in a number of ways. Their first line of defense is advertisement through chemical and vocal means. When the pack regularly traverses its territory, the alphas scent-mark. Urination not only serves as an eliminatory function; it pro-

1.1. A scent-post marked in February 1947 by timber wolves within the Willow wolf pack range. Note the scrape. (Photograph courtesy of Daniel Q. Thompson.)

vides olfactory cues as well (see 1.1). Wolves' feces also produce odors that serve as signals. A space unoccupied by wolves will be smell-less; an occupied territory will be literally filled with wolf odors. Scent-marking also provides olfactory cues to wolves within the same pack; for instance, the frequency of marks peaks during the breeding season, indicating the transferrence of profound feedback information between wolves in breeding condition.[27]

Howling serves a variety of functions. It furnishes information on the positions of pack-mates while they travel separately within the territory. Howling between pack-mates supplies information to neighboring wolves on the extent of territory and the frequency with which the resident pack patrols various portions of its space.[28]

Early in their development wolf pups become fearful of strangers, and as adults they usually avoid contact with unfamiliar wolves.[29] The olfactory and vocal "net" encompassing resident pack territories reinforces this behavior. Thus wolf packs arrange themselves in *exclusive territories*, and the borders of neighboring packs seldom overlap by more than a mile.

Occasionally, however, wolves ignore these basic tenets of wolf spacing. When scent-marking and howling fail to keep nonpack wolves out of the territory, the alpha wolves attempt to locate these intruders and chase them away. They resort to physical fights only when other means of expelling trespassers have failed. In these events the trespassing individual(s) may be killed. Young wolves (yearlings or young adults) that have left their natal territory in search of their own space and a prospective mate frequently die in this manner. On rare occasions when a wolf population experiences severe nutritional stress, whole packs trespass into neighboring territories in search of food, and wolves so killed are often eaten.[30]

Eventually the young replace adults in the population. Maturing wolves either disperse from their natal pack or remain within it, taking a chance that an opportunity will arise to replace the breeding adult(s). Dispersal is far more commonly the option employed by young wolves lucky enough to survive to that stage in their development.[31]

As "surplus" animals, dispersers risk a high death rate, but they are vital to the continued welfare of the population, because they are readily able to colonize patches of unoccupied suitable habitat and replace breeders within packs that recently lost an alpha. Some dispersers colonize packs adjacent to their natal territory. Others may travel 100–500 miles in search of breeding opportunities.[32]

When these dispersers range about, they search for space devoid of wolf sign or for cues that wolves of the opposite sex may be present. A flurry of activity commences when a pair becomes established. The newly formed pair scent-marks at high rates and travels about, staking out their territory. Their survival as a family unit depends upon their ability to claim a space sufficiently large to supply them and their future offspring with the food and cover they will require. In the upper Great Lakes region individual wolf packs occupy territories of between 25 and 150 square miles.[33]

Wolf Population Dynamics

Age ratios and mortality rates provide biologists with insights into the relative stability of wolf populations. Fewer than 50 percent of the wolves in stable wolf populations are sexually mature, adult wolves. In expanding populations pups may compose as many as 50 percent of the wolves. In stable populations the proportion of pups approaches 40 percent. In heavily exploited populations the pup proportion may be as little as 30 percent, and yearling wolves can be almost absent.[34]

Overall mortality rates determine whether a wolf population remains stable, increases, or decreases. In most recent studies, wolf survival rates have ranged from 35 to 75 percent annually. Wolf populations tend to falter when yearly mortality rates exceed about 40 percent.[35]

Wolf Studies

Much of our understanding of wolves has been obtained through detailed studies of their ecology in the past 20 years. In fact, the first serious studies of wolves in North America began around 1940. Adolf Murie conducted revolutionary work in Denali National Park (1939–44). Milt Stenlund (1952–54) provided a foundation for later work conducted by Dave Mech and others in northeastern Minnesota (1968 through the present). In Isle Royale National Park, Durward Allen began work in 1958 on a project that continues to this day. And Doug Pimlott and George Kolenosky introduced the howling censuses and radio telemetry in Algonquin Provincial Park, Ontario, between 1958 and 1965.[36]

These pioneering studies focused on the internal dynamics of wolf populations. By the late 1960s information was being obtained on age and sex ratios of wolves, reproductive success, social organization of packs, and special arrangements of pack territories. Similar information was being assembled on the ungulate prey of wolves. These elements of wild animal populations were considered crucial to understanding how each species functioned and how predator and prey interacted.

Science, such as it was, first met up with the wolf in Wisconsin back in 1876. In the centennial year of our nation's birth an article appeared in the *American Journal of Science* describing two extinct species of wolf and deer from bone fragments recovered from the lead region of southwest Wisconsin. This paper, obscured by the passage of time, was written by pioneer scientist J. A. Allen. How he came by the bones, exactly where they were originally uncovered, and the antiquity and exact identity of the species involved became a mystery for the better part of the twentieth century.

Presumably an early-day lead miner, or "badger," discovered the bones in limestone fissures from which lead and zinc ore was extracted, and they eventually found their way into Allen's hands. Allen claimed the wolf's bones were found near the Blue Mounds.

These dire wolf bones—if indeed they were from the prehistoric dire wolf (*Canis dirus*)—are among the northernmost remains associated with dire wolves in North America. To confuse matters another scientist published an account 50 years later claiming that the bones uncovered by lead miners near the Blue Mounds were those of a timber wolf. And, of course, no clear record survived regarding what happened to the bones that Allen had obtained from that curious lead miner who found those relics.[37]*

Between the time that Allen described his bones and the 1940s, no scientific inquiries were conducted on the wolf's ecology in Wisconsin. Throughout that period a war was being waged on the living wolf, *Canis lupus*. When science finally became reacquainted with Wisconsin's wolves, the curtain of annihilation was falling unerringly upon them. This campaign of obliteration can be traced all the way back to a time soon after the French missionaries had charted the riverine highways that criss-cross the land beyond the lakes.

*In the 1970s leg bones were found in the Harvard Museum of Comparative Zoology. They were attributed to Allen, evidently originated from the Blue Mounds, Wisconsin, and were identified as belonging to the extinct dire wolf.[38]

2

From Wilderness to Civilization

In 1634 explorer Jean Nicolet, who worked in the service of Samuel de Champlain, founder of Quebec and partner to the French fur trade, waded ashore at the head of Green Bay. None could have known, including the Winnebago Indians who greeted the strange Frenchman, that this day would spawn a great and profound change upon the land that sprawled westward from the shores of the mighty Great Lakes.

Jean Nicolet is credited with the discovery of a land that would eventually become the state of Wisconsin. Early explorers Jacques Marquette and Louis Jolliet, led by Winnebago guides, established the link that connected the western Great Lakes and the Mississippi River for New France's fur trade. While they canoed upstream along the Fox River from the Green Bay their guides spoke of a much larger, south-flowing stream that came within a mile of the Fox river. This river they called the Miscousan. The French traders adopted the phonetic spelling, Ouisconsin.

The gentle, rolling land drained by these rivers also came to be known by the Frenchmen as Ouisconsin. Several hundred million years ago it was an ancient sea bed. Roughly 9,000 years before European "discovery," a great continental glacier receded from Ouisconsin, leaving behind massive, barren glacial deposits of boulders, cobbles, and sand. To the east and north in the basins of old fault lines in the earth's crust the glacial melt waters formed the great lakes that would eventually provide a highway for the host of early-day explorers and traders who followed Jean Nicolet.[1]

Vegetation quickly reclaimed the postglacial landscape. By the time Marquette and Jolliet discovered the inland passage for New France, immense forests of pine and maple dominated the landscape from whence the river Ouisconsin arose, and lush expanses of prairie and oak savanna cloaked the rugged hills where it emptied into the mighty Mississippi.

The French explorers and traders found Ouisconsin's climate similar to that which they were accustomed in Quebec. Temperature extremes of 112°F and −60°F made life in the out-of-doors intolerable on occasion, but the land claimed four seasons of roughly equal duration. Winter winds were dominated by polar air masses. During spring and fall these masses often collided with the ebbing and waning of the warm, moist Gulf currents, providing about 30 inches of rain per year. Summer winds were occasion-

14

ally dominated by hot and arid currents spawned over desert regions 1,000 miles to the southwest, and these winds created droughts.

The wives of the few hardy fur traders that settled here raised crops of maize and squash after the customs of the Indian women. The growing season varied geographically in Ouisconsin, ranging from about five months in the southern oak savanna to less than four months in the deep hardwood forests of the north. This variability was caused in part by winter frost in soils and annual snow depths, which ranged from around 40 inches in the south to over 110 inches along the Lake Superior shoreline.[2]

Although uncommon, droughts were intensive enough to affect stream flow and lake depths roughly once in every 35 years, and hence did affect the traders' lives on occasion by making portages longer and more grueling along the route to Montreal.[3] Droughts profoundly influenced the Ouisconsin landscape, because they created the proper conditions for fire. Woody vegetation that encroached upon the southern prairies was eliminated by periodic fires, started either by lightening or deliberately by roving bands of Indians.

Prairie fires were cause for much excitement during the early days of settlement, as one witness at Kenosha attested:

> After the first frost in the autumn of 1835 had killed the millions of tons of grass west of us, we began . . . to see the rising smoke at a distance. The Indians probably had fired the prairies as early as they could for hunting purposes. . . . About 9 o'clock in the evening, it reached the woods which extended back from the lake for a half mile when the rich foliage from the fallen leaves fed the flames to a great height.[4]

Only a few woody plant species, such as the oaks, persisted in the presence of the rapidly moving, intensely hot fires that swept the prairies. Testifying to the hardiness of the oaks are pioneer accounts such as the following from Lima Township in southern Wisconsin's Rock County: "The surface is greatly rolling, covered mainly with burned white oak openings. . . ."[5] These openings were also called oak savannas.

Extending a hundred miles or so southward from the shore of Lake Superior and westward from Lake Michigan stood an immense forested region. Along the southern and eastern flanks this forest was composed of beech and maple trees. Farther north great stands of hemlock and yellow birch blanketed the landscape. Scattered throughout the region were large tracts of red and white pine groves. In the very far north, in shallow depressions left by the glacier, spruce bogs remained as vestiges of a cooler era. Interrupting the continuous forest were only the occasional openings created by violent windstorms or forest fires.[6]

In the years before Jean Nicolet stepped foot on Ouisconsin soil the land

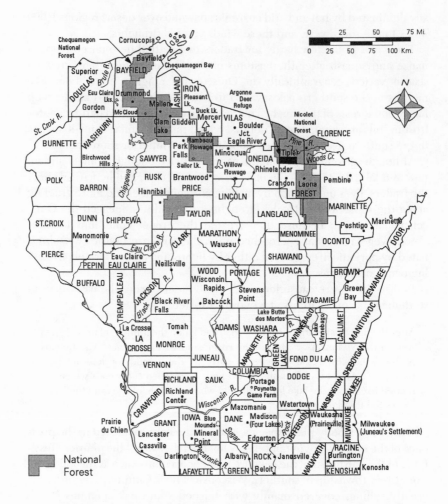

Map 2.1. Wisconsin: National Forests and important places mentioned in the text

was inhabited by various tribes of Indians. Bands of Potawatomis, Sauk-Fox, Winnebagos, and Menominees occupied the eastern forests along Lake Michigan and the southern prairies adjoining the Illinois country. Ojibwas (or Chippewas) and woodland Sioux frequented the cool Lake Superior forests and prairie borders along the St. Croix and upper Mississippi rivers. In the time before the Europeans arrived, the native people gathered wild herbs, nuts, and berries, and sought the flesh of animals with crude, Stone Age instruments that they created.

Like their European conquerors, Indians exploited the natural resources around them, but because they lacked the technology of the industrial age, these Native Americans existed in a harmonious state with the resources they harvested and utilized—that is, until the tools of the Europeans were introduced to them.

Fifteen years after Nicolet departed from the mouth of Green Bay, two enterprising fur traders, Pierre Esprit Radisson and Medard Chouart des Groseilliers, paddled ashore at the head of Chequamegon Bay and established the first trading post on Lake Superior near present-day Ashland. Thus began the fur trade era which would dominate the upper Great Lakes region and pit mighty European powers against one another during the next two centuries.

The Montreal-based French fur trade monopolized the region until 1759. Following the French and Indian wars from 1756 to 1763 the British-based Hudson's Bay Company empire established itself as the primary economic enterprise within the region. Under British rule, Ouisconsin became spelled in the manner of the English: Wisconsin.

Fur traders established permanent posts at Fort Michilimackinac, Green Bay, and Prairie du Chien, and situated many additional temporary trading posts closer to the roving bands of Indians, their only constituents, especially in later years when the furbearer stocks were systematically depleted.[7] Exploitation of furbearers and the Indian bands themselves intensified while rivals like the Northwest Fur Company and X. Y. Fur Company vied for trade with the Indians.

Armed with firearms and steel traps supplied originally by the French and now by British fur traders, the Indian population began to impact resources on a regional scale. Bison were among the first casualties of the European-Indian contact. Shortly after 1800 bison became extinct east of the Mississippi. Only 33 years earlier Englishman Jonathan Carver described the herds of buffalo he saw grazing near present-day Eau Claire while canoeing up the Chippewa River:

> Came to the great meadow or plains. Here I found excellent good land and very pleasant country. One might travel all day and only now and then see a small pleasant grove of oak and walnut. This country is covered by grass which affords excellent pasturage for the buffalos which here are very plenty. Could see them at a distance under the shady oaks like cattle in a pasture and sometimes a drove of a hundred or more shading themselves in these groves at noon-day, which afforded a very pleasant prospect for an uninhabited country.[8]

Bison were even declining in numbers in the Minnesota prairie country by 1800. Fur trader Thomas Anderson, who wintered along the St. Peter's River (now known as the Minnesota River) during the winters of 1805 through 1808, encountered buffalo there. By 1823 the slaughter extended as far west as the Red River basin south of the present-day Winnipeg, where a buffalo wool "factory" was being operated. This phenomenal depletion of buffalo was caused primarily by the local Indians, who were supplied with the necessary weaponry and taunted by the prospects of trading bison robes for trinkets. The last native bison that roamed Wisconsin were dead by the time Wisconsin Territory was opened to settlers.[9]

Early Accounts of Wolves

It was about this time that the fur traders give us the first historical accounts of wolves. Trader Peter Pond commented on the food habits of wolves while encamped in the vicinity of the St. Peter's River in neighboring Minnesota during the late 1770s. He wrote, "Woolves are Plentey—thay follow the Buffaloes and often Destroy thare yoang & Olde Ones in winter."[10]*

In the year 1803 fur trader Michel Curot occupied a post along the Brule River at the Nebagamon Rapids in Wisconsin's present-day Douglas County. On October 20th of that year Curot recorded in his journal that a cache of seven fawn skins containing wild rice was dug out and eaten by wolves. Nearly two weeks later, on the 6th of November, Curot wrote that an engagé by the name of Smith brought in "a deer that a wolf had strangled the day before."[11]

Following the War of 1812 the British ceded territorial rights in the upper Great Lakes region to a fledgling United States. However, the British remained influential in the fur trade business until the 1820s, when the American-based American Fur Company, backed by the establishment of U.S. Army forts throughout the old Northwest, became the dominant, albeit short-lived, fur company in the region.

Between 1818 and 1836 Wisconsin was recognized officially as part of Michigan Territory. Few Yankee settlers knew of the land called Wisconsin, which would shortly attract thousands of pioneers. In the 1820s Wisconsin was still inhabited only by fur traders and Indians, men in the army who guarded the trade routes from within their isolated outposts, and various entrepreneurs like John Fonda, who left descriptions about the wildlife he encountered.

In the summer of 1827 Fonda ferried supplies by boat on Lake Michigan between Green Bay and Juneau's Settlement (later known as Milwaukee). One day the howling of wolves attracted his attention to a "large doe that

---

*Though barely literate, Pond's observation of wolves taking the young and old has only recently been reiterated through scientific studies in the middle half of the twentieth century.

the brightness of the morning sun prevented us from seeing before. She was swimming out to sea . . . I have often killed deer in the water, after having put hounds . . . to drive them down, but never before had I hunted with wolves." Fonda drew his boat alongside the deer and dispatched it with a shot from his rifle.[12]

During that winter, Fonda carried mail between Fort Dearborn (Chicago) and Fort Howard (Green Bay). He noticed with peculiarity that the Indians in the vicinity of Juneau's Settlement were nearly starved despite the teeming abundance of elk.[13]

Within another decade the elk had almost vanished. Land-hungry sod busters eagerly poured into the southern portions of what was already unofficially recognized as Wisconsin Territory following the conclusion of the Black Hawk war in 1832. The southern and eastern flanks of what would shortly become the great state of Wisconsin were quickly transformed from the idle prairies and desolate expanses of forested wilderness into bustling little farming communities. Juneau's Settlement, Prairieville (Waukesha), and Four Lakes (Madison) were among the hundreds of communities that sprouted and flourished. Gone were the bison and elk upon which the Indians and wolves had depended, but the wolves remained.

By 1834 John Fonda had settled at the Bloody Run Coulee across the Mississippi River from Prairie du Chien in present-day Iowa. One day he saw a deer come down the coulee. He waited and, sure enough, after a few minutes had elapsed a gray wolf appeared.[14]

Fonda's knowledge of wolves was gained from keen observation skills that came from years of living in the wilds. This sense was shared by few other immigrants and Yankee settlers. Some did, however, take advantage of the wolves' hunting practices as Fonda had a decade earlier in the waters of Lake Michigan. One early morning in 1835, Darlington (Grant County) settler J. R. Schultz was awakened by a ruckus outside his cabin. ". . . he cautiously opened the door. . . . to his surprise he found a splendid buck that had jumped over the railing in seeking protection from a large wolf, which was glaring at his intended victim from outside, being unable to climb the fence." Schultz immediately shot the deer, and let the wolf escape.[15]

Schultz' experience was not unique. In the Neillsville area one old-timer recollected the 1840s: "Deer could be shot from the door of O'Neill's cabin and wolves would frequently chase them around into the clearing, the deer escaping by taking refuge in the dam behind the mill."[16]

Most, if not all, pioneers who relocated to Wisconsin Territory felt that wolves, like all predators, were pesky, and they dispensed with them whenever and wherever they could. (See appendix B.) And with just cause, because in these early years the settlers relied on a handful of farm animals for food and transportation. Most could ill afford to lose their precious livestock to predators. Markets were nonexistent, and neighbors were separated by miles and miles of desolate wilderness.

Robert L. Ream recounted his attempts at raising hogs in Dane County during the summer of 1838. "I procured some pigs . . . and kept them penned close to the house near the old cabins, but in spite of neighbor's dogs and all the care I could bestow on them, they were carried off by the prairie wolves."[17] A British visitor commented on the condition of the Wisconsin frontier in the winter of 1841. While the visitor boarded with a settler along the Fox River near present-day Burlington, a gray wolf was so bold as to raid the farmer's calf stable.[18] In nearby Rock County during the spring of 1841 Samuel Chapman remarked that wildcats and wolves ". . . have more than once taken my fat little pigs from my door and were unwilling to give them up even when followed in hot pursuit."[19]

Wisconsin was given territorial status in 1836 and was admitted into the Union in 1848. The area along the Illinois border was quickly settled by pioneer farmers, who plowed under the tallgrass prairie, cut away the oak groves, and with tireless labor harnessed the land. Between 1836 and 1850 Wisconsin's population swelled from a modest 11,683 to over 300,000 people. Agriculture became the strong arm of Wisconsin's economy.

By 1855 frontier towns extended up Lake Michigan from Milwaukee and along the Mississippi and Wisconsin rivers as far north as Hastings and Stevens Point. The impact on wildlife was becoming more pronounced. Deer, turkeys, and other edible game were being depleted in many southern locales by area settlers who hunted them at will to supplement their diets. The wolves and other predators became even more annoying in their depredations when wild lands were converted to agriculture and their native prey became scarce.

The last great invasion of bears occurred on Madison area farms in 1844.[20] They were rarely encountered afterward in the settlements east and south of Madison. However, the big timber wolves and smaller coyotes, or prairie wolves, as they were called by area settlers, proved to be more difficult to get rid of. One evening upon returning home, Y. T. Lacy, who farmed near Albany in Green County, noticed a disturbance "among his sheep and upon going into their yard found a large gray wolf helping himself to some very choice mutton. Mr. Lacy ran to the house, got his gun and killed the depredator. He weighed sixty-five pounds."[21]

A hundred miles to the north and west, Mrs. T. C. Higgins found herself in a similar predicament. One evening in 1861 she found a dozen wolves "contemplating an attack on a calf" in a pen on the family farm in the town of Poridge Creek (Eau Claire County). A few years later, and only about 30 miles from Mrs. Higgins' homestead, the last bands of wild elk in Wisconsin were hunted down in the hill country south of Menominee. In November of 1866 local hunters pursued a band of 12 for 15 miles, dispatching 9 of the herd.[22]*

The end of wolves in Wisconsin's southern settlements soon followed, despite a last rallying depredatory offensive by the beasts. Wolves menaced sheep herds in Waukesha and Door counties in the summer of 1866, and in the spring of 1867 Daniel Garner lost several sheep to wolves on his farm near Lancaster in Grant County.[24] Newspaper accounts, too numerous to mention, reported depredations on sheep near southeastern Wisconsin communities from Stoughton and Sun Prairie to Watertown, Palmyra, and Cambridge between 1878 and 1882.

The greatest share of problems was probably caused by those pesky little prairie wolves, but a few accounts provided sufficient details to satisfy any doubts that the culprits were the bigger timber wolves: "A large timber wolf visited the premises of C. F. Lang in the town of Koshkonong last Saturday";[25] "Some parties captured a large gray wolf on Mr. Dowley's farm some three miles from town [Janesville]";[26] and "Mr. O. Brooks of Janesville killed a grey wolf in Dane County last week that weighed fifty-three pounds."[27] These incidents, which occurred in the early 1880s, were the last records definitely attributable to timber wolves in southern Wisconsin.

The Cost of Progress

Settlers seeking a better lifestyle were not the only people interested in what Wisconsin had to offer. By the 1840s New England's great lumbering enterprises were at their peak. Already, astute businessmen were eyeing up the potential profits to be made by harvesting the vast forests that blanketed much of the upper Great Lakes region. Prompted by their expectations of a diminishing supply of good pine in the Northeast, some entrepreneurs moved their enterprises west to Michigan and Wisconsin. Logging boomtowns sprouted up overnight on the banks of numerous rivers throughout Wisconsin between the 1840s and 1880s.

Initially rivers were dammed and used to transport logs downstream to riverside mills. When the pines were cut away from the riverbanks, oxen and horses were used to haul the timber to the rivers for transport to the mills. Eventually the lumber barons would operate private railroads, transporting wood products from the pineries to distant mills. Timber was gold,

*The last elk was killed west of Stevens Point in 1868.[23] Elk were reintroduced unsuccessfully to Trout Lake in Vilas County from Yellowstone National Park in 1913 and 1917. By 1962 this herd had died out.

largely because of the great demand for lumber to house the swelling stream of immigrants in such frontier towns as Chicago, Milwaukee, St. Paul, and St. Louis.

In 1870 the lumber industry was climbing to the pinnacle of its importance in Wisconsin; nearly 70 million board feet of lumber were produced in that year by the state's mills. In 1899 Wisconsin's lumber production peaked at 3.5 billion board feet, and Wisconsin held the title as the world's largest lumber producer. In that same year the world's last wild passenger pigeon was shot near Babcock in central Wisconsin. Only 25 years earlier a large concentration of nesting pigeons, utilizing the branches of oak trees, had stretched for 50 miles between Tomah and Wisconsin Rapids.[28]

Stump farmers followed the lumbermen, clearing the cutover country of slash as they attempted to farm the northern "waste" lands. Many "bush farmers" found it easiest to set fire to the slash to make way for the plow. Occasionally these fires got out of hand. The Great Peshtigo Fire in 1871 burned an estimated 1.25 million acres of forest and cutover land, and claimed the lives of over 1,200 settlers. Other notable fires scoured the northern landscape at regular intervals from the 1880s to the mid-1930s.[29]

By 1920 most of the pine was gone, and Wisconsin's lumber industry turned to maple, hemlock, and second-growth pulp to survive. Lumber baron giants such as Philetus Sawyer were worth millions as a result of the ruthless exploitation of Wisconsin's pineries. When the supply of trees was sapped from the land many of the giant lumber corporations simply moved their operations westward in search of new "inexhaustible" supplies of timber.[30]

Without much fanfare, the last timber wolf in central Wisconsin was killed in Washara County in 1914. Long gone were the Indians, the prairies, and the bison and elk that had lived there. And the beaver, jealously coveted by the French, British, and later the Yankees, were nearly extinct in the state, reduced to a few scattered colonies in the far north. Among the cutover areas the last fisher, wolverine, and marten disappeared by 1925. Cougar exited from the state in 1908.[31]

But among the slashings of the north and within a few fragmented pockets of wild land in the west-central part of the state, the elegant white-tailed deer remained. And within isolated stretches of the deer's far northern domain the big wolves survived. Because of this, most twentieth-century Wisconsinities regard the wolf as a creature that has always been restricted to the north woods.

3

Wolves and Humans

Among the other evidences of the rude and primitive conditions of
the town, was the almost unceasing howling and barking of wolves at
night, around and within the very borders, sounding, at times, as
though the whole town was invested by scores of the brutes, much
to the annoyance and alarm of timid strangers.
(A description of the village of
Mineral Point in the 1830s,
from *Wisconsin Historical
Collections,* vol. 6, edited
by L. C. Draper.)

Wolves have interacted with humans in Wisconsin since
the retreat of the continental glaciers some 10,000 years ago. The first humans who associated with wolves within the geographic area of Wisconsin
were the American Indians. Undoubtedly all the tribes inhabiting the region had wolf clans. Clans were organized societies that tribal members
belonged to through birth or ritual induction or both. Like other prominent
animal figures the wolf ascribed to its followers certain mystic and real powers, and thus held significance in the Indians' spiritual, cultural, and func-
tional relations within their tribes.

The Wolf Clan was once important in Winnebago society. Their origins
myth states that the Wolf Clan people came from the water. When they
reached shore the wolves transformed into human beings. In one version
the clan encountered bear tracks on the beach and thus became closely
linked with the influential Bear Clan people. Water was very sacred to Wolf
Clansmen, and because of their origins Wolf Clansmen were often called
upon to calm the wind when parties of Indians were traveling across large
bodies of water.

By the time the Europeans arrived the Wolf Clan's role was fading in
importance among the Winnebagos, though it possessed some political and
social function. Their duties closely followed those of the Bear Clan, polic-
ing and enforcing discipline in the encampments.[1]

Little is known of the reverence the Indians may have held for wolves. A
small paw bone from a wolf that probably was part of an Indian's medicine

bag was found in an eighteenth-century Fox Indian archeological site near Lake Butte des Morts.[2] Wolves were held sacred at least occasionally by the Potawatomis, according to northern Forest County resident Loren Fishel. In 1924 Fishel decided to try his luck at wolf trapping. He enlisted the aid of local Potawatomi chief John Shopodock. Chief Shopodock thought it was bad medicine to trap and kill wolves himself but didn't mind directing others in their pursuit. He showed Fishel an old logging bridge across Mc-Donald Creek that the wolves used in crossing, and Fishel succeeded in capturing a wolf there.[3]

Although the Indians looked upon the wolf from both a utilitarian and spiritual perspective, the European and Yankee settlers that arrived here less than 150 years ago believed wolves were an annoyance to be gotten rid of. Wolves and humans encountered each other often and in many ways while Wisconsin's human population grew. Early trappers and settlers utilized wolves in one form or another, and wolves proved both an economic boon and liability to the early settlers. Their howling was viewed by some as musical, and by others as demonical. Sometimes wolves' dinner fare was usurped by ravenous humans; at other times wolves selected farmers' choice mutton or hunters' wounded deer. Wolves were feared too, especially by immigrant settlers who brought with them Old World traditions steeped in lurid tales of wolf attacks.

To be sure there was a little give and a little take in each of the many interactions between these two very successful species. Sometimes the humans benefited from chance encounters with the other species, whereas on other occasions it was the wolves that benefited. The relationships that existed between wolves and humans were many and varied. The following accounts depict the manner in which these master predators—humans and wolves—interacted on the Wisconsin landscape.

Food and Clothing

During the winter of 1807–08, fur trader Thomas Anderson established winter quarters on the bleak and barren prairies about 50 miles above the mouth of the St. Peter's River (now the Minnesota) in neighboring Minnesota. The region was entirely devoid of game that winter, and the traders were resigned to eating the flesh of anything they could catch, including predators like wolves and, in this case, coyotes:

> . . . I could take my share of all [predators] except the wolf. My cook said he would dress a piece, and dish it up so I would like it; so he cut off a choice bit from one just brought in and put it into the bake-kettle, seasoning it with pepper, salt and mustard, adding some Stoughton bitters and a glass of high wines to give it the taste of chicken. But with all this knowledge of refined

cookery, I could not stomach what tasted to me like a mouse-nest; for when better food cannot be had, the wolves live on mice. The men, however devoured it as voraciously as cats would their victims.[4]

Wolves unwittingly provided food for men on more than one occasion. Wolf kills were appropriated by hungry people; however, scavenging by people was a more common practice during the settlement era than in the twentieth century.

Several passages exist from records left by fur traders of voyageurs stealing wolf kills. On a blustery day in late March 1805, Northwest Fur Company trader Thomas Connor, stationed at the outpost near Cross Lake just across the state line in present-day Pine County, Minnesota, penned: "saw a Wolf that devoured a Deer. ran up & started the Wolf. brought the deer [to the post] which makes us an excellent feast."[5]

In December of 1832, Abraham Godin, discontent with his employer, John T. DeLaRonde of Portage, ran off into the wilderness and became hopelessly lost. "He came to a lake and found dead fish; and soon reached another lake where the city of Madison now stands. From there he walked two days without food; and then, fortunately, he found the carcass of a deer that the wolves had left from which he got a supply, such as it was, that lasted him for two days." Godin was eventually found near death by a Winnebago Indian named Big Fox, who nursed him back to health and ironically returned him to his employer.[6]

In February 1835, Father Samuel Mazzuchelli accompanied a fur trader in a sleigh down the Wisconsin River from Fort Winnebago (Portage, Wisconsin) to Prairie du Chien with the intention of establishing a missionary at the latter place. Along the way, "they scared two wolves from an antelope just killed, and so enjoyed the game themselves."[7] (The "antelope" was more likely a deer than a pronghorn.)

The only contemporary scavenging incident took place near the mouth of Fourmile Creek in Iron County, Wisconsin, in late February 1945. Wisconsin Conservation Department deer biologists Clarence Searles and Armin Schwengel located the fresh remains of a buck killed by two wolves they had been following. Searles related:

> That was the only time that I think I misbehaved during the time that we were on this project. . . . Looking over the animal . . . [we found] one ham was totally undisturbed, and I skinned it out and cut it off. And Schwengel and I took it back, and I cooked it for dinner. So we had wolf-killed venison. I think we were one of the few people who had eaten wolf-killed venison.[8]

Wolves were also known to raid fur traders' caches and usurp deer wounded by hunters who could not retrieve them. Recall trader Michel Curot's report that a cache of wild rice was raided by wolves in the fall of 1803 along the banks of the St. Croix River in present-day Douglas

County, Wisconsin.[9] During the November 1949 deer hunting season Julius Pfiffer shot and wounded a buck late in the afternoon south of Doublebend Road in northeastern Forest County, but was unable to track the deer because of failing light. "Upon taking up the trail the following morning he found . . . tracks in the snow [which] indicated that a pack of five or six wolves had attacked the wounded buck finally killing it. The deer was badly chewed. . . . [and] in too poor a condition to take home."[10]

The only account of the hides of wolves being used as clothing came from trader John Fonda during the late 1820s. He wore a buckskin shirt and leggings, elk skin moccasins, and a "wolf-skin *chapeau* with the animal's tail still attached."[11]

Wolves as Pets and Beasts of Burden

Wolf pups were occasionally sold and raised as pets by people who found and raided wolf dens. The Petts brothers of Alvin in northern Forest County found a timber wolf den in 1923 or 1924 along the north fork of the Pine River. They took three pups from the den, set a trap, and succeeded in capturing the bitch wolf. After hog-tying the wolf they took her remaining three pups to the family barn. The pups were kept there and fed for three weeks on porcupines which the brothers shot. The old female "started getting mean" after adjusting to the presence of people, so she was killed and bountied.[12]

Four of the pups were sold to southern Wisconsinites. The remaining two were sold to a colorful figure, "Barefoot Charlie Schroeder," from nearby Eagle River. He raised the two wolves, and they became a notorious fixture around the Schroeder homestead. One of the wolves would visit local logging operations and was crafty enough to open worker's lunch pails and steal their lunches. Both would lay in the sand rut road in front of Barefoot Charlie's home and barely move for a car. This reluctance to move eventually claimed the life of one, and the other was later trapped and bountied as a wild wolf.[13]

The use of wolves in place of dogs as a pulling team was a bit unusual. Nonetheless, James A. Danrel, a Cayuga (Ashland County) resident, trained several wolves to the harness, and in 1912 he mushed the team to Chicago for display.[14]

Wolves and Dogs

Dogs were often employed in hunting wolves, but it was the exceptional dog that would participate in such sport against so formidable an opponent.

In the 1840s, along the frontier north of the Illinois border, one pioneer commented on the manner used to condition dogs to the chase:

A good wolf-dog . . . was almost literally worth his weight in gold. Wolves when caught were often partially disabled, and then turned over to the dogs by the settlers, in order to accustom the latter to the sight of their foe, and many were the disappointed looks that crossed weather-beaten countenances as it would be found that "Tige" or "Watch" would, instead of boldly attacking, drop their caudal appendage and incontinently quit the field.[15]

By the 1920s hunting timber wolves with hounds had become a specialized pursuit. Well-trained, pedigreed dogs were required for the pursuit to be both enjoyable and successful. This kind of hunting presented a challenge because of the huge territories roamed by the wolf packs, the difficulty in accessing remote areas to retrieve dogs, and the real possibility that dogs could be harmed if they encountered the entire pack (see chapter 6). If the hunters were unable to follow closely behind, the wolves would turn on their foes and kill them.

Several hunting dogs used in the warden-sponsored Wisconsin Conservation Department wolf hunts in the late 1930s were killed. One dog was killed while pursuing wolves near Garland Springs in Vilas County in March of 1936: "The hunters had a demonstration of the power of the big Vilas County wolf when one of the dogs caught up to the pack and lost its life. Powerful wolf-jaws crushed the dog's head and ribs as it tried to flee from its huge adversary."[16]

The loss precipitated a drive to collect money to reimburse the owner for his dog. The following item appeared in a 1936 issue of the *Wisconsin Conservation Bulletin:*

Dog Insurance

Due to the danger to dogs of citizens engaged in the wolf hunt, Warden Louis Oshesky has started a wolf hunters club. Fees are collected from members to be used to reimburse owners whose dogs had the misfortune to get too close to the timber wolf pack. The club started out with the liability of compensating Joe Pekarek for the loss of a $50 hound killed by a member of the pack.[17]

When another dog failed to show up for two weeks after a 1938 warden-sponsored wolf hunt in the Argonne Deer Refuge, it was presumed killed by wolves.[18]

Dogs sometimes aided their masters in bringing a wolf in for bounty under unusual circumstances. In 1944 while driving the family tractor, 16-year-old Kenneth Black of Harshaw (Oneida County) discovered a wolf fighting the farm dog. ". . . he heard his dog growling and barking in the brush near the field. He . . . went into the brush to investigate, and found his big collie fighting a timber wolf. Kenneth . . . seized an iron bar, and waited his chance. When the opportunity occurred he cracked the wolf over the head and that was the end of the fight."[19]

Bert Biller related the following tale, which allegedly happened to him while on an excursion in the Robago Lake country in western Florence County in the 1930s:

> Another time while hunting gensing, I had our small collie dog with me. . . . I hadn't seen the dog for a long time and began to wonder what happened to him. . . .
>   . . . out of the brush burst the collie, running as fast as his little legs could carry him. About six feet behind was the largest Timber wolf I ever saw. How the dog kept ahead of him I don't know.
>   I shot the wolf in the neck with my .35 Remington automatic. . . . He was stone dead and never moved.
>   The dog and wolf had had a fight in the woods because the wolf had a piece of skin from his eyes to the tip of his nose peeled off and his face looked like a big turkey gobbler. It wouldn't have surprised me if my dog had attacked the big fellow, bit him in the face and then took off for me with the wolf mad as a hornet. . . . I hate to think what would have happened if that wolf had caught my little collie.[20]

There are very few records of wild wolves and dogs interbreeding. One attempted mating was recorded in Wisconsin. The romance developed in December 1946 and January 1947 on the east edge of Oneida County's Willow wolf pack range and may have involved an outcast member of that pack. The female wolf apparently "courted" a male Chow-mongrel dog on the Ernest Anderson farm near Skunk Lake, Oneida County:

> Anderson said that his dog had been enticed away from home several times during the past two months. Each time the dog would leave home for a day or two and run in the woods with his untamed mistress.
>   Events that led to the termination of the romance began at 10 o'clock Tuesday evening, Jan. 7. The wolf approached the vicinity of the Anderson residence in the town of Little Rice and howled for King. The dog failed to respond and the wolf left.
>   About 11:30 o'clock the wolf returned and again summoned King. Anderson, who had retired, arose and the noise he made frightened the predator. The wolf again departed, but evidently was curious as to why King failed to keep the appointment. She returned to within thirty feet of the Anderson house at 12:30 A.M. Wednesday. Anderson took a rifle, went a few steps from the house and ended the romance with a single shot.
>   The wolf was unusually large for a female of timber wolf species and was quite old, a point arrived at after inspection of the predator's teeth, which were badly worn.[21]

This same wolf was seen nearby at the Herman Witt residence, acting friendly with their dog early in the morning two days before that fateful

3.1. An old female wolf shot January 1947 east of the Willow Flowage by Ernie Anderson while the wolf was "courting" his farm dog. (Photograph courtesy of Daniel Q. Thompson.)

night (see 3.1). Biologist Dan Thompson, who investigated the incident, stated the wolf was thought to have been raiding garbage dumps in the Skunk Lake area just north and east of the Willow pack's territory. She was reportedly in excellent condition, having a half inch layer of skin fat despite her advanced age and eating habits.[22]

Economic Assets

Wolves were a valuable commodity to the persons who pursued them because of the state, county, and sometimes township bounties offered for their destruction (see chapter 5). Bounties offered many people an easy way to make big money quickly. During the Depression of the 1930s many northern Wisconsin residents turned to the woods as a both a source of sustenance (meat) and cash (trapping) in order to support their families. From 1930 to 1957 the state paid $20 for each adult and $10 for each pup wolf or coyote killed. This represented considerable earnings; throughout the 1930s and 1940s northern Wisconsinites typically earned between 18¢ and 75¢ in hourly wages (between $25 and $90 per month).[23]

The value of wolf pelts fluctuated quite a bit. In 1926, when Walt Rosenlaf began trapping, wolf hides were valuable and, combined with the bounty, offered such an irresistible opportunity for making easy money that he decided to pursue trapping seriously. ". . . I caught two coyotes on my way home [from school]. . . . I got $15 a piece for the hides and $30 bounty on them. My brother come home that night from Michigan, working in a lumber camp at one dollar a day."[24]

During the 1930s, the average coyote or wolf pelt brought $3.98. However, between 1945 and 1960 pelt prices fell to a range of 36¢ to $2.38, averaging a mere 85¢. As Rosenlaf put it, "I used to have piles of them wolves and coyotes. They weren't worth nothing to me. I mean, sometimes I'd skin 'em or [sometimes] not."[25]

Perhaps a bit unusual was the following transaction, which took place in a Mercer area tavern. During the winter of 1942 Ray Sensenbrenner caught five wolves up in the Pardee Lake country of northeastern Iron County, Wisconsin. "The Capones and bunch were still living yet, and Ralph Capone came up and bought one [hide]. What the hell, they all had money you know. He peeled off a hundred dollar bill and says to me, 'Keep the change, Ray.' Those were the days."[26]

One winter day in 1948 Wisconsin Conservation Department biologists Jim Hale and Bill Feeney discovered where the Scott Lake timber wolves had rolled and played amongst the abandoned structures at the Scott Lake Civilian Conservation Corps camp in Forest County. In several places quantities of wolf hair were lying about, which the two men enthusiastically collected and tied into flies for trout fishing. They were undoubtedly among a minority of Wisconsin fishermen to make such use of Wisconsin wolf hair.[27]

Economic Liabilities

Although livestock losses to predators were annoying, and for a time in the 1800s considerable, the annual revenue lost because of depredations was never assessed or made public. Official appraisals of depredation damage to the farming industry were unwarranted, because it apparently was never considered "epidemic."

Wolves were first labeled as destroyers of game, specifically deer, during the 1860s in the heyday of Wisconsin's market hunting era. The market entrepreneurs exploited wild animal populations at profit and shipped their carcasses en masse by rail to feed the hordes of hungry immigrants in the bustling frontier towns. Although these hunters were methodically annihilating the state's elk and deer herds, they viewed their business as "progressive" and, at the same time, condemned the predatory nature of the wolf as "destructive." To the market hunting industry the wolf and other predators were an economic liability. Reports such as the following emanated from the hunters' camps and frequently circulated among the state's newspapers: "The hunters complain bitterly of their [wolves'] villainous conduct in driving all the deer off. . . ."[28] Reports of wolves' impacts on deer became a popular news item by the turn of the century. For instance, in February 1897: "This winter the wolves are very numerous in Marinette County, and it is reported they cause more havoc among the deer than do the hunters who violate game laws."[29]

The government's first official stance printed as circular number 58 by the U.S. Bureau of Biological Survey was issued in 1907, and it corroborated the opinions expressed in the newsprint. It was entitled "Destruction of Deer by the Northern Timber Wolf." The opening statement, a product of the naivety of wildlife biology investigations (at that time in their prenatal stage), became firmly ingrained in the minds of sportsmen and conservation officials alike, and reinforced a formidable philosophy which would dominate the politics of big game–predator management for half a century and beyond. Biologist Vernon Bailey wrote: "Timber wolves have become so numerous and destructive to game in the Upper Peninsula of Michigan and extreme northern Wisconsin and Minnesota as to threaten to exterminate the deer."[30]

The wolf's predatory nature was not only condemned by the hunting community, it even raised the ire of powerful business people in the tourist industry, who recognized the value of deer in attracting tourist dollars. Both groups despised wolves. But gradually a strong animosity grew between these two influential voter groups, largely because the tourist "Bambi lovers" believed hunting seasons were too liberal, resulting in an overharvesting of deer that could threaten the tourist trade.

Pro-hunter newsmen occasionally slipped little statements into articles in an effort to draw attention away from the hunting issue. For example:

> Did you notice the extraordinary number of timber wolves that were shot by deer hunters this season? Evidently these beasts like the abundance of deer they find in northern Wisconsin so they are staying here with us. One of these marauders will do more deer killing in one winter than ten score of hunters in an open season.[31]

Highly emotional verbal warfare such as the following excerpt, entitled "Going Like the Bison," which appeared in the Minocqua's *Lakeland Times*, became commonplace in northern newsprint when the two groups exchanged rhetoric:

> I do not believe we should tolerate a few men [hunters and wildlife officials] who have no interest in our welfare to say what to do with our deer. The deer are as attractive to the tourists from the cities as our lakes. They will go miles to see deer, and the deer are becoming fewer each year. In a few years they will be gone like the bison of the plains. Let us stop this slaughter of our deer, until such time as they become pests instead of pleasures.[32]

The growing conflict between the hunters and tourist industry culminated after the end of the 1943 deer hunting season. The wolf turned out to be a pivotal figure. If there was anything over which the two groups met eye to eye, it was the fact that wolves killed deer and thus cost both interest groups "deerly" in lost game and revenue.

Wolves caused a few other economic problems. The following item, entitled "Many Queer Accidents, Hwy. Report Shows," appeared in a 1939 issue of the *Lakeland Times:* "A car struck a wolf. The wolf's body disconnected the battery cable. Another car smashed into the unlighted car."[33]

Howling

The wolf's howl can carry over distances as great as six miles.[34] Because of their large territories, wolf howling helps pack-mates keep in contact with each other. Early settlers were often greeted by the nightly howling serenades of wolves. Of course, most didn't view howling from the wolf's standpoint, but according to their own predilections. Not surprisingly, many found these sounds disturbing.

New arrivals to the early Wisconsin settlements found accomodations lacking. On their journeys most pioneer families camped where nightfall overtook them. The Rosaline Peck family found themselves within three miles of where Madison would shortly stand, but on the evening of April 14, 1837, the area was yet undeveloped. They "rested comfortably, til near 3 o'clock on Saturday morning, when we were awakened by a tremendous wind storm, and howling of wolves, and found snow five or six inches deep. . . ."[35]

One year later, Robert L. Ream and a Mr. Wells encamped at Grand Springs on the Sugar River while en route to the Madison area:

> We built a large log fire (to keep off the wolves, as Mr. Wells said), and fried our bacon and boiled our coffee. The aroma . . . must have soon filled the atmosphere; for the prediction of Mr. Wells was verified in an incredibly short space of time, by the surrounding of our camp with prairie wolves in droves. They commenced such a snarling, fighting, barking and howling, as I have never heard before or since. They made the "night hideous," and kept up the music with a thousand and one variations until morning's dawn.[36]

At the very early age of 13, John C. Barland and his 10-year-old brother, Tommie, were employed to run supplies to the lumber camps along the Eau Claire River. Like the Peck family and Ream party, they were in the habit of camping overnight along the routes to and from the logging camps they supplied. One night the young boys encamped in the gorge along Fall Creek. The howling of wolves caused them to snuggle up close together and wait out the night.[37]

Wolf howling was considered an acoustical pestilence by residents scattered across the countryside settlement farms. During the 1840s in Wood County, Reverend J. S. Hurlbut recalled that wolves would sometimes "surround dwellings and make night hideous with their howls. . . ."[38] In 1847, settler John Greening wrote a description of the Mazomanie area: "I have heard wolves howl in the edge of the woods at night and then the neighbor's dogs begin to bark, and all up and down the settlement. I have lain in bed and heard the most horrible din between the two for hours together."[39]

For a brief period in Wisconsin's history when hordes of settlers were flocking to the area, tent towns popped up literally overnight. The character of the wilderness they invaded had changed, but some of the crucial elements of the wild land remained for a spell.

One newly arrived settler commented on the living conditions of immigrants at the frontier town of Kenosha during the winter of 1835–36:

Not very spacious rooms did the boarding houses furnish then. . . . one of the boarders . . . tells me that the sleeping chamber was so low that they had to put their heads out of a hole in the roof to get room to draw on their pantaloons, while at night the sleepless wight would sometimes entertain himself by looking out of this hole and hearing wolves howl along Main Street.[40]

Even some of the larger "towns" of that early era were not without wolf music. As late as 1873 the city of Beloit experienced similar annoyances: "Our Beloit neighbors find great difficulty in keeping wolves away from the city; they are nightly invested with the noisy "varmints" who keep up an incessant howling. . . ."[41]

Well into the twentieth century, residents in certain Wisconsin towns could hear wolves howling. Gordon Sorenson, recalling the days of the 1930s in Drummond (Bayfield County), stated, "On cold winter nights they [the timber wolves] could be heard from town."[42]

Reminiscences of wolves howling were, to some, more pleasant. By far the most out-of-character comment of its day was made by one Almon Welch, who reflected over his early manhood as a settler in the 1830s in Waukesha County:

The happiest days of my life were those when I could take enough "grub" to last a week, and with my axe go into the woods rail-splitting, sleeping on logs at night, lulled by the howling of wolves.[43]

Recalling the days of his youth in Glen Flora during the early 1900s Evander Noble claimed:

Across the railroad tracks . . . was a series of dry knolls with heavy, thick timber on both sides. This seemed to be a popular rendezvous for wolves.

The Soo Line Limited arrived at Glen Flora about midnight and when it blew the whistle for the Range Line crossing it started a chorus from a large pack of wolves. It was intensified when the whistle blew for the Glen Flora station, but after it passed, that endless forest reverted to its usual silence—and we could go to sleep again.[44]

People seldom saw wolves, and the only reminder of their presence was their howling. The eerie wailing startled many an unwilling human bystander, because it most often occurred at night when the human spirit is most frail. Even so, some managed to find humor in the experiences.

Take, for instance, warden Warren Holger and special warden Joe Ziburski. These two officers had spent the better part of an especially dark evening in the fall of 1950 parked off an isolated stretch of Iron County fire lane in an area actively patrolled by deer poachers. They sat concealed beneath the canopy of the maple forest, emersed in the black, foggy night, veiled in silence within the depths of the forest. Around midnight their solitude was suddenly interrupted by the distant howl of a timber wolf. A little later it howled again, closer. "We sat there and could hear this timber wolf coming over from west of us. Every little bit, she'd stop and let out a beller. She came right to Highway 51 and she stopped. . . . After about five minutes or so she turned around and went straight back where she came from. You could hear her going until you couldn't hear her anymore." Holger and Ziburski sat there for a while afterwards. Then Holger, half grinning, turned to his partner and said, "If I wouldn't be here what would you be doing now?" Joe chuckled and said, "Hell, I'd be heading to town!"[45]

Encounters

Fairy tales, folk yarns, and Hollywood dramas have perpetuated the impression that wolf attacks on humans were (and are) common. However, since the advent of death certificates there have been no verifiable records of unprovoked attack on humans by wolves in the North American continent (including the recent "attack" of a Duluth, Minnesota, youth).[46] These records neither confirm nor deny that wolves may have preyed on people—at least occasionally—during the settlement era. In the absence of irrefutable facts we are left to decipher the verbal and written accounts of those who settled the wilds.

Wisconsin has its history of folk yarns and tales of wolves and people encountering one another. Ever prone to imagination, many old settlers probably misinterpreted wolves' actions during their encounters. What actually transpired when wolves and humans bumped into one another?

One dark night in 1836 Isaac B. Judson was making his way from Milwaukee to Waukesha when he was set upon "by a pack of wolves of unusual fierceness. Fortunately, he had a large cloak for protection against the cold, which, when the wolves became uncomfortably close, he would shake vigorously." This temporarily frightened the wolves, and in this manner he inched his way to McMillan's hotel in an exhausted condition.[47]

In the southwest corner of Wisconsin the following stories were related by Mr. Charles Rodolf and Mr. Daniel Burt:

> The wolves were not dangerous, though in the winter of 1837–38, I was followed by a drove of them for about twelve miles, from near Gratiot's Grove til I reached the Pecatonica [River]. The night was dark and they rushed several times near the wagon, but by swinging the whip at them I caused them to retreat.[48]

Daniel Burt told a similar tale about what befell him while walking from Cassville to Patch Grove.

I had not traveled over two miles before I came upon two large gray wolves, that appeared more fond of my company than I was of theirs. They continued to follow me, keeping from fifteen to twenty yards in my rear, with no signs of withdrawing. I unfortunately had no fire-arms, my only weapons being a dirk-knife with a five-inch blade, and a stout stick. These I carried ready for instant service, and thus we traveled over the hard white crust, the wolves keeping about the distance named above. Occasionally I would turn on them with my knife and club and a yell that would not have disgraced a Souix Indian, when they would retreat for a short distance, but as soon as I turned they would turn also, and again follow me. At times . . . I could not keep my feet, these white-teethed howlers would rush upon me, sometimes coming within five or six yards before I would regain my footing, when they would again retreat. . . . I found, much to my pleasure that my repeated assaults was [sic] telling on my adversaries, and as I discovered they were losing courage I regained mine and turned on them more frequently. After having followed me a distance of some seven miles, they gradually allowed the distance between us to increase until finally we parted company for good, much to my relief. . . . Having passed the greater part of my life upon the frontier, I have always regarded this as the most thrilling of my experiences.[49]

During the winter of 1837 Alexander Pratt and two companions were traveling between Blue Mounds and the "First Lake" (in what is now Madison) when their compasses failed. Darkness descended upon them as they reached the Catfish (Yahara) River. One partner was late making it into camp, so Pratt and the other member of the party went out in search of him.

. . . it soon became so dark, that we could only proceed in the direction from whence we came by feeling the footprints of our pony in the snow. . . . The wolves commenced howling around us, evidently intending to give us their hand, without a formal introduction; and at times they would approach so near us that we could see their glaring eye-balls through the darkness. In this manner we felt our way back for the distance of about a mile, when we met our companion who was completely exhausted.[50]

Benjamin Piper saw two big gray wolves skulk across the moonlit path ahead of him one night in 1841 when he was returning to his home from Watertown in Jefferson County. The two wolves disappeared in the brush and commenced howling and did not stop until he reached the clearing in front of his home.[51]

On occasion enterprising pioneers pitched fire brands at wolves when packs appeared uncomfortably close. One evening in 1837 Ralph Ostrander made camp in a downed treetop east of the Rock River near Aztalan while journeying to Milwaukee. After building a fire to dry his clothes, he discovered wolves nearby and, by throwing fire brands amidst the bunch, secured his escape to Pratt's tavern.[52] Sheboygan County settlers A. G. and Mrs.

Dye recounted that "wolves often prowled about. On different occasions Mrs. Dye went to the door and threw fire brands among them in order to frighten them away."[53] From neighboring Minnesota John Wilcox was reputed to have thwarted the advances of three wolves by dropping burning birch bark in his trail. "The wolves did not follow beyond the fires. . . ."[54]

Settlers occasionally found wolves annoying in unusual ways. In making the journey west from Milwaukee one evening, Rufus C. Dodge decided to make camp on the west bank of the Bark River. The next day he discovered that wolves had rummaged through his baggage and nearly devoured his blacksmith's bellows![55] Another settler, E. S. Purple, "had a portion of a leg of a new pair of boots eaten away by wolves" while en route from Milwaukee to Prairieville. "No man who saved his own legs from the wolves, complained if he did lose the legs of his boots."[56]

A Mr. Waterson from Royalton, while hunting one day in December 1853 near White Lake in Waupaca County, "was entirely surrounded by a pack of wolves in broad daylight. By great caution he . . . [made] good his retreat."[57]

Two chilling encounters occurred at opposite ends of the state. The first took place in Grant County in 1857:

> . . . Mr W. T. Patton . . . while returning home from Lancaster . . . was met in the road by five large wolves. They refused to give the road and from appearances of the plainest kind were about to attack him, but he beat them off with an ax handle, which he was fortunately carrying in his hand.[58]

The other encounter occurred during a winter evening in 1868 when the Williams brothers crossed the frozen St. Louis River en route from Fond du Lac, Minnesota, to Superior City, Wisconsin. After reaching the Wisconsin shore they struck out on a trail through the forest.

> While resting here we heard far off the sharp bark of some wild animal, and soon the sound came nearer and we started on a run, and had just got off the trail and on an old Military Road when we saw that the animals were timber wolves and very fierce looking, and we could see their eyes flashing while they howled.
> . . . our only defense was crying out with all our might and that seemed to keep them away. We struggled along falling often in the snow. Finally William became so exhausted that he would fall helpless and lay in the snow and we would leave him, hoping that the fear of the wolves would [arouse him] . . . but he would not stir, so would have to return and help him along. We told him the wolves would eat him but his only answer was "I cannot come, let them eat me" and in this way we struggled along, the wolves in the meantime keeping us company. . . .
> Finally we came to a clearing and the wolves left us. . . .[59]

In the year 1860 a stranger passing through the Black River Falls area lost an arm in a hunting mishap. Wolves tracked his blood, and it was believed he would have been devoured by them had a person in a nearby house not let him in and offered him shelter. One cold winter night around the turn of the century immigrant teamster Morris Thieme, while hauling logs east of Park Falls, Wisconsin, was beset upon by a pack estimated to contain 25–30 wolves. The wolves chased him out onto the ice of Ess Lake, and although he turned the team loose, the wolves abandoned the chase.[60]

A most peculiar incident occurred in Iron County, Michigan, during the winter of 1938–39 and was reported in the *Florence Mining News:*

> William Maruska, of Duluth, credits a flashlight with saving his life on a harrowing hike from Paulding to Watersmeet recently. . . .
>
> Dogged by timber wolves on a forest trail, Maruska kept the animals at bay with flashes from his flashlight while he traveled the 15 miles on foot.
>
> ". . . There were three of them," he said. "All big animals, the wolves were almost upon me before I saw them. I thought I didn't stand much of a chance. . . . I had to do something quick for they kept closing in. The only weapon I had was a small flashlight. I pointed it at them and pressed the switch. Instantly they wheeled and ran, but not far. . . . No more than a hundred feet away, they stopped and when I turned the light away, they closed in again. . . . The wolves tried to approach me from either side. There was some quick work with the flashlight as I switched it from one side to the other. As the moments passed, I became afraid that the batteries in my light would become exhausted. I had been using the light a lot in my work.
>
> "Fortunately, the batteries were fresh when I got them and the beam remained strong and bright. If it had gone out on me, I feel sure I would have been torn to pieces."[61]

Oneida County resident Ed Epler related an incident involving deer hunting partner James Donnelly which occurred in the Fourmile Creek country in northwestern Forest County around the 1940s. Jim was sitting on an old fallen log, and he resembled an old stump more than a man. Once when he gazed behind him he spied a big timber wolf returning his stare. He very slowly raised his rifle, took aim, and pulled the trigger, but the gun did not fire. Away went the wolf, and Jim remarked, "With my gun frozen that wolf could have killed me!"[62]

In any one of these encounters had the wolves been serious about making a meal, the outcome would have been quite different. But then again, these tales would have died along with the victims.

Wolves were thought to exhume bodies at grave sites and scavenge the remains of people. However, the only hint of body-snatching comes from an intriguing story around 1814, shortly after the British overran the U.S. garrison at Prairie du Chien. It seems one Antoine Dubois and a man named Champignier were sent out to Giard's Coulee several miles west of the fort in present-day Iowa to obtain a supply of meat. Both were shot by a villainous Souix, and Champignier was killed outright. Though mortally wounded, Dubois

> made a trail of gun powder, some five feet from the dead body of his companion, completely encompassing it, well knowing it would prove a protection against wolves; and then he made his way, as best he could, to Prairie du Chien. . . . When a party repaired to the spot . . . they found Champignier's body untouched by the wolves, though the tracks of these animals were plenty *outside* of the powder line, but none *within*.[63]

Among the Wisconsin folklore about actual wolf attacks, only two accounts of any merit have surfaced, but because of the lack of any "official" investigations, sketchy details, and poor record keeping, they must remain unsubstantiated. The culprits of the attacks in these accounts were not identified beyond a doubt as timber wolves. They may have been dogs, coyotes, or other beasts. However, the following accounts indicate there were, after all, many hazards associated with taming the wilderness.

The March 12, 1873, issue of the *Evansville Review* in Rock County reported: "A man by the name of King was attacked by three wolves between Haynesville and Edgerton one night last week, and was so badly injured that his recovery is doubtful."

On the evening of January 16, 1902, farmer Olaf Halesrud, who resided north of La Crosse, was attacked by "wolves" raiding his hog pen.

> Thursday evening Halesrud was awakened by a low howling in his barnyard. A disturbance among the pigs and other animals quartered there prompted Mr. Halesrud to make an investigation. . . . From the pig pen a dark object slunk off and Mr. Halesrud found two of the pigs dead, one half devoured.
>
> There was a growl and Halesrud looked around to see two balls of fire glaring at him in the darkness. Presently another pair of eyes a little further off reflected the light of his lantern and he come [*sic*] to the realization that he was being surrounded by wolves. Determined to gain the house before it was impossible Halesrud started on a run to the residence which was about 150 feet distant. Before he had gained twenty feet there was a snapping and snarling behind him and he turned to be confronted by nearly a dozen yelping barking wolves. One made a lunge for his throat. The farmer tried to protect himself with a small club which he had snatched up. The wolves were evidently to be re-enforced, judging from the barking which was now plainly audible in the distance.
>
> Several times Mr. Halesrud was forced to the ground with the wolves upon him but each time he fought them off and regained his feet, fighting his way inch by inch toward the house. The door was finally reached and half fainting he staggered inside and shot the bolt.

Mrs. Halesrud, who by this time had been aroused from her slumber helped her husband to the bed and dressed the gaping flesh wounds which practically covered his body. Although Mr. Halesrud's condition is serious it is thought he may recover.[64]

Local townspeople organized a hunt, and two hounds belonging to D. Costley were killed while pursuing wolves believed to have been involved in the attack of Halesrud. It was later reported that Halesrud died from his injuries.[65]

The account of a more recent attack filtered in from the deer hunting camps following the 1939 hunting season. "Ira Klabunde of Two Rivers went home with . . . a dead timber wolf. His first shot at the wolf was not fatal and the beast attacked him. Klabunde exhibited fang marks on his rifle stock as evidence of the battle it took to subdue the wolf. . . ."[66] Klabunde, who was hunting somewhere in the vicinity of Minocqua, was apparently not injured.

Wolf Tales

Wisconsin and Upper Michigan are replete with horror stories of wolves attacking and killing many an unsuspecting wayfarer. These tales can be dismissed as products of imaginative minds. What probably begins as a fireside tale, firmly ingrained with realistic, elemental ingredients (such as place names and third-person accounts) is readily absorbed by many a gullible listener. And so the stories circulated throughout the communities like wildfire.

. . . the timber wolves in northern Wisconsin and Michigan's upper peninsula are not man-killers, says the department of conservation game men after investigating the latest "bad wolf" story. A report of mysterious origin recently had it that a timber wolf had attacked and eaten a lumber jack four miles south of McMillan in Luce County. On hearing the report, the state conservation officers from Newberry investigated, but in checking the county coroner, sheriff's office, physicians, and undertaking parlors, they were unable to find any clues of the supposedly missing man or as to how the story of the wolf attack originated.[67]

Some stories are so terrifyingly believable they made it into newsprint. The following account appeared in the February 19, 1873, issue of the *Evansville Review:*

Wolves are becoming so numerous in the Northern Pineries that they attack lumbermen as they pass from the different camps. A pair of boots were recently found near Sherry's mills with the feet still in them; particles of clothing, etc., showed the horrible work of these rapacious, hungry brutes.

The newsmen in this case were probably duped. This was a common tale, and although the pattern of events remains unchanged in different versions of this tale, both the victims and locations differ. Apparently a Swedish immigrant met the same brutal fate near the Sunshine River in Minnesota's Chisago County, "and is said to have been wholly eaten up, not a bone being left, except his feet, which were gnawed as far down as the wolves could reach into his boots; only shreds and small scraps of his clothing were found."[68]

Northwestern Vilas County had its own boot story, as related by Ray Sensenbrenner:

A guy was supposedly killed and eaten by wolves north of Winchester. Those people up there, called the Shack People, were real poor. Supposedly, one cold winter night one went into Winchester for supplies. When he failed to return they went out to look for him. All they found were his rubber boots. The wolves had eaten all of him except for his feet which were inside his rubber boots.[69]

Russ Olson of Mellen, Wisconsin, rationalized such incidents. Occasionally cadavers would be found in the woods which the wolves may have eaten from, providing the basis for this type of story. "So the timber wolves got the credit for it. Whether they did it or not—and whether he was killed that way. You know, everybody gets heart-attacks or sick. The guy was probably dead . . ." before the wolves found him.[70]

The most sensational of the stories that originated in the north woods involved a huge pack of timber wolves chasing a supply sleigh hauling meat to the winter logging camps. Ed Epler related the least farfetched account, which is said to have taken place along the Fourmile Creek area on the Forest and Oneida County line:

. . . Ed Grattan . . . and one of his teamsters brought two sleighs to town for supplies. One sleigh was loaded with groceries and the other carried a ton of beef hind quarters. Unfortunately, Mr. Grattan was detained at a bar by a group of friends until it was too late to get back to camp before dark.

When they got to Steve Aldrich's farm on the Military Road, they were warned by Steve that there was a large pack of wolves near Four Mile Creek. Steve invited Grattan to stay overnight but Grattan thanked him and drove on.

The load of beef was in the rear when the wolves attacked. The driver threw off a hind quarter of beef and drove on, and each time the wolves attacked he threw off another until the entire load was gone.

When they went back the next morning they found that all the beef had been eaten. They estimated there were at least twenty wolves in the pack that ate that sleigh load of beef![71]

If there was a shred of truth to the story it probably revolved around the disappearance of a considerable amount of beef meant for the logging camps. One might well be more suspicious of the teamsters or supply manager than the beasts of the forest.

Arthur Latton's humorous version also involved 20 wolves with insatiable appetites. It seems, however, in this version the teamster was reluctant to yield up his cargo and resorted to shooting the wolves, one by one, when they repeatedly closed in on the sled. Each time a comrade fell, the others would quickly turn on it and devour the hapless wolf before resuming their attack on the team. At the end of the story but one wolf remained who still had a craving for beef.[72]

Russ Olson's version, which he heard as a child, occurred near the Cold Springs Quarry–Mineral Lake region of Ashland County. In this instance the prized commodity wasn't beef quarters but a barrel of sauerkraut. Olson, who couldn't remember the teamster's name, believed the story as a child, but "crossed that one off" when he got older.[73] Our hats are off to the brave soul who, in thwarting the voracious wolves, refused to yield any of the precious cargo to them and undoubtedly prevented a holocaust the north woods hasn't witnessed since the Great Peshtigo Fire. Had the 20 wolves finished that barrel, enough methane gas would have permeated through the timber lands to set the whole Lake Superior basin ablaze come the next noon hour when the lumberjacks lit their pipes!

Respect and Fear of Humans

Most experienced outdoor people agree that wolves have a profound respect for humans and act reserved when encountered. The following account demonstrates how a man's ingrained fears and imagination distorted reality during an innocent encounter on the ice of the Cisco Lake chain in Michigan's Gogebic County during one winter in the early 1930s. An ice fisherman claimed that he had been chased from his fishing shanty and treed by a pack of wolves. The shaken fellow reported it to the Michigan Conservation Department, and they sent Clarence Allen to inspect the situation. "I looked at the tracks and I seen the story. Hell, they didn't go nowhere near his shack. He just seen them and thought 'Here they come!' and he left and went up a tree. They were more scared of him than he of them."[74]

Like Clarence Allen, fellow trapper Walt Rosenlaf knew well the habits of timber wolves and felt there was little for a person to fear when in wolf country. Rosenlaf had several unusual experiences with wolves during his trapping career on and south of the Willow Flowage in Oneida County between 1930 and 1949.

> People say wolves . . . eat you up. . . . Oh, and how many timber wolves I seen. They used to follow me up there on the Flowage. I [used to] go way back up there where the Tomahawk River comes into the Flowage . . . and I'd ski back. . . . [Frequently] it was already getting dark when I was up there yet, and I'd ski all the way [back] to Willow Lake.
>
> One time I looked back and there was two timber wolves coming right behind me. I didn't have my gun. They went right by me and they just turned their head . . . when they went by, and looked at me. So, I wasn't scared of them either.[75]

In Traps

Many animals are fairly aggressive when trapped or cornered. However, most trappers agreed that trapped wolves were not vicious to approach, although no one quite trusted them. In fact many trappers didn't waste ammunition but clubbed the wolves they caught instead. Rosenlaf stated "The timber wolf when in a trap is ashamed of himself[.] never try to fight you they more or less just give up."[76]

Russ Olson wanted to get a picture of a live timber wolf. One day he was given the opportunity when he found a wolf in one of his traps. The wolf, disconsolate, lay down and steadfastly refused to stand and pose for Olson and his partner, despite their best efforts to coax it. Russ said he finally "went over there and jerked him up by his tail and my partner took his picture."[77] (see 3.2).

During the winter of 1922 Walt Rosenlaf's father set a trap for a timber wolf north of Brantwood in Price County. A violent snowstorm struck and prevented him from checking the trap. When he finally returned there was no trace of his trap; something had taken it. About two weeks later he decided to check out the carcass of a sick horse he had shot for a farmer, and there he found the tracks of a wolf dragging a trap. He

> . . . trailed him and got him in the deep snow miles from where he took after him. He said the wolf just gave up so he looked him over [and] saw he had chewed all his teeth [off] on the steel trap. he didn't have no rope so he took some willow wood, they are limber and you can wind 'em and make a good rope out of [them]. he made lines out of one on each side of the wolves [sic] head to steer him. he then took the trap off his foot. he was going to drive the

3.2. Trapper Russ Olson holds the tail of a live timber wolf caught in a trap in the Ashland-Iron county area. Note the submissive ear position. This photo was taken in the late 1930s. (Photograph courtesy of Russ Olson.)

wolf home[.] the snow was deep and he was on skies [*sic*], but the wolf never moved from the spot so he had to club him to death and drag him. . . .[78]

Regarding the reactions of trapped wolves upon seeing their captors, Frank Tomaier of Glidden said, "Wolves and coyotes are cowards. I've had a big one up in Duck Lake [Iron County, Wisconsin] sit back and howl right next to me. . . . Wolves never lunged."[79] Russ Olson said, "The big ones— they didn't dive around or anything. The minute they'd see you, they'd be watching you. They either sat or lay down. They wouldn't get up or offer to fight. I imagine that if you got close enough so that they wouldn't make a mistake they would have nailed you."[80]

Walt Rosenlaf also experienced the howling of several wolves when he was near them, ". . . otherwise, they're not vicious." He recalled:

One young timber wolf I had . . . caught underneath a spruce tree in a blue-
berry swamp. . . . I used to . . . club my wolves with that ski pole I had and
then choke them so I wouldn't get the fur bloody. I had a 30-30 that morning
with me. This wolf was not a big one so I decided to club him and skied right up
to the edge where he had the circle [the extent of the chain on the trap] around
that tree, and I stepped on that circle thinking it would hold me, and I went
way down. That swamp was soft underneath!

   That was . . . the [only] wolf that ever jumped at me, and I had that ski pole
in my hand and I stuck it in his mouth when he come at me. . . He bit that
hardwood pole . . . and just crushed it. . . . I crawled out of there and used
the 30-30. I didn't want to take any chances.[81]

During the final years of the species' existence in Wisconsin and Upper
Michigan, individual wolves showed remarkable fear of man. After a hundred years' exposure to every conceivable device ever contrived for their
demise, some wolves became crafty and downright paranoid when they
encountered human scent or sign. These wolves sometimes went to extreme lengths in avoiding humankind.

Biologists Clifford Bakkom and Ralph Hovind had a taste of how a pair of
wolves evidently reacted to the fresh trail made by the two biologists in
February of 1946. They had been trailing the pair of wolves in the Willow
Flowage area and didn't know at the time that the pair of wolves had circled
back and was heading nearly on a collision course with the biologists. "They
[the wolves] took a logging road and followed it until they came to our tracks
made 15–20 minutes before. The tracks showed that the wolves retraced
their steps a short way and headed straight west to [an] open swamp where
the wind covered the[ir] tracks." Hovind sketched a map in his notebook
showing that the wolves were heading north into a gusty 20-mile-per-hour
wind out of the northwest. The wolves approached the biologists' trail to
within 10 feet but turned around, apparently in fright.[82]

Dan Thompson noted that the Willow wolf pack avoided a small pulp-
cutting operation in November and December 1946 in the central part of
their territory, where he most often noted wolf activity. While the pulp-cut
was in operation, "the wolves had traveled on the fire lane above and below
the pulp cutting, but had avoided the fire lane in the area of disturbance.
The pulp cutters made daily car trips . . . and were present in the woods
only during daylight hours. However, this disturbance was evidently
enough to make the wolves divert from their most frequently traveled
route."[83]

Regarding wolves in Michigan's Upper Peninsula, Adolf Stebler commented:

   In their travels these wolves generally appear to avoid sites of logging operations. This tendency was apparent in both the Cusino and the Hulbert areas

during the winter of 1950. . . . Except upon one occasion at Mahoney Lake in mid-February, . . . the Cusino wolves are not known to have cruised through the sites of any of these logging operations. . . . There was also a small logging operation in the northern part of the Hulbert area. . . . This site likewise seems to have been avoided, for so far as is known, the Hulbert wolves by-passed it rather than cruise through it.[84]

Thompson similarly noted avoidance of a stretch of fire lane within the Willow wolf pack's territory during the summers of 1947 and 1948, when the lane was used as a detour route for a highway that was being repaired.[85]

Occasionally wolves were reluctant to cross or walk on plowed lanes. Stebler remarked, "A travel trait often manifested by wolves is their apparent hesitancy to cross roads from which the snow has been plowed. . . ." He reported examples of this behavior in the Cusino wolf pack in both 1938 and 1950. However, he also stated, "On the contrary, the Hulbert wolves crossed a plowed road regularly throughout the 1950 winter." He also mentioned that the Cusino wolves had used a plow trail in January of 1936.[86]

On the 11th of March 1945, while biologists Clarence Searles and Armin Schwengel were following the tracks of nine wolves on a north-south fire lane southeast of Duck Lake in Iron County, Wisconsin, they had an opportunity to interpret the wolves' behavior on encountering an idle cabin owned by Dr. Benjamin Dike. At the time, the wolves were traveling north; Dike's cabin was located on the west side of the lane. ". . . At Dike cabin 2 animals went in on the west side of the lane apparently investigating rabbit tracks. On their return to lane 1 animal passed within 20' of S.E. corner of Dike cabin. Although the animals had followed the west side of lane up to Dike [cabin] they crossed to east side while passing the cabin. . . ."[87]

During winter, trappers frequently set traps and caught wolves in the snowshoe trails they had established. Some wolves learned to avoid all such trails. Adolf Stebler did not notice such avoidance tactics in the Cusino, Michigan, wolves in 1938, but apparently witnessed this trait in that pack in 1950. He mentioned, "Wolves usually seem to avoid stepping in a snowshoe trail. Instead of doing so, they will either travel more or less parallel to it or they will leap over it."[88]

Trapper Ray Smith observed similar behavior on the Florence-Forest county line in northeastern Wisconsin. "A timber wolf, he won't walk in your snowshoe trail, he'll cross it. But when he comes to it, he'll usually stop about thirty feet before he gets to it, and then he'll run real fast and jump sixteen feet and he'll go over it."[89]

Smith remembered well the last time he noted such behavior. It was the last time he saw a timber wolf track, and the incident took place on the creek behind his property during the late 1950s. He had been beaver trapping along the creek and had a well-worn horse-sled trail established.

> We got a big snow, must have snowed 15–16 inches. Anyway, when I went down to place my [beaver] trap a timber wolf had crossed the creek. . . . he come to that trail, and it was all snowed over [so] you couldn't tell where the trail was. The timber wolf knew there was a trail there, and he wouldn't cross it. He come to it in four different places, but he would not cross it.

Smith went back and fetched his hounds and set them on the wolf's trail. A week later the hounds were found near Smokey Lake, 20 miles northwest of Smith's home across the border by a Michigan resident.[90]

Harried, harassed, and hunted down to the last of their kind, these last few survivors harbored a paranoid mistrust of anything tainted by human scent. And for good reason; after all, they *were* survivors.

Wolves and humans have shared a long and varied relationship in Wisconsin. In the time preceding settlement, wolves were largely ignored but were sometimes killed for their pelts or for food and clothing. While settlers transformed the wilds into farm and field, wolves became an annoyance. Some found solace in the howl of the wolves while many others felt their livelihoods and even their lives were threatened by the presence of such beasts. With the spread of civilization across Wisconsin, the wolf's range receded northward, and the animal's influence on human affairs waned. The wolf's role as master predator was diminished by a superior and formidable predator whose unrelenting pursuit of the wolf was responsible for the ultimate demise of Wisconsin's original wolf population. The complex relationships that existed between man and wolf were shaped in part by the former's burning ambition to subdue the untamed Wisconsin landscape.

4

Tales from the Trapline

Very soon after settlements appeared, local municipalities were formed, and among the first order of business was the establishment of bounties to help rid the frontier of unwanted predators. People who collected these bounties were a varied lot. Some had chance encounters with bears, wildcats, or wolves that ended fatally for the critter. Others went forth with a sense of purpose, methodically searching for sign of these predators, making it their business to pursue, hunt, and trap their quarry.

Most who tried to earn a buck by collecting bounties failed miserably. Those who were eminently successful earned the admiration of their fellow citizens. The prestige of these individuals inevitably increased as predator stocks declined, partly because of the lengths to which they went to capture the last local bear, wolf, or wildcat.

Who were these men? What motivated them to pursue this type of career? Unfortunately, history has left us with only bits and pieces of the story of bounty trappers on Wisconsin's frontier. However, some of their successors survived to modern times in the cutover country of the north, providing a picture of the personalities of those wild bounty men.

Of the many thousands of people who at one time or another killed wolves during the settlement of Wisconsin, Rueben Fulson, or Fulsom, stood out in the crowd as a person seemingly possessed of his sport and at the same time mesmerized by the animals he pursued. He was known to folks in the Green County community of Albany as Old Ruby, the Wolf Hunter.

Ruby was of Canadian descent, arriving in Green County by way of New York State in either 1841 or 1842. His background was largely unknown, adding to the mystery of his peculiar ways. Rumors indicate he came from reputable stock, but his education was interrupted by his hunting pursuits at an early age. Some say he was married fully three times and a technicality in his fourth marriage ceremony caused an annulment with the result that both members of the nuptial party departed ways. Others claim a union with the regular army caused Ruby to immigrate to Wisconsin.

Whatever the case, Ruby found it easy to ply his trade in the bustling farming communities sprouting up along the Sugar River. Wolves abounded and many a farmer's stock fell prey to their predatory ways. Ruby was able to support his addiction to hunting through the bounties that had been instituted to combat wolf depredations. Ruby supposedly made his home in a small cave amongst the rocks along the left bank of the Sugar River just northwest of the village of Albany. Many townspeople pitied the recluse for his habits, and offered him both food and shelter during periods of inclement weather. He was described as a kind and inoffensive man, though "he seemed to live and move in a world of wolves, became wolfish in nature, looked and talked like a wolf."[1]

Ruby was reputed to have caused a large share of the reduction in numbers of wolves in Green and neighboring Rock County and was held in high esteem by the settlers of that region. He died in 1875.[2]

Ruby wasn't the only wolfer with eccentric habits. Others were scattered up and down the frontier. Wolves were sometimes brought in live by local trappers and arrangements were made as soon as possible for a wolf and dog fight. The following incident occurred in a Grant County frontier prairie town in 1838. The unnamed narrator was a foreman on a jury deliberating a case which seemed hopelessly hung:

We should have hung there until this time, probably, but for a couple of huge, gray, timber wolves, that old "Wolf-catcher Graham," had brought into the town plat, securely caged in his wagon. Everybody then attended court, and everybody brought his dogs. The old wolf-catcher set up a loud cry, saying he would let out a wolf against all the dogs in creation, if the people who desired the sport would pay him $20 each for his wolves, and allow him the scalps. The money was raised quicker than you could count it. We would have almost paid the national debt to see a wolf-fight. The first wolf—and he was an old settler, I tell you—was let loose in the yard, right under our window. We ran to it, and climbed on each other's shoulders. Such snapping, barking, growling and bristling you never heard or saw. Dogs and wolf were piled up almost to the upper story, in a living, biting, snapping, rolling, tumbling, and boiling mass. Some of the dogs were thrown *hors du combat*, but others took their place. . . . In the dog and wolf revolution, the latter actually entered the sacred halls of Pepper's tavern, where all our fair female population were gathered and gossiping. Such a scattering, screaming, fright, running-up stairs and jumping on beds was never seen or heard of. But the poor wolf, as if he understood the tenderness of the female heart, galloped up stairs too; on the bed he jumped with tongue protruding, and with beseeching looks, prayed for mercy. But up rushed the dogs dripping with blood; now mad with fury and blessed with victory, they scaled the parapet. A universal and deafening hubbub ensued. Men rushed in with clubs, seizing a dog or two by the tail, and tossing them out the window, and sometimes punching the wolf, that by this time had learned that the generous dimensions of female apparel offered him the safest retreat.

But, not withstanding the poor wolf's surrender and meek behavior after he entered the forbidden halls, he was slain without mercy. There is not a living man, or woman, or animal, that witnessed that scene but if they are still alive remember it to this day. I am satisfied that jury never would have agreed in that case had it not been for Graham's wolf.[3]

Not everyone who set traps for wolves approached the level of sophistication attained by the professional trappers. Failures probably far exceeded those who reached the ranks of old man Graham, and history doesn't easily surrender records of man's shortcomings.

Mr. Foreman . . . had set a number of traps in a circle, with a bait in the center, to catch a wolf. A Mrs. Powell lived near where the traps were set, and her little dog got into one of them, and of course set up a dreadful howl.

Mrs. Powell went to the rescue of her pet and got caught in a trap herself, and of course there was more music. A large black dog belonging to Pierce Bradley . . . then thought it best to go and see what was the matter, of course he got caught, and then the chorus was complete. Fortunately, the outcries brought Mr. Foreman to the rescue, and he set them all at liberty.[4]

Poor Mr. Foreman would have done well to call upon Ruby Fulsom, who lived not 20 miles south of the village of Exeter, where this incident took place.

The job attempted by thousands like Foreman and accomplished by men like Fulsom and Graham was a necessary part of the process of taming the wilderness. Predators had no place in a civilized society. They were a menace to area farmers and, by some accounts, were considered dangerous.

Early in the twentieth century the motivation for killing predators such as wolves took on a new dimension. Sport hunting of game emerged from the more earnest subsistence and market hunting days of the past. Concomitant with the development of this visionary approach towards hunting arose a philosophy that through removal of predators game populations would increase.

Now, brother hunter, what have you and I contributed to the cause of substantial protection of these fast disappearing creatures of the forest? Very little. We have, on the contrary, hunted and killed them for years and years—and got nothing in return. . . . Why not, instead of killing off all the game, do some real man's hunting by killing off the foxes and wolves? It's real sport and can be much enjoyed by every red-blooded hunter and every wolf you kill you will save at least one deer. It will prove enjoyable, profitable, and at the same time save the fast disappearing game. The farmers and settlers will welcome you and bless you and when you next go on your annual hunting trip you will find game more plentiful, and much of the disappointment caused by failure to get your game, removed.[5]

This thoroughly adopted motto—Remove all predators and game will increase—became the vision of the sport hunting fraternity.

Although modern-day trappers were firm believers in the predator removal philosophy, their motivation to trap predators came as much from the matter of realizing profits from the sale of furs and receipt of bounty claims as from their duty as faithful sportsmen. To many people who lived on subsistence incomes, trapping became a serious business and, to quite a few, a principal means of living. The good trappers who thoroughly knew the habits and traits of the animals they sought used these insights to turn a profit.

This intimate knowledge caused many wolf trappers to have a soft spot in their hearts for these beasts, at least in the trappers' later years, despite their perceptions that wolves were a menace to the deer herd. Russ "Hoot" Olson spoke the sentiments of many: "The timber wolf is an animal I had a lot of regard and respect for. They really were a beautiful animal."[6]

Walt Rosenlaf was a serious fur trapper. He was raised in the farming community of Brantwood in southeast Price County. Lured by the ease of making money (compared with the demands involved in other forms of employment), Walt was already a seasoned trapper by the time he finished grade school in 1926. He caught his first timber wolf in 1930 while staying at a logging camp up in the Willow country, after being urged to trap wolves because of their abundance. At first glance he thought the animal in his trap was a police dog, and for a few moments he debated whether he should take it. But he shot it and collected the bounty. Walt's skills as a timber wolf trapper improved rapidly, and within two or three years he was catching three or four annually. He respected the timber wolf's strength and cunning, and thoroughly enjoyed the challenge in capturing them.

Rosenlaf's trapline ran from Highway 8 to the Willow Flowage in southwestern Oneida County. His trapping pursuits frequently took him away from home and family. During the winter months his wife took care of the farm chores, because he often left at 6:00 in the morning and wouldn't get in until 9:00 or 10:00 at night. He rarely carried a lunch or water bottle with him but admitted his tongue was hanging out when he got home.

During the fall he would park his car at the gated lane at Bass Lake and, with packsack strung on his back, walk the eight-mile trap-line through the woods to the shores of the Willow Flowage.

I had a piece of tin out there from an old shack and I'd lay underneath that tin at night. . . . Wolves would howl close . . . at night and coyotes [too] . . . but they never bothered me. . . . the deer were the only ones that would come right up next to that tin and they'd stomp their feet down.[7]

The next day he would complete the circuit, carrying out his assorted, cumbersome booty.

In them days we had to carry them out. I had a great big pack sack with heavy leather straps on it. Sometimes it was so heavy I didn't dare put it down. I'd back up on a stump and lean [into] it [to take a break]. If I put it down, I couldn't put it back on again. That was over hundred pounds I was carrying a lot of times.[8]

One fall he had an especially thrilling encounter. He was unarmed on this occasion.

I remember one night especially. I had one female [wolf] in a trap [after killing it.] I was coming back. . . . it got dark on me, and I had about three miles to go along the edge of that Flowage. . . . I had a little flashligh with me.

. . . This other wolf, must have been the partner [to the dead female Rosenlaf was carrying], and he pulled alongside of me not too far in the woods and he'd howl every now and then. And you know, it kinda put the chills in your back. . . . He never come close enough so that I could see his eyes or nothing.

Rosenlaf finally reached the Willow River stream bank and took his boat to the opposite side, where his auto was parked, and thus lost his escort.[9]

During the winter months Walt used skis, and extended his trapline to include the northern shores of the Willow Flowage. He pursued muskrat, weasel, and mink for their valuable furs, and sought bounty on fox, bobcat, coyote and timber wolf.

Walt Rosenlaf knew his business, was good at it, and his success attested to his abilities. He was a trapper from the old school; he worked long hours, endured many physically trying moments, and typically worked alone.

During the winter of 1937–38 Rosenlaf was trapping in the area south of Clam Lake. While there he most certainly crossed paths with another trapper, George Ruegger. Ruegger was born in Illinois in 1881 and, at 12 years of age, hired out to work on a local farm for nine dollars a month. A large skunk colony was continually raiding the chicken coop, and one day after George succeeded in killing one of the skunks, a fur buyer happened by and told him skunks were worth money. "I pricked up my ears when he spoke money, for $9 a month wasn't much." He soon caught seven skunks and sold them for a dollar each.[10]

In 1906 he bought a 30-day homeseeker's ticket, and looked over the Sawyer County area. Liking it, in 1908 he moved his family to Radisson.

Of all the outdoor activities Ruegger engaged in, he described wolf trap-

4.1. George Ruegger inspecting a fawn succumbing to starvation March 1941 near Palmer Lake, Vilas County. (Photograph courtesy of Wisconsin Department of Natural Resources Photo Archives.)

ping as his first love. He had a 23-mile circuit in the woods around Radisson, and during the winter he worked it on snowshoes.

In 1928, by good fortune, he reported some game violations to warden Ernie Swift. Thus began a beneficial association with a man who was destined to become a top administrator in the Wisconsin Conservation Department and who would possess considerable influence, especially among the ranks of the powerful warden force. Swift was, to say the least, awed by the character of George Ruegger. As a field warden he had associations with George; recalling these, he reported that Ruegger would turn over information on violators, accompany the warden to their premises, confront the accused violator, and say " 'I don't wish to have you accuse a neighbor of giving information to the Conservation warden, and create any ill will. Therefore, I came along to tell you that I am the man who told him.' "[11]

During the early 1930s the government became involved in controlling wolves primarily as a result of the growing popularity in sport deer hunting. This brought government administration in close contact with wolves for the first time (see chapter 6). By the winter of 1935–36 (if not earlier)

George Ruegger was employed by the Wisconsin Conservation Department's warden force on a case-by-case basis as a depredation control trapper in response to complaints of timber wolves killing deer and of black bears doing damage to sheep and apiaries. He worked as a government trapper at least until 1938.[12]

Poynette Game Farm Gets Some Wolves

By 1935 public demands for control of wolves because of their depredation on deer caused the Wisconsin Conservation Department to become involved in control trapping. P. C. "Jake" Jakoubek, head of beaver control, was given the responsibility of wolf control activities at the direction of chief warden Barney Devine.

In late February 1936, Devine instructed Jake to get some wolf traps in the Boulder Junction area of Vilas County in response to deer damage complaints received from warden Hartwell Paul. After appraising the situation Jake informed the chief warden that it was not advisable to set traps there because a team of 40 hunters with dogs was actively hunting the wolves, and he was concerned that the traps would freeze up because of the warming trend in the weather. As an afterthought, Jake wrote: "Should it be agreeable to you, I might suggest that we go into that territory just before the snow leaves and see if it would be possible to track some female to her den and try to take some timber wolf cubs for the game farm."[13]

On March 5, 1936, Devine responded: "I believe, and I am sure the Director would approve, that you should make every effort to obtain a pair of wolf puppies for the State Game Farm. Naturally, too much time and money cannot be spend [sic] for this work; but you should make every effort to locate a den."[14]

In the meantime two pregnant female wolves in the Vilas County pack were killed by the hunters. Whether Jake and others searched for a den is not known, but it is certain that no wolf pups were obtained that spring.

However, Jake's idea did not die. In fact, after Jake had failed to obtain pups, the Conservation Department approved of an attempt to capture, alive, some adult wolves for display at the Poynette Game Farm. During the fall of 1936, Jake "heard of a pack of timber wolves in eastern Price County, so it was decided he would give them a whirl."[15]

Jake enlisted the aid of George Ruegger to assist him in the task of live-trapping some timber wolves for the game farm. On December 28, 1936, Jake reported that they had located wolf trails in the Sailor Lake region of Price County and had set seven traps. ". . . but on account of the snow leaving us I was obliged to pick them up again. We will reset them as soon as we get a fall of snow."[16]

In early January, Ruegger was hired as a state trapper for a period of 90 days. He was allowed a salary of $3 per day and an expense account not to exceed $100 per month. He was instructed to assist Jake in the live-trapping operation and work on any damage complaints that might be received. In addition Devine said he would "appreciate any . . . pointers you may give the wardens . . . on the trapping of timber wolves."[17]

Jake and Ruegger's trapping campaign was plagued by bad weather. The two had hopes of being successful after resetting their traps following a five-day rainy spell over Christmas, but reported ". . . as there was not enough snow for the wolves to trail, they did not come near our sets. . . ."[18] The weather was dismal and the wolves were not cooperating. On February 1, Jake was forced to report, ". . . we have had rather poor success with the wolves so far. They have ignored our sets; however, we hope with the new snow, they will start trailing, which will make our operations considerable [sic] easier. . . . We are changing our system and have twenty-one sets made."[19]

Conditions continued to worsen. On February 11th Jake wrote:

> I am almost ashamed to report on my wolf-trapping operations, since we have been unable to catch one, although, we did have a hold of one which went through during the snow storm and was caught only by a toe. The experiences we have gained in this time, of course, is worth something, and I am very confident since the new snow that the wolves will trail. I believe before the month is over we will be able to get them.[20]

Shortly after they began trapping, Jake considered how the two could safely handle a timber wolf in a trap. He wrote to Devine: "I have been at a lost [sic] to know just how to handle a live timber wolf, but I have an idea it will require a good strong muzzle. I am wondering if it will be possible for me to have such a muzzle made. I ordered two from the catalog and found them just about poodle size so we cannot use them."[21] Devine replied, "I believe a harness make[r] might be able to construct the type of muzzle necessary to take care of a timber wolf. . . . You should be able to have one builty [sic] locally."[22]

Jake had the fire control crew at Park Falls construct a wooden crate for transporting the wolves down to Poynette, but he still faced the problem of how to subdue a wolf to get it out of the trap.

On Saturday morning, the 18th of February, the two men finally caught a timber wolf.[23] Ruegger recollected the incident:

> "I had one trap fairly close to the road and one day when Jake came down to the camp I asked him to look at it. He forgot about it and I didn't feel right about

this, as I sometimes have a feeling when I am going to catch something in my traps, so we went back to look at it.

"I went down into the woods and sure enough, the trap was gone. Hiking back up to the road, I told Jake to go back and get the crate and I would follow the wolf. I hadn't gone very far from where he had got into the trap until I found him with his toggle tangled up in some popple trees."[24]

Contending with the problem of extracting the wolf from the trap became a sudden reality for the two men now. Ruegger continued:

This was my first experience in trying to take a timber wolf alive and for the life of me I couldn't figure out how we were going to get him out of the trap and into the crate.

"While Jake was gone, I commenced to experiment and as I circled around him, he would show his teeth and say 'Whuh.' When I threw snow at him, he would jump and snap. Finally, I got close enough to give him a good poke in the ribs with my walking stick and he just wilted. I was surprised and thought he was being tricky, so did it again; he just laid there trembling. When Jake finally came with the crate, he was still lying down and I guess Jake thought I had been pretty rough with him.

"For awhile then we tried to get the wolf into the crate without getting too close but it didn't work, so I went up and took the trap off him and pushed him in. I had mittens on. He rolled his eyes at us and then looked the crate over, all the time not moving, and it seemed as if he said 'They got me.' The odds were too great against him and he knew it."[25]

The next wolf they caught gave them another problem.

"We got her in a trap about three miles off the road and didn't have a crate for her. It would have made mighty tough traveling to get her out that way anyhow. I punched her in the ribs the same as the other and, you know, her reaction was just like his. When she was laying down there we shoved her into a packsack and buttoned her up and took turns carrying her out to the road. One of the boys put a collar on her and hauled her down to Poynette in the back of his car. When they give up, they give up in earnest."[26]

Fire control employee George Fleming was one of the boys who drove the wolves down. He remarked that every time the truck came to a stop the wolf would stand up, and when the truck took off the wolf would lie down.[27]

The third wolf they caught was in bad shape. Some time before, the wolf had been caught in a snare and in his struggles he eventually broke the cable, but the wire had become embedded in his neck. Ruegger recalled, " 'He wasn't able to breathe through his nose at all, but through a hole in his windpipe which had been cut by the snare. For the life of me I can't figure out how he ate.' "[28]

The two trappers accumulated roughly 680 trap nights before they captured their first wolf. On March 3, 1937, Jake decided to terminate live-trapping activities. "Considering trapping conditions, I believe we were quite fortunate in taking three wolves. However, one of them is in bad shape and probably will not survive. Nevertheless, the female we obtained last Sunday and the first male caught I believe will make a splendid pair for the farm" (see 4.2). That spring two wolf pups were born to the female at the Poynette Game Farm (see 4.3).[29]

During the next several years the wildlife pathology staff at Poynette conducted a few experiments with the game farm wolves. In 1940 wolf blood was given to University of Wisconsin professor Wolfe "to be used in the precipitin test for his classes and any other instances where it may be used, such as court cases."[30]

In 1941, Dr. Chaddock, pathologist of the Wisconsin Conservation De-

4.2. One of the live-captured timber wolves shortly after its arrival at the Poynette Game Farm, in March 1937. (Photograph courtesy Wisconsin Department of Natural Resources Photo Archives.)

4.3. A female timber wolf with two pups at the Poynette Game Farm in June 1938. (Photograph courtesy Wisconsin Department of Natural Resources Photo Archives.)

partment, wrote a report on the preparation of wolf scents useful in trapping wolves. He undoubtedly collected the droppings and urine from the game farm wolves. He also experimented with wolf scent as repellant for deer. In October 1940 Dr. Chaddock mailed several ounces of scent to wardens, "to experiment with it to prevent deer damage to crops." He advised the men to apply three or four drops per acre distributed in three or four locations and note any effects it might have.[31] Ironically, the Wisconsin Conservation Department supported eradicating wolves because of their alleged damage to the deer herd and yet valued their urine in repelling deer that were damaging crops.*

Records on breeding and the fates of the animals held at the Poynette Game Farm were never kept. Occasionally, the number of captive Wisconsin wolves on display at the game farm dwindled to the point where replacements were necessary.

The state never repeated its live-trapping program using special contract employees. Local wardens were apparently instructed to make contacts with wolf trappers and offer them an additional sum of money beyond the bounty for live wolves.

*The results of Chaddock's experiments have not been found.

In September 1946 an arrangement was made with local Glidden trapper Billy Bay to capture some timber wolves for the Poynette Game Farm. Sometime before the 19th of September, Bay captured a pup on the west fork of the Chippewa River southwest of Glidden. Around the 18th of October he trapped an adult wolf "in the neighborhood of Forest Wonder Lodge in Iron County and notified the [Conservation] commission that he had a good specimen. Wardens then went to the trap and took the animal in a cage. Later it was taken to Poynette to the the state Game Farm."[32] Bay sold the live wolves to the state for an unspecified amount.

Wolves were also purchased from Joe Heizler and Stan Kolnik, two local Phillips trappers.[33] In the 1940s and early 1950s it was still easier to procure wolves from the wild than to trade with zoos for captive-born wolves.

Deadly Conviction

Clarence Allen of Marenisco was one of the state of Michigan's depredation control trappers. On one occasion in about 1946, the Michigan Conservation Department received complaints of timber wolves killing deer in a big yarding area south of Sandstone Rapids near Ewen. They called Allen in on the case, and he agreed to take the job on the condition that the department would provide assistance in removing the carcasses of any wolves trapped.[34]

During the second week of this campaign Allen caught "two of them big devils." After dispatching them and placing them in a secure place, he hiked the eight miles to town and called the wardens. About two days later, upon returning after a full day in the woods, he found the two wardens waiting for him in his cabin. One of the gentlemen insisted that they get the wolves yet that day. Allen remonstrated, "Do you know how far down in there they are? From here it's about six miles, it's getting late, and it's going to get dark before we get outta there. It's a job draggin' them things." The warden remained firm. Allen shrugged his shoulders, grabbed his cap and coat, and said "OK, I'm a younger man than you guys and if you can stand it, I can."

The trio found the two dead wolves and began the grueling task of bringing them out. Allen dragged one and the wardens handled the other, one pulling while the other pushed with the aid of a forked stick. The physical strain was having an effect on Allen. Exerting every muscle, enduring the pain, Allen kept running one thought through his mind, "I'm young and in shape. I CAN TAKE IT." It seemed that every time he got to the top of a hill the two wardens hadn't even reached the bottom of the last one yet.

In this manner the procession advanced—the moon coming up, colder than heck, and the two wardens getting farther and farther behind. Finally when they were within two miles of the cabin Allen turned around, found the wardens, and said, "You guys are getting tired, I know you are. You were tired when we started. Leave them here and I'll come and get them the rest of the way."

The three cached the wolves and began the last leg of the journey back to the cabin. On their return Allen and the two wardens struck up a conversation. After some distance Allen realized that the older warden wasn't answering. "What the hell happened to Barney?" Repeated yells brought no replies, and Allen was forced to make his way back, thinking the old coot had keeled over from a heart attack. He found the old warden sitting on a log.

"Oh, Jesus. I'll never make her."

"Jeez . . . Barney, you've got to make her. I can't carry ya'. You sit here, you'll freeze to death!"

"I'll never make it. I'm just pooped right out."

"I know—I tried to tell you. You know the old saying 'There's no fool like an old fool,' and I believe that's what you are!"

Allen grabbed him by the arm, and in that manner the two made it back to the cabin. Going inside, Allen ordered the warden to take his boots off and get to bed. The old man had the audacity to say, "Oh no. I've got to go to town tonight."

That was the last straw. Allen snapped at him, "What the hell's the matter with you—you crazy? I'm going to be the boss now. You get them boots off and get into bed."

The other warden was supportive. "Step on him. He doesn't know when he's had enough."

Allen watched over Barney while he took off his boots. When Barney removed his stockings, Allen noticed that the skin of his toes lying beneath his snowshoe straps came off with them. Allen didn't say anything, and the old warden didn't seem to be aware of it.

Years later Allen found out just how costly that night's adventure had been. Warden Barney Lindgren's injury never healed. Shortly after, he was diagnosed as diabetic, his gangrenous foot and leg had to be removed, and he died soon thereafter.

Wolf trapping attracted independent people who tolerated rugged conditions and loved the challenge of adventure. The rugged life of 1840s-vintage Green County along the Illinois border appealed to Rueben Fulsom. A century later that same sense of adventure lured men like George Ruegger, Walt Rosenlaf, Clarence Allen, Billy Bay, and many others into the wilds of northern Wisconsin and Upper Michigan to do their part in extending civilization up to and beyond the shores of Lake Superior. Their experiences were many and varied, as time and circumstances dictated. What made them different from all others was their thrill of pursuit and the challenge to catch another wolf.

5

The Bounty in
Wisconsin and Michigan

The old Chevy pickup pulled into the parking lot behind the 1930s-vintage Wisconsin Conservation Department ranger station. Two men dressed in suspendered wool pants, flannel shirts, and mackinaw jackets got out. One went to the office door while the other stood by the tailgate peering intently at some objects in the bed of the truck.[1]

A few minutes later the fellow emerged from the ranger station with the local conservation warden, who was carrying a clipboard on which were attached some official-looking papers. Warden McKeague looked in at the cargo in the pickup, then dropped his cigarette butt on the ground and crushed it with the heel of his high-laced, black boot. "Where'd yah get 'em?" The driver replied, "Over toward the Willow between the Spring and the Kaubashine. One's a dandy. Made quite a fuss trying to git outta the trap. Ripped up quite a swath through the alders, but the chain held him secure once he wrapped hizself up in a clump o' downed spruce."

The two men dropped the tailgate. The warden leaned over and, while the three separated the carcasses of the wolves from the three coyotes, Charlie Gustafson offered, "That's a mighty big one there. You got a scale? I bet he's over a hundred. Other one's no doubt a pup-o'-the-year. Scrawny thing but still's bigger'n these here coyotes. Damnedest thing. Caught two coyotes and this pup within a hundred rods all on the same night."

Warden McKeague unsheathed his buck knife from the leather case on his belt and laid it down next to the carcasses. Each wolf and coyote was turned over on its back and the inside of the back leg was slit from groin to hock. Next a series of holes was punched in the ears of each wolf and coyote using leather-punch pliers. Picking up the clipboard, the warden scribbled down some notes and then asked the fellows in to complete the forms.

"Did ya catch all of 'em in roughly the same section?" McKeague asked. Gustafson replied, "Two coyotes and the pup were up on section 13 on the pine ridge south of where the Kaubashine empties into the Tomahawk. The other coyote hit on a set over near Smith Lake in section 5. The big timber we caught night before last between Spring and Swamsauger Creek. Near as I can tell it was somewhere around section 25." The warden jotted the information down on each of the forms, then concluded, "O' course you boys are familiar with this formality. Jes' sign here and in about 30 days you should be getting your $90 in the mail from Madison." The two fellows signed for their money on their respective bounty affidavits, immediately below the fine print that read in part: . . . *I have not spared the life of any wildcat or wolf in my power to kill.* . . .[2]

The word *bounty* is defined as a reward or premium, especially one given by a government for killing certain animals. The first wolf bounty law in the United States was adopted by colonial Massachusetts in 1630. Politicians were quick to learn the influence bounty laws had on their livelihoods. It is no surprise then, as biologist Stanley Young put it, that "in no other country have laws for the riddance of wolves passed in such numbers or amended so frequently."[3] The various statutes and amendments pertaining to Wisconsin's own bounty system provide a veritable nightmare for the legal historian attempting to make sense of this rich effluent of legislation.

It is impossible to give a detailed historical account of the Wisconsin and Michigan bounty systems, because the statutes pertaining to bounties were generally divided among several provisions and were subject to the vagaries of political appropriations. Conflicting statutes, repeals (sometimes occurring twice in one legislative session), and poor record keeping add to the difficulty of making sense of this political football. As with most other states, bounties existed at several different levels in Wisconsin and Michigan, and often times simultaneously. At any one time there may have been township bounties, county-financed bounties, and state bounties. In addition, occasionally groups of individuals would support private bounties through subscription.

One such example comes from Waukesha County's town of Summit. In the post–Civil War depression year of 1868 sheep farmers there were plagued with problems, and wolves were implicated as the culprits. "No sooner was this discovered, than a subscription was taken, and a bounty of $100 per wolf was offered for every wolf killed in the town; and very soon after a permanent bounty of $50 was voted by the town, and an additional bounty of $25 was offered by the county."[4] Thus $175 could be collected in bounties for each wolf killed within the town of Summit.

Multiple bounties were levied on wolves right on up to the end of the bounty era. In the 1950s in Michigan's Chippewa County a five dollar bounty was paid by Hulbert Township and another five dollars was offered by a local hunting club in addition to the state bounty.[5]

The Wisconsin Bounty System

1835–1957

So far as can be determined, the first bounty offered on Wisconsin soil was passed by the territorial government in 1839, offering a three dollar bounty on wolves. A year before statehood, in January 1847, the Waukesha County board declared that a "bounty on wolf-scalps of every description, should be and the same is hereby fixed at, three dollars each."[6] That October the same county board increased the bounty to five dollars a scalp.[7]

Wisconsin became a state in 1848, but it wasn't until 1865 that the first bounty was enacted by the state legislature. Presumably, township- and county-financed bounties were in vogue before that time.

Wolf depredation upon settlers' livestock during the 1830s and 1840s undoubtedly precipitated government-supported bounties, as the following narrative demonstrates: "The wolves continued to annoy the people of Madison very greatly, until we petitioned the county authorities to pass a note affixing a bounty on their scalps. The Board of Commissioners finally yielded to this request, and established a bounty."[8]

Wolf depredations on livestock diminished gradually as these animals were eliminated from the farming regions. By the early 1930s wolves were restricted to only a handful of localities in the northern portion of the state, and their effect on farmers' stock further declined when these marginal farms were abandoned. During this time justification of the bounty system focused on the issue of saving the deer from the menace of wolves, thereby assuring that more deer would be where they properly belonged—before the sights of sportsmen's guns (see chapter 6).

Cost to Taxpayers

Bounties have long been labeled government give-away programs. It is impossible to determine how many taxpayers' dollars were spent on various township, county, and state bounty laws in existence between 1848, when Wisconsin became a state, and 1957, when the timber wolf bounty was removed. On the state level alone, records surviving to the present day do not, for the most part, differentiate the amounts spent on fox, bobcat, lynx, coyote, and wolf, but include all in one lump sum (figure 5.1). Betwen 1865 and 1944 the burden of the bounty system to state taxpayers was $2,332,440. During the next nine years, 1945 through 1953, the amount was fully half that which was spent in the previous 75 years, $1,100,217.50, of which $522,640 were paid on coyotes and wolves.[9]

Although bounty payments were the same for coyotes and wolves, the amount paid per animal varied by year (figure 5.2). Before 1880 the state

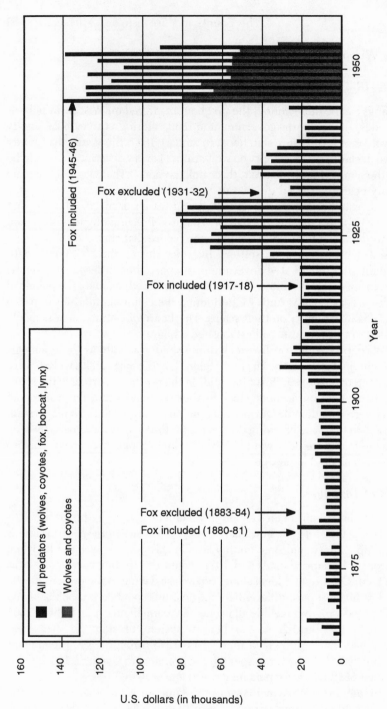

Figure 5.1. Bounty costs in Wisconsin, per year, 1865–1957

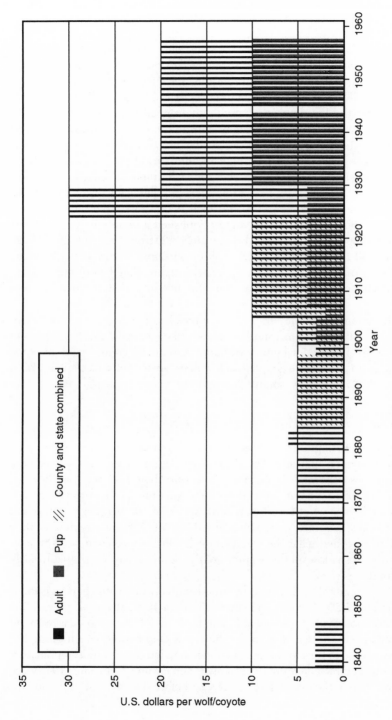

Figure 5.2. Bounty amounts paid per wolf or coyote in Wisconsin, per year, 1839–1957

65

paid a $5 bounty, except during 1868–69, when they offered $10. In 1880–81 the legislature again allotted $5 per wolf or coyote but increased it briefly to $6 between 1881 and 1883. From 1883 through 1897 the bounty was $5. Between 1898 and 1901 the bounty dropped to $3 per wolf or coyote.

In 1901 the legislature initiated a differential bounty, separating pups from adults. By statutory law young-of-the-year were legally declared pups from "the 1st day of March to the 1st day of November." This period was later shortened to March 1 through September 1 (1940s and 1950s), allowing pups to be claimed adults earlier each fall (trapping peaked in October; see chapter 8). The state paid $3 for each pup between 1901 and 1904; $2 from 1905 to 1906; $4 from 1907 through 1929; and $10 per pup from 1930 through 1956. For adults the state established a bounty of $5 from 1901 through 1904; $10 from 1905 through 1922; $30 from 1923 to 1929; and $20 from 1930 through 1956. During all or portions of four particular years (1868, 1879, 1943–44, 1953), the state failed to establish or appropriate funds for bounties. (See the section "Bounty Repeals in Wisconsin," below).

The amount of money spent for bounties by the individual counties undoubtedly fluctuated in a similar manner. Between 1883 and 1922 the state legislature honored a bounty payment only if the county paid an equal amount. In 1895, for example, each wolf or coyote netted a claimant $5 in state and $5 in county bounty (figure 5.2).

Numbers of Wolves and Coyotes Destroyed

Records were kept on the numbers of wolves and coyotes bountied in Wisconsin between 1930 and 1960. Unfortunately, no distinctions between the two species were made by officials who verified bounty claims, but between 1947 and 1956 a separate list of the numbers of timber wolves was prepared. It is not known whether officials verifying claims were asked to determine the species, whether some volunteered the information, or whether they merely recorded what the claimant declared the species to be. Although this casts a shadow on the accuracy of the figures, they are probably fairly accurate.

The number of these canids bountied annually fluctuated between about 1,000 and 2,200 before 1943 (figure 5.3). In 1935, the peak year, 2,324 wolves and coyotes were taken. The peak may have been caused by an abundance of these canids, or by the Great Depression, which prompted many people to turn to trapping to obtain needed cash, or by a combination of these factors. The numbers of wolves and coyotes taken after 1945 were almost double the take in an average year before the outbreak of World War

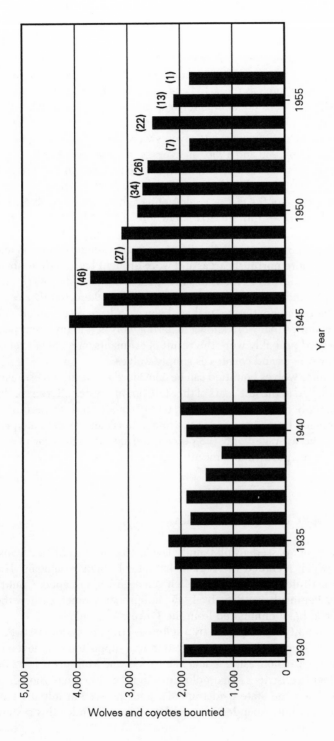

Figure 5.3. Number of coyotes and wolves bountied in Wisconsin, per year, 1930–57
Note: The numbers in parentheses represent the numbers of known timber wolves bountied in that year. These numbers correspond to Table E.2, the "total take" column.

II. A sudden surge in the number of unemployed, composed largely of discharged servicemen, may have accounted for some high bounty years in the postwar period, such as the 4,134 claims processed in the nine-month season of 1945, but does not adequately explain continued high takes that persisted until 1953, when bounty claims returned to pre–World War II levels. A total of 54,743 wolves and coyotes were destroyed for bounty in Wisconsin between 1930 and 1956, an average of 2,105 per year.[10]

In the eight years between 1947 and 1956 state bounty claims were processed on 176 "timber wolves." These figures have to be closely scrutinized, because some of the claims could not have been timber wolves. For instance, timber wolves did not exist anywhere close to five counties that claimed to have bountied 13 of these animals (Chippewa, 4; Juneau, 1; Polk, 3; Portage, 2; and Shawano, 3). Possibly they were killed by hunters and trappers in the more northerly areas and were brought back to their home counties before claims were filed, despite the fact that bounties were supposed to be claimed in the county the animals were taken. In other cases the list did not contain timber wolves known to have been killed and bountied in counties that were known to harbor wolves.[11] Many discrepancies in the record probably were the result of claimants and officials referring to timber wolves and coyotes as simply wolves.

The 176 timber wolves bountied can be considered a maximum estimate of the wolves taken in the last years of the state bounty system. Even so, the proportion of timber wolves in the annual take of coyotes and wolves during that period ranged from 1 percent of the total in 1947 and 1950 to 0.4 percent in 1953, and averaged only 0.8 percent during the eight-year period between 1947 and 1956, when some attempt was made to segregate the two species.

Michigan Upper Peninsula Bounties

The U.S. Congress passed a wolf bounty law in 1817 in the old Northwest Territories, which included the region that later became Michigan. The first bounty instituted by the state of Michigan occurred in Lapeer County in the Lower Peninsula in 1838. By 1935, and probably much earlier, the timber wolf had been eliminated from the Lower Peninsula.[12]

Michigan's bounty was replaced by a state-paid trapper system between 1922 and 1935. This predator control system was supported by a levee of $15 from every $50 of nonresident deer license fees and $1 from every $2.50 of resident deer license fees. An employee of the U.S. Bureau of Biological Survey supervised the state-paid trappers, and the system initially employed 3 trappers but expanded to 26 in later years.[13] Under this system

7,663 coyotes and 855 wolves were destroyed. The total cost of the state-paid trapper system was $538,542.52, or and average of $63.22 for each animal killed.

On January 1, 1935, the trapper system was replaced by a new bounty law, which remained in effect until 1960. From 1937 to 1959 female wolves brought in $20 apiece, and males were worth $15. During this period 707 wolves and 111,569 coyotes were destroyed at a cost of $11,375 and $1,899,280, respectively. Each wolf killed cost $16.10 and each coyote cost $17. The total cost to state taxpayers from 1935 to 1960 was $2,449,197.50.[14]

The proportion of wolves in the total take differed greatly under the two systems. During the state-paid trapper era 10 percent of the animals destroyed were wolves, whereas only 0.7 percent were wolves following restoration of the bounty in 1935. The latter percentage calculates to a ratio similar to the one observed for the two canids in Wisconsin between 1947 and 1956. Trappers were instructed to focus their efforts on wolves under the state-paid trapper system, hence the greater proportion of wolves in the take relative to the bounty era. (see chapter 6).

Fraud

Just as quickly as bounties were adopted, schemes were developed by enterprising citizens to bilk the coffers of the bounty system. Fraudulent practices plagued every bounty system ever devised by lawmakers.

The first Waukesha County bounty established in January 1847 was not without its problems. "This resolution brought many a dollar to the pockets of sharp hunters, as the county paid nearly as much for dog scalps as for wolf scalps. It requires a keen man to discover the difference between a wolf scalp and the scalp of a pup."[15] Many an unscrupulous character used this time-tested weakness in the bounty system to defraud taxpayers' dollars, right up to the glorious end of the bounty era. Claiming dog remains as a wolf's was the oldest trick in the book, and one of the easiest to get away with too.

Usually high bounties were an open invitation to swindlers. The 1868 composite bounty of Waukesha County and the Town of Summit, established through private subscription, township, and county action, offered $175 for each wolf killed.

No sooner had this bounty become a settled thing, than hunting wolves became a good business, and forthwith, several men went at the work of extermination . . . Very soon after this the wolves in Summit were *non est.*, but the hunters were equal to the emergency. Therefore, wolves were hunted from adjoining localities, and chased into Summit to be killed. One in particular was

worried and hunted, for several hours, back and forth between Summit and
Ottawa [townships] . . . until finally, he was shot in Ottawa, and dragged over
into Summit to die.[16]

The bounty system was plagued with problems of fraudulent activities,
and like most other government "give-away programs," lawmakers were
utterly helpless in combatting the onslaught of such illegal activities, try as
they might, and try they did on numerous occasions. The bounty was extremely popular, because it ostensibly supported a noble cause which, to
the public, was akin to mother, country, and apple-pie. If there ever were
anything a politician is allergic to, it is adverse public sentiment. The legislature's ineptness in dealing with bounty problems stemmed from an inabil-
ity to take a unified stance on the issue confronting them. All too many of
the body's members were more concerned with appeasing public sentiments. The result was a patchwork bounty system and an endless game of
charades between the state's lawmakers (at the township, county, and state
levels) and those enticed to make a buck the dishonest way.

Perhaps the most ludicrous example of political absurdities was a case
where a suspicious county clerk submitted a scalp to the secretary of state
for closer scrutiny. "It was the scalp of a dog and no more resembled a wolf
than a poodle resembles a St. Bernard." The secretary refused to process
the claim and advised the county clerk to do likewise. After some little
"investigation" the county board adopted a resolution declaring the animal
a wolf and instructed the County Clerk to pay the county bounty.[17]

The Wisconsin State statutes generally specified the procedures to follow
in applying for bounty claims. The step-by-step provisions specified what
body parts were necessary to be exhibited as proof, and spelled out limitations in the time that could elapse between the death of the beast and the
filing of the claim. It also specified to which government official the beast
had to be presented for verification, and what steps that official must take to
mark the beast against repeat presentations.

Throughout the history of the bounty the claimant had to take an oath
that he had not spared the life of any predator within his power to kill.
Taking a sworn oath did not deter some from falsifying information. Not
surprisingly, by 1878 state newspapers carried statements such as: "The
wolf harvest has been quite plentiful this season and the lucky hunters are
correspondingly happy. *Professionals seldom kill the female*" (emphasis
added).[18] The craftier hunters knew that each female that bred produced on
average five or six more wolves to be bountied.

In early February 1879 newspaper correspondents reported on a new
twist in "farming" wolves. On February 13, 1879, the *Beloit Free Press* remarked, under the title "Wolf Culture": "Senator Bailey . . . instructed that

the state should look into whether or not people are raising wolves. . . . Another individual has been cornered down to a disclosure of his occupation in wolf raising within a few miles of the capitol city."

Another article, which appeared in the *Evansville Weekly Review* on February 19, 1879, stated: "Wolf raising in Wisconsin is becoming quite an enterprise. . . . Various parties are engaged in the business and succeed in making it quite profitable for the amount invested." For some people the sworn oaths did not stand in the way of making money. Farming wolves for bounty provided a healthy income.

One of the easiest ways to defraud the state was to present animals for bounty that were not in fact wolves or other bountied species. In order to accomplish such masquerades, unscrupulous individuals needed to work around two provisions of the bounty law. These dealt with the parts of the body that were required to be presented as proof, and the length of time that was allowed between the time of death and when body parts were no longer acceptable for presentation. The second provision was, of course, entirely dependant upon information supplied by the claimant under oath. There was no real way to verify on which date an animal had died.

Guidelines for these two provisions were fairly lenient (in favor of the claimant) early in the history of bounty laws in the state of Wisconsin. However, as time progressed and more improprieties were uncovered, these clauses became stricter. The 1865 law provided a 20-day grace period between killing and filing the animal's ears and scalp for claim. In early 1866 some honest citizen was denied a claim because on the bounty affidavit he reported that more than 20 days had elapsed since killing the wolf. The *Janesville Daily Gazette* in mentioning this incident stated, "It is urged by many that the clause in the statutes giving only twenty days to report should be repealed."[19]

The time limits had to compromise between the constraints that were most practical for people to abide by and sufficient strictness to guard against the possibilities of defrauding the system. Understandably the crude methods of transportation in that day made it difficult to file bounty claims expediently. Up until at least 1870 people had to come to the county seat to file claims with the county clerk or circuit court.[20] But the passing of time also increased the possibilities of fraudulent activity. For instance, an enterprising citizen could kill a dog that did not even remotely resemble its wild cousin, but with time and the help of the sun and flies, especially in the summer months, any county clerk who wished to keep his or her appetite would gladly verify the claim of a scalp or carcass well along in putrefaction with only the slightest inspection.

Citizen unrest over the 1866 claim denial may have prompted the state legislature to lengthen the time allotment. Under provisions of Chapter 138 of the Laws of 1870, a person had 30 days to present the scalp with ears attached to the county clerk. By 1878 the law was as lenient as it would ever be, allowing 60 days to process claims, much to the chagrin of county and state officials who were given the task of verifying claims. By 1907 a person had only six days to apply for bounty. However, between around 1917 and 1921, under an elaborate certification process, a person had six days to deliver the entire carcass to the town chairman, but had an additional 20 days to have it certified by the county clerk. After 1923 the grace period was six days and the entire carcass had to be presented to either the county clerk or a game warden (see 5.1).

One of the bounty provisions described the portions of an animal needed to verify a claim and what officials had to do to prevent those portions from being resubmitted. According to 1870 and 1883 statutes the scalp and "ears entire" were necessary, and upon inspection the official was supposed to destroy it. The 1907 statutes specified that the "scalp of said animal with both ears and both upper eyelids entire" had to be presented to the town chairman within six days between 8:00 A.M. and 5:00 P.M., and then to the county clerk or register of deeds within 30 days. The scalp was then destroyed in the presence of three people. Under the 1917 provisions a person needed to present the entire skin with skull attached at the nose in a "well-preserved condition." If the clerk or register of deeds could not identify the specimen they were to send it to the Wisconsin Conservation Commission, who would make the decision. Upon determination the skin was sent back and the skull was supposed to be destroyed or deposited in "some scientific museum." The county clerk had to remove and destroy the skull and slit the scalp, not less than six inches, between the ears.

In 1921 people filing claims had to exhibit the entire carcass within eight days to the town chairman, who would punch three holes through the right ear, "not less than one-eighth inch in diameter." Within 20 days the person had to deliver the town chairman's certificate and the hide to the county clerk, who would complete the paperwork and punch three holes in the left ear. By the late 1940s any person filing a claim had to exhibit the entire carcass with hide attached to the county clerk or game warden, who would punch both ears and slit the inside of the right leg.

L. B. Nagler, the chief clerk in the secretary of state's office, who had charge of bounty claims, described some of the major weaknesses of the bounty law and gave an account of some of the fraudulent cases he had witnessed in an article that appeared in *LaFollette's Weekly* in March of 1913. He stated that the law mandated the county clerks to "pass final judgment on bounty claims but does not compel the hunter to exhibit more than the scalp. Identification in this manner is not certain." He went on to say:

5.1. In order to claim a bounty, trappers were required to present the *whole carcass* to the county clerk or game warden, making it necessary to carry each timber wolf carcass out of the brush. (Photograph courtesy State Historical Society of Wisconsin, neg. WHi [X2] 15560.)

Perhaps not one person in fifty has ever seen a live wolf and not one in a thousand can distinguish the scalp of a wolf from that of a dog or a fox. I once presented the scalp of a red fox (*Vulpes fulvus*) to an experienced woodsman and hunter who pronounced it a "Black-tip wolf"; and he admitted that, as town chairman, he had issued certificates for bounty on many of them.

The "black-tip wolf" is a nature fake. "Wolves" with black-tipped ears are red foxes.

A consignment of thirteen scalps on which a hunter claimed bounty for three mature wolves and ten pups, amounting to $140, was received by the secretary of state in July, 1911, and identified as one young coyote, two young red foxes, one black squirrel, one fox squirrel, and eight gray squirrels. The scalps were in an advanced state of decomposition—a common trick to prevent, or at least discourage, the rough examination. Herein lies another weakness of the Wisconsin law, namely, the time limit in which claims for bounty may be presented. . . . It is an outrage to require an official to make a critical examination of a six-day-carcass or a thirty-day-old scalp in midsummer.[21]

Nagler reported that, in still another ingenious scheme, an Indian from Jackson County killed a wolf and proceeded to turn the entire hide into a series of scalps, collecting the bounty on each of the manufactured assortments. A subsequent investigation uncovered the fraud in two similar cases.[22]

On some occasions town chairman and county clerks were tempted into joining forces with unscrupulous citizens, and in this manner bilked the bounty coffers, splitting their profits. Early in the history of Wisconsin's bounty law the legislature realized that such temptations created a dangerous weakness in the system, and they enacted provisions for penalizing those caught in such ventures of collusion. For instance the 1870 statutes provided a penalty of one to three years. In 1898 the sentence was reduced to one year and a fine of $500. This remained essentially the same in the 1925 statutes. The most typical form of such conspiracy involved recycling dead animals wherein the official conveniently forgot to destroy or mark the scalps or carcasses and falsified records to obscure fraudulent activity. Nagler reported:

A man in a northern county received a certificate from a town chairman for one wolf and one wildcat. He changed the figures to read "12 wolves and 10 wildcats" and collected $300 bounty. In this case the county clerk was also implicated. He certified that he had examined and destroyed 22 scalps. The clerk emigrated to Central America and the hunter spent a two-year vacation at Waupun.[23]

In regard to another case Nagler stated:

In 1906 the county of Jackson allowed $7,780 for wolf bounty on 389 mature animals. The next year, under the administration of an efficient county clerk, over 300 fraudulent claims were rejected, only 67 were genuine, indicating that about $6,000 was collected on fraudulent claims in one year in Jackson County alone.[24]

In the latter years of the bounty, problems in verifying animals were limited primarily to pups, and occasionally to dogs that resembled adult wolves and coyotes. Wisconsin Conservation Department employee George Fleming, having participated in the capture of several wild wolves for the Poynette Game Farm (see chapter 4), complained that many a police dog was ignorantly passed off as a wolf on bounty affidavits.[25] The problem was considered large enough to warrant the 1948 Pittman-Robertson–funded cursory investigation of police dog, wolf, and coyote back hairs to learn if any distinguishing characteristics existed. "Bounties have been paid on police dogs, and large coyotes have often been classed as timber wolves. . . ." The conclusion of the small study was not promising: "It was hoped that some structural difference might exist in the hairs of each species, but none was found."[26]

The hair study was probably the first and only serious attempt made by the department to find a method of distinguishing between dogs, wolves, and coyotes. Nearly 15 years earlier the department had issued a strange news release on the topic of differentiating between dog and wolf pups:

> Its not always easy to distinguish between dog and wolf pups, according to conservation department authorities, but definitely its not true that the former lap water like cats, and the wolf pups drink water in the same manner as horses.
>
> Instead, young of both species lap water, except that wolves tend to lap more slowly, and to take more water at each lap.[27]

But, of course, this little gem of wisdom wasn't of much help to officials looking at a squirming pile of dehydrated puppies or, worse yet, their rotting corpses, when they attempted to learn whether they were being duped.

In early April 1953, a citizen presented Oneida county clerk Lloyd Verage some puppies for bounty, claiming they were coyotes. The clerk handed them over to warden Harley McKeague for identification. McKeague, in turn, handed them to game manager Cliff Germain, who had no little task in solving the problem. "We have a good library of books here which I thought would solve the problem, but they helped only a little. Textbooks give many . . . characteristics to aid in identifying, but they refer mainly to adult animals." He felt that the ear shape, uniform coloration, and pelage pattern indicated they were coyote pups, but added:

> To cinch this case, I asked Bill Waggoner, the warden supervisor in this area, to give us his opinion. Boys at the Trout Lake area often bring in coyote pups in the spring up there. He said these look just like all the coyote pups he has seen.

In view of the above, unless we had some good reason to believe that someone was trying to dupe us, we must conclude they are coyotes.[28]

An example of one of the more perplexing vexations to confront officials occurred in May 1937.

> County clerk George E. Costello and conservation warden Arthur Baie of Marinette county, were confronted with the question, "when is a wolf cub not a wolf cub?" Harry Chapman, town of Niagara, brought in a wolf for which he had filed a bounty claim. The wolf had a litter of five unborn cubs. The question was whether or not Chapman was entitled to the $10 bounty on each of these pups.
>
> The statutes were consulted but they aided little in solving the matter. The Chief Warden was consulted in Madison via long distance telephone. He ruled that Chapman had $70 in bounty coming, the usual $20 for the wolf, and $10 each for the cubs.[29]

Use of Poisons

Strychnine, a toxic substance extracted from the seed of a tropical tree, was probably the only poison to come into widespread use in Wisconsin. By 1860 it was an extremely popular poison used by professional "wolfers" on the North American plains to secure winter peltries. The first American firm to manufacture the poison was Rosengarten and Denis of Philadelphia in 1834.[30] Poison was used primarily to curtail depredations on livestock, and minimally to secure pelts for sale in the fur trade.

The first mention of poison as an aid in eliminating wolves in Wisconsin comes from the town of Madison during the late 1830s or early 1840s. It seems William Lawrence found steel traps an encumbrance in ridding the locality of the irritating prairie wolves, so he resorted to the use of poison. "By a skillful distribution of strychnine, he succeeded in soon bringing in a large number of scalps, and leaving a large number of their carcasses on the townsite, and in this manner a quietus on their further depredations and annoyances."[31]

The following scene took place on a farm in the town of Bridge Creek in Eau Claire County in early March of 1861:

> Early in the evening, Mrs. Higgins heard an unusual noise in the calf pen, and upon going out found something like a dozen wolves contemplating an attack upon the calf. Upon her approach, they retreated a short distance. Mrs. Higgins is a good shot with a rifle and she first determined to shoot at least one of the intruders with her husband's loaded rifle; but upon reflection she con-

cluded to put strychnine upon some meat she had in the house and give it to her unwelcome visitors. She did so and upon the return of her husband, who was absent the forepart of the evening, he found twelve wolves lying dead within a few rods of the house. [32]

Poison was occasionally used as an aid in obtaining quantities of furs for the fur trade. However, by the time strychnine came into widespread use the fur trade was declining in Wisconsin, and wolf pelts had a relatively low market value. Nonetheless, a few "trapper" entrepreneurs used poison. One Luke Wright was using strychnine to obtain wolf pelts for the fur trade on the Black River drainage before 1866. "He would take the 'pluck,' heart, liver and lungs, of a deer, and sprinkle them freely with strychnine. This would be scattered around where wolves were likely to roam. This result was a plentiful supply of wolf pelts, with a minimum of labor." [33]

Around the turn of the century Albert Nemmick used strychnine in the Delta area of western Bayfield County. The numerous logging camps provided him with a steady supply of worn out or injured horses, which he would pick up, dispatch, cut up, and lace with the poison for distribution along his trapline. In this manner he obtained wolf pelts, although he claimed he lost twice the amount he secured because many managed to crawl off before dying. [34]

Perhaps the most insidious side effect of strychnine was its ability to cause secondary poisoning, especially through plants upon which afflicted animals drooled in their death throes. On the Great Plains this poison retained its deadly property for years and killed many an unsuspecting buffalo, antelope, and pony, raising the ire of the plains Indians. [35] Such problems were not unique to animals, nor were they restricted to the prairie regions. The following clipping appeared in the March 22, 1860, issue of the *Eau Claire Free Press:*

> J. C. Thomas, familiarly known as "Blue Tom" died on Friday at Rose's logging camp, Little Falls, on the Chippewa River, from the effects of eating of parsnips taken from the garden where strychnine had been thrown for the purpose of poisoning foxes and wolves. He got up from the dinner table after partaking of them and in less than half an hour was a corpse. Another man by the name of Multy came near dying from the same cause.

Laws governing the use of poison were adopted only one year after the first state bounty was instituted. Chapter 45 of the Laws of 1866 restricted the use of poison for wolves and wildcats from January 10 to February 20. In 1871, for some unknown reason, the Chapter 45 poison provisions were repealed. Chapter 19 of the Laws of 1875 allowed the use of poison for wolves and wildcats from November 10 to December 20 but required public notification of the intent to use poisons. Beginning in 1879 and appearing at least through 1883, state law specified that public notice must be posted in three locations in each township identifying the locations and dates for each bait placed out. It further specified that no baits were to be placed closer than 80 rods from a house. The season ran from November 10 through February 20, and each individual had three additional days to remove baits. The provision also stipulated that users of poison were legally responsible for damages caused. Between 1899 and at least 1901 the season was extended to March 1 with the usual three days to pick up baits; but no other restrictions were noted. The 1905 statutes do not mention poison. The last year in which poisons were mentioned was 1917. That year the season lasted from December 1 to March 1. Notices like those in place in 1879 were necessary, and the restriction of 80 rods from habitation was in force.

The reason for eliminating the use of poisons remains obscure, but in light of the serious attempts by the legislature to regulate its use from earliest times, it is certain that poisons were ultimately considered a public health hazard too lethal to remain a legally sanctioned device for use in destroying what were considered noxious animals.

Bounty Repeals in Wisconsin

During the 92-year span of state-sponsored wolf bounties in Wisconsin, only four major bounty repeals totaling four years (not including the final repeal in 1957) were instituted by the state legislature and/or administration. For unknown reasons bounty bills were not enacted nor were appropriations made in 1869 and for a few short months in 1953. In the latter case a special legislative session recreated a bounty bill which passed over the veto of the governor, indicating that a good deal of pro-bounty lobbying took place.

The critical newspaper expose of fraudulent activities associated with the Wisconsin bounty system in early 1879 was obviously the leading cause for the March 5th repeal that year. State lawmakers, quick to forget and undoubtedly yielding to public pressure, reenacted a similar bounty bill within one year.

In 1943 the annual bounty bill was not enacted by the state legislature, but its members inevitably acquiesced under nearly constant pressure, and in March of 1945 the bounty was reinstated with the consent of Wisconsin Conservation Department officials, including noted ecologist Aldo Leopold. Twelve years later, on June 6, 1957, the Wisconsin wolf bounty was finally, and permanently, repealed (see chapter 6 for additional details).

Bounty Repeals in Michigan

Several times bounties were repealed during the history of the wolf bounty in Michigan. In 1921 the bounty system was repealed and replaced by a state-paid trapper system administered by the U.S. Bureau of Biological Survey until 1935. A similar program initiated in Wisconsin in 1930 failed miserably (see chapter 6).

During the mid-1940s several nationally recognized wildlife authorities began voicing concern over the loss of big predators such as wolves and over the wisdom in bountying the remaining populations in the upper Midwest into extinction. Opposition to bounty repeals was intense in Michigan, as elsewhere. In an effort to sidestep controversial bounty repeals the establishment of "wolf refuges" was suggested as a manner of preserving populations of wolves.

Early in 1947 the Detroit Sportsmen's Congress proposed establishing a wolf sanctuary in Porcupine Mountains Wilderness State Park, a massive, rugged escarpment along the Lake Superior shoreline in the northwest corner of the Upper Peninsula. In response, Michigan Conservation Department Game Division chief Harry Ruhl pointed out that such a sanctuary would be inconsistent with the state bounty. He further mentioned that plans were afoot to open state parks to hunting and trapping, and such a sanctuary would complicate policy.[36]

The move to establish a wolf sanctuary in the Porcupine Mountains surfaced again in January 1948.[37] Opposition to the proposal began to solidify. By April various Upper Peninsula sportsmen's groups were issuing public statements against the Porcupine Mountain wolf sanctuary. The Blue Lakes Sportsmen's Club, based in Houghton, issued their stance:

> Members believe . . . the great potential tourist rendezvous of the Porcupine Mountains country would be virtually a no-man's land.
>
> . . .
>
> Blue Lakes' members believe the Porcupines to be a virtual museum of copper and silver mining history; and ornithological paradise; a rendezvous for many of the most highly desirable forms of mammalian life in the state. They do not, however, want to see it become a wolf's stamping ground.[38]

In March of 1949 an internal review of the situation was summarized for Game Division chief, Harry Ruhl. The report's summary read, "So long as wilderness areas such as the Porcupine Mountain State Park exist in Michigan the wolf will be with us too."[39]* Apparently the department chose not to

---

*Several people questioned whether wolves yet remained in the Porcupines by the late 1940s. Long-time trapper Clarence Allen felt they had been largely eliminated from that area by the late 1930s.[40]

support active efforts to preserve the wolf in the Porcupines (and elsewhere in the Upper Peninsula), and left the species to its own devices. To be sure, in 1960 the Porcupine Mountains "wilderness" was still around, but the wolf was not. Proponents of the wolf sanctuary turned their energies instead towards Isle Royale National Park.

In the meantime, Lee Smits, an influential executive at ABC in Detroit, informed Game Division chief Harry Ruhl in April 1948 that he intended to seek a resolution from the Michigan United Conservation Clubs to remove the bounty on timber wolves. As a peace offering, Smits wanted to know if the Michigan Conservation Department would be willing to supply qualified employees to respond to depredation complaints. Ruhl warned that regardless of any peace offerings Smits was likely to meet with considerable opposition to his plan.[41]

During the early 1950s several outside organizations pressured the conservation departments in Michigan, Wisconsin, and Minnesota into removing bounties on wolves. In 1950 the American Society of Mammalogists adopted a resolution informing the three states of their concern over the lack of protection for the eastern timber wolf. They urged the three states to abolish den hunting and destruction of young wolves. Michigan Game Division chief Ruhl responded by mentioning that wolves were highly controversial animals, but informed the society that he had passed their resolution on to the Michigan Conservation Commission. Internally, Ruhl sent a cover memo with the resolution to Secretary of the Michigan Conservation Commission W. O. Osgood, stating that the resolution should be presented to the commission "on an informational basis." He pointed out, once again, that this was a legislative matter and that it was inconsistent to pay a bounty and not have den hunting.[42]

In early 1951 the Michigan Conservation Department once again received a petition, this time from the Michigan Academy of Science, Arts, and Letters, urging that the department develop a plan to ensure the preservation of the timber wolf, recognizing that the estimated five wolf families in the Upper Peninsula were in great danger of extirpation. Game Division chief Ruhl responded that he did not object to the resolution (though he did take exception to the notion that there were only five families, which he took to mean pairs, remaining in the state). He drafted a letter asking that the academy take the lead in efforts to remove the bounty, because the department was in an awkward position of being in support of the legislatively mandated state bounty. It was suggested that public education could be a tool "to overcome the present feeling against the timber wolf."[43]

In 1952 the Michigan Conservation Department prepared a report for the commissioners reviewing the state's bounties. The report stressed that the near extinction of timber wolves was not caused by the bounty. "The disappearance of large tracts of wilderness areas has been responsible more than anything else for the disappearance of the wolf."[44] Biologists of that day neglected to see that a major benefit of wilderness areas did not relate to any inherent physical feature causing wolves to *prefer* them, but rather to the fact that people, the only major enemy of wolves, were largely *absent* from such areas. Thus, wilderness provided wolves a certain degree of sanctuary from the constant harassment of humans, especially during bounty days, and positively influenced their chances of individual survival.

The department acknowledged:

> Many individuals and quite a few organizations feel that the wolf should be preserved for aesthetic reasons. Others feel the opposite way and demand complete extermination. Undoubtedly, the former is the more desirable attitude. However, wolf numbers are so low that it is extremely dubious that they would increase or even survive under complete protection. There is not enough wolf range left to permit an increase.[45]

The report recommended:

> In view of the vociferous demonstration that greeted the attempt to release wolves on Isle Royale, it would appear that any attempt to remove the bounty on this species would only jeopardize chances for success with removal of the fox bounty. It is recommended that no action be taken in regard to the wolf bounty.[46]

In this instance the wolf's future in the state was being bartered for a better policy on fox.

In 1959 the state of Michigan repealed the bounty on timber wolves, effective on March 19, 1960, and in 1965 placed them on the list of animals protected at all times.

In the time that elapsed since 1817, when the first territorial bounty laws went into effect, hundreds of thousands of wolves, coyotes, and individuals of other species were destroyed for the coveted, taxpayer-supported bounties within the areas that would eventually be known as Wisconsin and Michigan. From the start, government bounties were subjected to the onslaught of unscrupulous parties that would prove a nuisance for lawmakers up to the end of the bounty era. Beyond a doubt the bounty tided many a family over during hard times—an early form of social welfare. In the final analysis, the bounty accomplished its aim, the annihilation of the timber wolf, which ceased to exist within the confines of Wisconsin and Michigan by the time these states' bounties were finally repealed.

6

Deer, Wolves, and Politics:
Wolf Management in Wisconsin

The winter of 1935–36 was a hard one on the state's deer herd. Deep snows caused the deer to bunch up tightly in their yards while long cold snaps drained the warmth from their veins. Signs of trouble echoed from many areas of the North by those who were out and about. In those days, though, people knew little about such things as starvation among the deer. And they viewed predation as unacceptable, except in regard to their own activities, which weren't looked upon as predation but as almost a God-given right. They didn't realize that it was *natural* for yards, teeming with deer, to attract animals such as the big wolves. That winter what they knew was the wolves were prowling about the deer yards, deer were dying, and something had to be done about it.

One of those who had been out and who took stock in conservation efforts on behalf of the deer decided to see what he could do. On the 14th of February W. A. Bull, a resident of Cavour in Forest County, penned a letter to Wisconsin Conservation Department director W. H. MacKenzie:

> Dear Sir:
> I just came in from a trip up north up on Sec 4 38-15[.] on the way in I saw a number of places where deer had been chased by wolves out of their yards from on[e] swamp to anothe[r] in different places remains of deer killed by wolves. . . .

Bull, who knew that the Nicolet National Forest was closed to taking predators that year, requested MacKenzie's permission to trap the wolves and wildcats plaguing the deer yards in that section. He concluded by saying, ". . . I believe I could save some game between now and spring in that territory if I had a permit to trap there. Please let me know."[1]

From its beginnings, wolf management was inexorably linked to the sport hunting of white-tailed deer until the wolves were finally exterminated. Indeed, the notion of wildlife conservation had grown out of people's recognition of the recreational value of hunting such game species as grouse, waterfowl, and deer. But deer weren't always looked after in the nurturing manner of W. A. Bull and fellow like-minded sportsmen/

82

conservationists of the 1930s. In fact, during the settlement years of Wisconsin, deer were slaughtered by the thousands to supplement the diets of hungry settlers and line the pocketbooks of market hunters, who sold deer by the boxcar load to urbanites in eastern cities. As a result, deer disappeared from the southern prairie region of the state between 1845 and 1850.

The impact on the deer by the immigration of hordes of people into the central portion of the state during the peak of that region's logging boom between the 1850s and 1860s was no less disastrous. These were the glorious halcyon days of the market hunter. Most winters the logging camps hired full-time hunters to supplement mess hall larders. One James Terry, who was engaged to supply game for the two logging camps of John Sterling on the north fork of the Eau Claire River, brought in 38 deer one year and 47 the next.[2]

The market hunting industry quickly capitalized on the improved conditions of transportation when railroads penetrated the region. Over 3,000 deer were shipped out of Eau Claire during three winter months in 1866 on the railhead bound for Milwaukee. In January of 1856, the editor of the *Richland Center Observer* lamented: "Richland County . . . has furnished more venison for the eastern markets this winter, than has any other county in the State. Every few days, wagon loads of whole deer pass through our village for Madison and Milwaukee. We fear that our forest will soon be stripped of this kind of game."[3]

Perhaps as an outgrowth of the concern of some progressive Wisconsin citizens, the first deer hunting restrictions were enacted by the state legislature in 1851. However, the various laws enacted prior to 1890 were ineffective, because no law enforcement staff existed. In 1887, the governor appointed four wardens to the task of enforcing the state's game laws.

By the turn of the century the attitudes of most people had changed from one of outright utilitarian use and/or monetary gain to a more supportive role in preserving and enhancing recreational hunting opportunities of deer and other game species. The dawn of modern sport hunting and sportsmanship was at hand in Wisconsin. This movement represented the first significant step forward in wildlife conservation. The protective web that was to develop around the much-coveted game species, however, did not extend to less sought after species. In fact, it considerably diminished public opinion of predators, which were viewed as worse than competitors. Such creatures as wolves were labeled outlaws, destroyers of game—an attitude that has prevailed among some of Wisconsin's hunters up to present times.[4]

Between 1890 and 1920, the state's deer hunting laws gradually became more restrictive when people's exploitative attitudes gave way to the promotion of game conservation efforts (see 6.1). Although attitudes towards game species became enlightened during this transition period, attitudes towards wolves did not improve. Market hunters, sport hunters, and wardens alike condemned wolves as beasts of destruction and complained of their villainy in slaughtering deer. In 1893, state game warden Mackie reported that wolves and lynx were killing many deer in northern Wisconsin and urged that the bounty be increased.[5] This appears to be the first official statement in Wisconsin condemning the wolf and its predatory ways.

By the second decade of the twentieth century, the Wisconsin government began passively "managing" deer, even though no official agency (e.g., the Wisconsin Conservation Department) yet existed to provide active management programs. By decree of the Wisconsin legislature, areas were set aside as refuges for deer. In 1914 the first deer refuge was established within two townships in Forest County. Known as the Argonne Deer Refuge, the area was closed to all hunting and trapping, including the taking of predators. The practice of protecting predators persisted to the annoyance of the local citizenry and warden staff until 1930, when a federally subsidized control program was implemented and trapper Charlie Walker was hired to trap predators doing damage to the deer herd within the refuge.[6]

The predatory animal control program, a cooperative venture of the Wis-

6.1. The results of a successful deer hunt in 1903 originating from the Boyd Mason Resort west of Park Falls. (Photograph courtesy Wisconsin Department of Natural Resources Photo Archives.)

consin Conservation Department, Minnesota Conservation Department, and the U.S. Bureau of Biological Survey was developed to test whether government-employed trappers could reduce predator populations at a lower cost than public-supported bounties.[7] Supervised by Otto L. Coleman, an employee of the U.S. Bureau of Biological Survey, seven trapping districts were established in northern Wisconsin, and six trappers were selected and on the job by March 15, 1930. Charles Walker was stationed at Crandon; Stan Plis at Goodman; LeRoy Stabnow at Mellen; and Carl Mielke at Mercer. Various other employees were listed as stationed at Pembine, Eagle River, and Gordon. The details of the government trappers' jobs were outlined in a Wisconsin Conservation Department monthly survey report (note the emphasis on timber wolves):

> Each of these men who begin work on March 15 will be assigned to a district in the state in which there is a severe infestation of timber wolves. Because the gray timber wolf does more individual damage to wildlife than the coyote or other predatory animals, intensive work will be carried on against it in the beginning although the coyotes, bobcats, and other predators will not be neglected.
>
> Mr. Walker will work in Forest and Florence counties to begin with; Mr. Plis will start in Bayfield; Mr. Gratias in Douglas; Mr. Stabnow in Ashland and Iron counties; Mr. Jensen in Eagle River district; and Carl Mielke near Mercer.
>
> Each of the men appointed to a district is familiar with the locality and he will be given an outfit of traps and equipment and expected to go where he knows he can do the most good. The activities of the men will be judged by the number of wolves and other predators caught.
>
> All pelts taken by the state trappers will be turned over to the conservation commission, and will be sold at public auction. Trapping activities will extend throughout the year, end in the summer time when the pelts are valueless; the trappers will turn in scalps of the animals as their work will be determined largely upon the number of predatory animals they kill.
>
> Each of the men will work on the basis of a four-day trap line. He will have a base camp and three other camps. The first day he will go from his base camp No. 1; the second day to camp No. 2; the third day over different territory to camp No. 3; and on the fourth day, return over still different territory to his base camp.
>
> Whenever possible, trap lines will be so arranged that cars can be used to go from one central point to another, although most of the trapper's traveling will be done on foot following the actual trap line.
>
> Each man will have from 50 to 75 traps which he will set according to his judgment and knowledge of the country. These traps have been chosen after years of experience in federal work, and are No. 4 Newhouse with extra length chains, an extra swivel, and extra steel drags which were made especially for this work, and which have proved very successful in other districts.

Minnesota trappers and Wisconsin trappers will work in harmony along the borders. Trap lines will meet. In Minnesota there have been six men employed who have been located in the northeastern part of the state concentrated as in Wisconsin, in places of severe infestation of timber wolves. C. C. Skinner, assistant leader of the Biological Survey, is located at Duluth, and will spend most of his time supervising trap line districts in both states. Mr. Coleman's office is in Madison.[8]

The predatory animal control program was not without its problems. Predatory animal trapper William J. Kraemer, who replaced LeRoy Stabnow, fired for selling beaver to a fur farm,[9] posted a notice in the Mellen newspaper after it was discovered that some of his government traps had been stolen: "Investigation shows that some of these traps have been taken and it cannot be considered a joke. The penalty for such a theft under the federal penal code section 47 is very severe. I wish to notify the public to be more careful hereafter."[10] Because it was common knowledge that the control program was designed to measure the efficiency of government-employed versus citizen bounty trappers, the traps were probably taken by a local trapper who did not appreciate the government's infringement on his or her livelihood.

During the two-year period this program ran, 30 different trappers were employed and at least 5 were discharged for "inefficiency." Only 60 bobcats, 93 foxes, 1 bear, and 152 coyotes and wolves were taken by the predator control trappers between March 1930 and December 1931. The cost to taxpayers was $30.20 per bobcat, $12.08 per fox, and $181.20 per coyote or wolf compared with the respective bounties of $5, $2, and $30 per animal for these species.[11]

In his final report, Coleman noted that the Depression caused a surge in trapping activity; he went on to say, "It is not the animals taken by these trappers that affects our catch but the nuisance they create." During October, November, and December 1930 he reported that many traps were stolen, several cabins were ransacked, one cabin was burned, and Carl Spenser was shot from ambush on two occasions, perhaps by some "illegal beaver trappers that were known to be working his territory."[12]

Local antagonism towards the predator control program was expressed in other manners as well. Assemblyman L. S. Shauger introduced legislative bill 198A in 1931 to abolish the program, which he thought was wasteful and "one of the outstanding incidents of the state management of affairs that might be conducted by the individual" (through a state-supported bounty).[13]

Trapping activities of the predatory animal control program officially ceased on January 31, 1932, and four days later project leader Otto Coleman walked out of Room 406 in Madison's Pioneer Building for the last time.[14]

National Forest Predator Policies

In mid-December 1928, the National Forest Reservation Commission approved the acquisition of a 151,680-acre tract of land known as the Oneida Purchase within Vilas, Oneida, and Forest counties. Between 1929 and 1934 major land purchases for the Nicolet National Forest were completed.[15] Land acquisition for the Chequamegon National Forest was also completed during the early 1930s.

The U.S. Forest Service was responsible for the management of timber resources and wildlife habitat and the protection of watersheds. Management of wildlife on national forest lands, however, was made the responsibility of the Wisconsin Conservation Department. The Game Management Division of the Wisconsin Conservation Department was created in 1928,[16] and the warden field force was given the fledgling division's responsibilities of monitoring and inventorying the state's game populations.

In 1934, 1935, and 1936 all furbearers from beavers to timber wolves were protected with a closed season in Wisconsin's two national forests by mutual consent of the Conservation Department and the U.S. Forest Service. Mr. Earl Tinker, regional forester of the Forest Service, requested that predators be protected within the national forests in order to "achieve a better biological balance with the snowshoe hares."[17] Further, Forest Service personnel "recommended that they [wolves, coyotes, and bobcats] be left alone until more accurate details [on their ecology] have been obtained."[18]

During the severe winter of 1934–35 reports of starved deer began to filter down from the north (see 6.2). These first hints of deer problems were met with skepticism by Wisconsin Conservation Department staff officials. Then, alarmed by the results of the deer census drives made by Civilian Conservation Corps (CCC) crews, Forest Service personnel in the Chequamegon National Forest, recognizing the potential damage an overpopulated deer herd could cause the federal timber lands, made a request to the Wisconsin Conservation Commission (the governing board of the Wisconsin Conservation Department) for the removal of 14,000 deer, including does. The Forest Service request called for a radical turn-about in the structure of the deer hunting seasons. Since 1925, the odd-numbered years had been closed to deer hunting, and during the open season years, only bucks could be harvested. Furthermore, the recommended harvest quota for an area the size of an average northern county was over half the annual statewide harvest. The Forest Service request created quite a commotion amongst sportsmen and Wisconsin Conservation Department personnel.[19]

In response to the request, the commission sent "a few wardens to the Chequamegon, who reported after a cursory investigation that the deer were far less numerous than claimed by the Forest Service and the scarcity

6.2. Deer dead from starvation. (Photograph courtesy Wisconsin Department of Natural Resources Photo Archives.)

of browse was not acute." Additionally, Game Management Division director H. W. MacKenzie and law enforcement personnel resented Forest Service intrusion into the game management affairs of the Wisconsin Conservation Department.[20] The Forest Service request was summarily denied, but it effectively polarized the attitudes between the deer hunters and concerned citizens who had recently organized the Save the Deer Club. As Dahlberg and Guettinger put it, "Only six years before, in 1930, the Conservation Department had estimated the state deer population to be 25,000 animals. The refuge idea was just catching on and the idea that deer populations could be limited by the capacity of the range to support them was too revolutionary. 'Save the Deer Clubs' were hastily organized throughout the state in answer to this request for herd control." The hunters and "Save the Deer" proponents agreed that predators, particularly coyotes and timber wolves, were destructive to the deer herds, and they called for the removal of these animals. At odds with both interests was the Conservation Department, which sought an effective management program that would itself become, as the Forest Service had already, increasingly concerned with keeping the deer population in check with its range.[21]

Meanwhile, wolves were being blamed by the Conservation wardens for the destruction of some 200–300 deer along the Woods Creek drainage in the Nicolet National Forest of western Florence County during the winter of 1934–35. One of the wardens, Royce Dallman, reflecting back on the incident 40 years later, felt the deer were overpopulated in that region, had succumbed to starvation, and before being found by the wardens, had been scavenged by coyotes and wolves, which thus were blamed for their deaths. Bert Nixon, warden in Florence County, was able to hire a trapper who removed one wolf before the forest was closed (see 6.3).[22]

In January of 1936, chief conservation warden Barney Devine received several complaints of timber wolves destroying deer in the McCloud Lake area in the Chequamegon National Forest near Clam Lake. After requesting information from wardens Fred Minor and P. C. Peterson, who contacted local citizens for their opinions on the matter, Devine, perhaps because of the sensitivity of the public on the deer issue, decided to begin a trapping operation to remove the wolves. He temporarily appointed local trapper George Ruegger with the specifications to work with Peterson and

6.3. A timber wolf held by warden Bert Nixon, caught in 1934 by a hired trapper along Woods Creek before the Nicolet National Forest was closed to the taking of predators. (Photograph courtesy Nicolet National Forest Archives.)

warden Leon Plante in removing the wolves from the McCloud Lake area.[23]

The trappers' efforts were initially slowed down, because Ruegger was sick and unable to join forces with the wardens as planned. On February 21, 1936, Leon Plante reported that the control trapping had begun. "We have found evidence of one deer that the wolves might have killed some time ago." Additionally he reported, "I found one buck fawn deer that has probably died from sickness or starvation which I am sending to Dr. Graves at Poynette." Although the group shot at a wolf along a fire lane leading into the area and a wolf was temporarily caught in a trap, inclement weather forced them to abandon their efforts without success on February 26. Thus, in response to the complaints, the state initiated a control trapping program on federal lands closed to public trapping.[24]

Serious winter deer losses were reported from several areas in the northern part of the state in 1936, and the Save the Deer Club voted in favor of a closed deer season until 1938, alarmed that hunting was causing a decline in the herd.[25] The public was becoming increasingly agitated over the deer issue. Especially disquieting to Save the Deer Club members and deer hunters was the fact that predators were fully protected within the national forest lands. Hunter V. E. Cole from Tipler wrote in the *Florence Mining News:* "I am told the wolf is under protection in the interest of this re-forestry project." He went on to say that the damage done to the trees by the browsing rabbits and deer "would not begin to equal the value of the deer that are being slaughtered yearly, night and day by the hungry wolf." Expressing an opinion felt by many of the hunters, he stated:

> Every few years we have what is termed an open season on this wild game [deer], and the period of time in hunting comprises about twelve days, we are allowed one buck deer in this open season, if we fail to fill our license in that time we just simply move off the hunting ground, we can't afford to mix up with authority of the game warden. But the wolf is not restrained in his lawless work at any time of the year, he can take either sex, buck or doe, his license calls for this, those ivory fangs inside his upper and lower jaw means death to the harmless deer once this snarling brute is on the warpath.[26]

Although the two national forest lands were completely closed to the harvesting of all furbearers between 1934 and 1936, this was soon determined to be impractical, because "there was not much logic in having the national forests in a different status than the rest of northern Wisconsin," a fanciful twist of logic that would abrogate the last ditch efforts of the Conservation Department in saving the wolf from extinction in the 1950s. As a result, state and federal authorities eased restrictions on taking predators. The two national forest lands were opened to hunting coyotes and timber wolves during the November 26–28, 1937, deer season. Additionally, a hunting season on these canids was allowed between January 1 and March 15 and during the deer season of November 19–25, 1938, in the federal forests.[27]

Timber wolves were also felt to be a menace to the deer herd within the Argonne Deer Refuge in the Nicolet National Forest. In spite of the relaxed restrictions in controlling predators on federal lands in 1938, special permission had to be obtained to hunt wolves within the confines of the 72-square-mile refuge. After being granted permission, warden Royce Dallman staged a public hunt involving over 300 citizens during three weekends between January 9 and 23 with the resultant loss of one hunting dog (to wolves) and one timber wolf. "The Conservation Commission is determined to exterminate the wolves and will put in a state trapper after the wolf hunt next Saturday and Sunday."[28] In early February, George Ruegger made an attempt to trap within the Argonne Deer Refuge, but a warm spell that brought rain spoiled the trapping conditions. He left his set traps in the care of a local citizen to "pick them up in time."[29]

In 1939 the season on wolves, coyotes, and bobcats was opened during the November 25–December 1 deer season in the Chequamegon National Forest but closed during the remainder of the year. In addition to the above open season, there was a season from January 1 to March 1, 1940, for hunting in the Nicolet National Forest. No trapping was allowed in either of the forests.[30]

In 1941 the trapping ban on predators in the federal forest lands was lifted because of the difficulty of enforcing separate regulations for the National Forest. A season was established from January 1 to April 1 which permitted hunters to carry high-powered rifles in their pursuit of predators. Additionally, predators could be hunted during the deer season, November 22–30.[31] The controversial restrictions on predator harvests within the federal forests of the mid-1930s did not last, partly because of their unpopularity and the enforcement difficulties. The unrestricted "season" of 1941 remained in force until the late 1950s.

Wisconsin Conservation Department Wolf Policy

As mentioned earlier, widespread deer starvation was first brought to the public's (and the Conservation Department's) attention during the winter of 1935–36, creating quite a controversy for Game Management Division officials. Although the constituencies of the Save the Deer Club and the state's deer hunters did not see eye to eye, both parties believed deer predators should be eliminated. Members of the Save the Deer Club felt removal of wolves, coyotes, and other predators would enhance the survival of greater numbers of deer. This, in turn, would mean that more deer would be visible (and attractive) to vacationing tourists in the northern Wisconsin resort areas, thus solidifying their outdoor experience and boosting the business of the tourist trade. Similarly, hunters felt that the elimination of predators would increase the deer population and, in turn, the number of deer hanging on the deer camps' venison racks.

The Wisconsin Conservation Department policy towards predators was, itself, a product of its day, for the age of ecological concepts had not yet dawned (though the stage was set with current developments within the Wisconsin scenario). Indeed, in 1935 and 1936 the Conservation Department sponsored a predator control "game" at the request of the county game and fish committees and only sportsmen's organizations were allowed to compete. The organization that accumulated the greatest number of "vermin killed" points won the context.

Thus members of these organizations were encouraged by the department to kill predators wherever and whenever encountered. In so condoning this action, the department was reinforcing the notion that predators were vermin whose presence in the natural world was unhealthy and detrimental to the concepts of conservation.

Although some of the Wisconsin Conservation Department's policymakers may have had a more enlightened attitude towards predators, in general they probably kept their opinions to themselves owing to the overwhelming unpopularity of such thoughts. Most of the department's field personnel (wardens and forest rangers) were hunters who themselves despised predators, harboring the same feelings towards wolves as those of the general populace.

By the mid-1930s the wolf was emerging as a villain in a precarious position while tensions over the deer controversy mounted. The main ingredients in the political arena affecting the wolf were (1) growing unrest amongst citizens over the deer dilemma, (2) the "antiwolf" prejudices of the warden staff in general, and (3) the desire by local wardens to appease the agitated citizenry, with whom they had to interact with as neighbors.

The Conservation Department's separate and highly restrictive policy towards wolves and other predators in the federal forest reserves (a state bounty and unlimited harvests ruled elsewhere) was a source of constant nagging by riled citizens. Louis Spray, secretary of the newly formed Save the Deer Club, wrote to the director asking why "wolves are protected in the Chequamegon Forest." In response, game official Ralph Conway emphasized that exterminating predators was considered poor conservation, but "if in the judgment of the department the wolves are too numerous within such areas [national forests] the eradication of these animals would be carried out by hunting and not trapping." He pointed out that opening these areas to public trapping was frowned upon, because "trappers would be inclined to take other species of game also."[32] Conway's response meant that, when and where the Conservation Department sought help from the public in controlling wolves, the form of control would be hunting.

The department sanctioned citizen wolf hunts on a number of occasions, usually in response to angered citizens, especially those with political clout, as in the case of W. E. Williams, Lincoln County Game Advisory Committee chairman. In late January 1935 he wrote to W. F. Grimmer: "This deep snow [three feet] is causing this writer no little concern about the welfare of our deer. . . . the deer are certainly in immediate danger of extermination unless something is done for their protection from wolves."[33] Williams mentioned that he had brought this matter to the attention of the chairman of the Lincoln County Board of Supervisors with the suggestion that the county either hire its own hunters or increase the county bounty from $40 to $50. Grimmer issued hunting and trapping permits to three local citizens (Messrs. Krueger, Waldburger, and Wendt) and instructed employee K. C. Jakoubek of Tomahawk to run down and help them out (curiously no federal forest existed in Lincoln County, so hunting permits for bountying wolves should not have been necessary).[34]

Warden-sponsored animal hunts were instituted in several areas and became very popular annual events. The Argonne Deer Refuge in the Nicolet National Forest and the Garland Springs area in the Legion State Forest were the sites of annual warden-sponsored wolf hunts between the mid-1930s and at least 1944.

Sometime before the end of February 1936 warden Hartwell Paul organized a highly publicized "small volunteer army" to hunt a pack of nine timber wolves on state forest lands in north-central Vilas County. Complaints had been received that the pack had killed 17 deer. To facilitate the hunt, Chief warden Barney Devine offered Paul the use of the state's cabin on Wildcat Lake, "for the use of the men hunting timber wolves."[35] At the conclusion of the hunt, which ran through March, it was reported, "Six timber wolves have been disposed of in the Vilas County area and plans are already being discussed to dispose of the rest of the pack next season"[36] (see 6.4). The hunters returned the following winter; in February 1937, Ernie Swift directed that state crews were to plow out the Habrich Road to give the hunters and their hounds better access.[37]

On many occasions, however, game officials decided to respond to specific complaints by hiring a few local, trustworthy trappers. These fellows, although formally only on temporary assignment, were known as state trappers. Beaver-control supervisor K. C. "Jake" Jakoubek was assigned the added task of supervising the activities of the state's wolf trappers. Gener-

6.4. A 95-pound timber wolf shot March 1936 during a warden-sponsored hunt near Land O'Lakes, Vilas County. (Photograph courtesy Nicolet National Forest Archives.)

ally, he received orders from Barney Devine, chief conservation warden, who obtained word of complaints from citizens and/or wardens. In some cases Devine made specific inquiries to local wardens to verify complaints; at other times he sent word to Jakoubek to initiate trapping. Despite the fact that Jakoubek was responsible for control trapping operations, Devine apparently directed the hiring of most of the trappers. In 1935, Jakoubek requested the formation of a separate predator-control section, but this was declined because of insufficient funds.[38]

Trappers evidently were hired on a case-by-case basis, and state trapper credentials were issued each time the individual was hired. In 1937, the state's wolf trappers received "$3.00 per day salary and an expense account of not to exceed $100 per month." They were admonished to be frugal with their expenses because of budget constraints. Another stipulation was: "No bounty will be allowed on wolves caught to be skinned and skins [will be] turned in to the Conservation Department."[39]

Between December 1936 and January 1937 Ruegger and Jakoubek were assigned to live-trap timber wolves for display purposes at the Poynette Game Farm. Ruegger related that Jake had heard a pack of timber wolves working an area in east-central Price County within the Chequamegon National Forest, "so it was decided that we would give them a whirl." As early as February 1935 the local warden was pushing to have local citizens carry out control trapping on the federal purchase unit in Price County, because he felt the wolves would "do a great deal of damage to deer yarded in that locality if they aren't killed off." Two male wolves and one female were removed by Ruegger and Jakoubek (see chapter 4).[40]

During the winter of 1936–37 reports were again received of the ravages of wolves on the state's deer herds. The Civilian Conservation Corps' Camp Dunbar reported finding two deer killed in the Woods Creek area, and the local conservation warden was ordered to investigate. This was in the same drainage of western Florence County where warden Bert Nixon had reported the loss of 200–300 deer to wolves during the winter of 1934–35.[41]

In September 1937 conservation warden John Long wrote to Game Management Division superintendent W. F. Grimmer, and advised him that timber wolves had rapidly increased in the McCloud Lake region, which lay on federal land. He stated, "I don't believe that the U.S. Forest Service will seriously object to an open season on these animals at this time so long as you will grant them permission to control rabbits situated on their plantations."[42]

At the close of the 1937 deer season J. E. Bonnel, who owned a hunting camp in the McCloud Lake region, addressed a letter to the Wisconsin Conservation Commission complaining of the lack of deer in his area due to the abundance of timber wolves. Reacting to this letter Superintendent

W. F. Grimmer sought the comments of local wardens Fred Minor and Ben Waskow. Minor was aware that wolves existed in the area, and Waskow commented on what the local gossip indicated: ". . . at least two of these timber wolves [were] killed during the deer season. However, there has been no timber wolves bountied in Bayfield County to my knowledge for more than a year which leads me to believe that they are not as plentiful as Mr. Bonnel would have you believe."[43]

Despite the fact that both wardens failed to support Bonnel's complaint of an abundance of wolves, chief warden Barney Devine made arrangements to employ George Ruegger for a period of 60 days to carry out "a real trapping campaign in an effort to reduce the numbers of these animals." Ruegger control-trapped for the state in the area in early 1938. At the same time Walt Rosenlaf privately trapped three wolves there.[44]

The political sensitivity of the wolf demanded that the Wisconsin Conservation Department obtain information on the existing situation between deer and wolves on a yearly basis. For this the department relied upon its warden field force. In January 1935, Superintendent W. F. Grimmer instructed Jake Jakoubek to summon information from northern wardens on reports of wolf depredations on deer. Jakoubek sent a memo to wardens at Eagle River, Antigo, Sturgeon Bay, Marinette, Rhinelander, Oconto, Florence, Crandon, Wausau, and Shawano and received substantially the same report—that no complaints had been received by wardens from areas where wolves were still found. Warden Arthur Baie of Marinette went so far as to solicit information by placing a notice in the local newspaper. The one exception came from Florence County warden Bert Nixon, but Jakoubek wrote to Grimmer, ". . . I really do not see that there is much we can do about it at this time."[45]

In January 1936 chief conservation warden Barney Devine gave the following directive to various wardens: ". . . contact the best wolf trappers and hunters in your district and inquire whether or not they have observed . . . any place where these animals [wolves] had destroyed deer."[46] The five responses received were negative. Warden Royce Dallman, from the Argonne Deer Refuge in Forest County, stated that three deer kills he had inspected during the previous winter were all "crippled in some way."[47] Rhinelander warden Harley McKeague wrote, "I believe that dogs do more damage than wolves or bob-cats. . . ."[48] Devine commended Wabeno warden R. A. Keeney for thoroughness in reporting, and encouraged him to "continue to gather such information as this from time to time, selecting, as you did in this instance, responsible people when seeking information."[49]

The Wisconsin Conservation Department's surveys on timber wolf–deer depredation problems became an annual event at least through 1944. The surveys asked wardens to supply information on their own personal observations, and occasionally, as in the 1936 survey, to consult with local citizens.

The administrative stance towards predators in general during the 1930s was a product of its time. The state's predator policy was in line with the public's attitudes, and thus it was an acceptable policy. Regarding timber wolves, Conservation Department officials probably believed they were a menace to the state's deer herd, but found they were a particularly annoying pest because frequent public complaints demanded that campaigns, which increased expenditures, be waged to destroy wolves to appease the citizenry.

War on the Homefront: The 1940s "Deer War"

On June 12, 1940, the Wisconsin Conservation Commission authorized the implementation of the Deer Research Project with special appropriations of the federal Pittman-Robertson Act after their primary research proposal, a waterfowl project at Horicon Marsh, did not meet with the approval of the federal government. William S. Feeney was employed as the project's game biologist. Feeney's main job was to conduct an inventory of existing browse conditions in the deer yards throughout the north. The project became PR W-4-R.[50]

A small group of trained biologists, some with college degrees, marched off into the deer yards each winter from 1940–41 to 1943–44 under the leadership of Feeney. Their findings supported the fears of those few who realized that Wisconsin's deer herd was overpopulated and outstripping the forests of all palatable browse (see 6.5). Feeney summarized findings in July as follows:

> By those who have given it any study, it is well known that an important deer range problem has existed in Wisconsin for a number of years. . . . During the past four years . . . we have had the opportunity of observing unusually varied winters.
>
> . . .
>
> Regardless of the mild winter [of 1943–44], logging operations, and [artificial] feeding, the deer herds were currently way over the browse production capacity in 40% of the winter range.
>
> . . .
>
> There is *no* remedy beside starvation for getting a deer population in balance with its range, except to reduce the surplus by taking antlerless deer, with or without the taking of bucks. . . .[51]

6.5. Heavy browsing of red maple in the Palmer Lake, Vilas County, deer yard in 1941. (Photograph courtesy Wisconsin Department of Natural Resources Photo Archives.)

Predictably the findings of Feeney's work in the first few years were greeted with suspicion and disbelief by Wisconsin Conservation Department personnel. Feeney's lack of confidence in the abilities of the warden and ranger field force, largely an unprofessionally trained group, created a rift within the department. When asked by the chief warden during a meeting in Tomahawk in 1942 why the field force hadn't been contacted, Feeney replied, "Sometimes it helps to contact them and sometimes it is a headache, to be honest with you." He felt that most of the information obtained by the field force was unreliable.[52] As Flader so aptly put it, "It is easy to understand the resentment of many in the field force that Department officials in Madison should take the word of Feeney's research crews over that of long-time employees who were in their own estimation, intimately acquainted with and responsible for their own areas."[53] Feeney's claims insulted the integrity of the field force and further alienated his views from those of the public, backed now by the field force in mistrusting his evidence.

Possibly as an outgrowth of the intensity of the issue and the growing mistrust of Feeney's findings, the Wisconsin Conservation Commission appointed a nine-member team of interested citizens to the Citizens' Deer

Committee in the fall of 1942. Aldo Leopold, professor of game management at the University of Wisconsin–Madison, was selected as chairman. The committee members were to conduct individual and group investigations into conditions of the deer herds in their winter ranges, independent of the surveys conducted by Feeney's crews, and make a report on their findings.[54]

The winter of 1942–43 was a severe winter and many deer died of starvation. Leopold organized the committee members' inspections of winter yards and made announcements in advance, inviting the public to accompany them on their tours. The committee members, witnessing first-hand the starvation that Feeney had been proclaiming for two years, were convinced that action was needed immediately.[55]

On June 9, 1943, the Citizens' Deer Committee issued a majority report stating or recommending among other things that:

1. starvation in winter yards was occurring.
2. artificial feeding did not relieve pressure on preferred food plants.
3. if the herd weren't reduced it would decrease through starvation.
4. implement an anterless deer season.
5. "a low population of timber wolves [should] be deliberately maintained as insurance against undue congestion or excessive numbers of deer."[56]

Leopold was undoubtedly the driving force in recommending elimination of the bounty on wolves. As early as 1942 he had been tossing the idea around amongst his peers, reasoning that the removal of the wolf bounty would "restore at least in part, the natural machinery for deer population control." During the Conservation Commission meeting in May 1943 Leopold advised that the removal of the bounty was justified because the wolves had a "tendency to disperse the [deer] herds."[57]

In 1943 the state legislature's Joint Finance Committee, probably recommended against funding bounty bill appropriations, wooed perhaps by the Citizens' Deer Committee and most certainly by Aldo Leopold. The Wisconsin Conservation Department also had a hand in the matter. In an appearance made before the Joint Finance Committee and Governor-elect Orland Loomis, department representatives argued that the loss of the bounty would create no harmful effects on game populations. They pointed out that bounties were instituted by the legislature as a protective measure against depredation of settlers' livestock and did not originate as a game management item, and further noted that annual payments were declining, suggesting that "fewer of these animals were taken than in previous years and that should bounties be removed . . . the effects would not be injurious to other species of game. . . ." They suggested eliminating bounty appropriations as a means "to streamline the budget in keeping with wartime economy," and added that, if information revealed a need for reinstituting the bounty, "a subsequent legislature could again make an appropriation."[58]

In July 1943, the state legislature approved the state budget bill, which did not include appropriations for the bounty. This action spawned an indignant backlash by citizens, outraged with what they perceived as bureaucratic indifference to the classic deer-wolf, hare-coyote, pheasant-fox issue. By the end of the year the Conservation Department had received such a flurry of protest letters that it had to issue a news release stating, "The wolf bounty was repealed by the legislature and is the province of the state lawmakers rather than the Conservation Commission."[59]

Agitated citizens, of course, wasted little time with deliberations among conservation officials; they doggedly pursued their representatives, fortifying their stance with no idle threats. In response to the stiff dissatisfaction of their constituents, 10 northern assemblymen drafted a new bounty bill but failed to get it introduced on the floor until the close of the legislative session. Despite strong sponsoring,

> . . . all moves to have the bill introduced were blocked by the majority agreement to introduce emergency legislation only.
>
> During the final hour of the session usually devoted to indefinite postponement of all unpassed bills, Assemblyman John B. Chapple, Ashland, arose in his seat and asked unanimous consent to introduce the wolf bill. His move was received by the Assembly in a hilarious manner, and after the request had been objected to, . . . the bill was passed and on its way to the Senate.
>
> In the Senate the bill was received and passed within ten minutes, and within an hour . . . it was back and ready for transmittal to the governor's office.[60]

This action was heralded as one of the most successful acts northern legislators had ever experienced. But their achievements fell short of victory when acting governor Walter Goodland vetoed the bill. Public indignation was widespread throughout the north, and "one northern lawmaker remarked to reporters at the time the bill was up for consideration that his vote could very well mean the difference between his re-election and defeat. . . ."[61]

The deer season in November 1943 was split; between the 18th and the 21st, fork-horn bucks were legal, and from the 25th to the 28th, antlerless deer were legal. In the first doe season since 1919, 128,296 legal deer were harvested. The 1943 harvest exceeded the next highest kill (the 1942 season) within the previous 10 years by some 83,000 deer. Members of the

Save Wisconsin's Deer Committee, a newly formed organization, reacted strongly to the "slaughter" of 1943 and became an effective, highly vocal group by the summer of 1944.[62]

Immense public outcry following the 1943 slaughter alarmed Wisconsin Conservation Department officials. Assistant Director Ernest Swift commissioned his old friend and veteran trapper George Ruegger and department employee D. W. Waggoner to conduct a survey on coyote and wolf populations in Forest and Iron counties, to report, among other things, "population and damage as we see its signs only" during the latter half of March 1944. Swift obtained from Ruegger and Waggoner what Feeney could not corroborate or ethically condone:

> . . . the coyote population in Iron County is rapidly increasing and . . . this spring's crop will be out of balance. . . . The red fox population is on a definite increase. . . . wolves are found in all parts of the counties we visited. We did not study the food habits of wolves as we know deer to be their principal food. . . . in the area we visited the deer population did not seem to be out of balance with the general light to medium population. . . . in the study area in Forest County, wolves were found in numbers sufficient to do great damage to the deer herd. This area is now and has been a game refuge for years.[63]

In a cover letter of the report sent to Swift, Ruegger added, "The timber wolf is also on the increase and spreading out to territory that has not had timbers in it for some time."[64] Thus, not only did the Ruegger and Waggoner report refute Feeney's belief that predators were not harming the deer population, but on the basis of a cursory survey of one or two days' duration in each locality, Ruegger and Waggoner claimed that the deer populations were light to moderate in the very areas that Feeney had noted chronic overpopulation problems (i.e., the Argonne Deer Refuge and central Iron County). Ruegger was regarded by many to be a true and just character[65] and probably rightly so: "The investigation is headed by George Ruegger, probably the best wolf man in the state."[66] But Ruegger was also described as a man that was always looking for an excuse to kill wolves.[67]

In a separate action, the now annual Timber Wolf Warden Questionnaire was circulated among the warden force during the early part of 1944. The survey was devised by Wisconsin Conservation Department officials in Madison and consisted of the following questions:

1. Have timber wolves increased, decreased, same? List percentage in your county in the past year.
2. What are the estimated populations in your county?
3. What type of damage do timber wolves do in your county?
4. Can you estimate the number of timber wolves hunted and trapped in your county during the past year? If not why?

5. Is the timber wolf population or parts thereof in your county ranging into other counties? If so, what counties?
6. In your estimation is reenactment of the wolf bounty necessary for the protection of livestock, deer, any other?
7. Have you any particular recommendation on type and amount of bounty?[68]

Summarized, the report read:

Timber wolves were reported to be ranging in twenty counties, but only eleven of these have noted an increase in the population. A total of 314 was estimated in the state. From reports wolves are not numerous in the northern tier and range south as far as Shawano County on the east side. Skipping the central counties they dip down again from the Sawyer County area to Jackson County, but in reduced number. . . . To date, no damage was reported in nine of the counties but deer and livestock were being killed in the other eleven. *Little if any hunting or trapping was being done as there was no incentive. Thus all deemed it wise to place a bounty on them* in order to prevent livestock and game, recommending $10 to $50 be paid per head. Many wardens suggested payment of bounty on both pups and adults without distinction. [emphasis added][69]

Questions 3, 4, 6, and 7 were loaded, and the warden field force easily answered in an according manner. The conclusion that little or no hunting and trapping of wolves had occurred contradicted a statement made by Conservation Department biologist Dan Thompson: "During this bounty free period, there were no indications that wolf hunting for sport in any way diminished, the Wisconsin Conservation Department [trapper questionnaire] data even suggested that the coyote and timber wolf kill increased."[70] Backed by the Ruegger and Waggoner report and the recent Timber Wolf Warden Questionnaire, opinion amongst administrators must have leaned heavily towards the public's in support of reenactment of the bounty.

Meanwhile the public, which had been brewing over the wolf-deer issue for years, now was faced with the slaughter of 1943 and removal of the wolf bounty. By spring 1944, public emotion over the issue of wolves versus deer had reached a fever pitch. Irate citizens sought numerous avenues as outlets for their pent-up anger over what they viewed as an untenable situation. Letters poured in to the department, to elected officials, and to newspapers. The public's intense animosity was further fueled by a lack of trust in the Conservation Department and the department's frequent conflicting statements on the numbers of timber wolves present in the state. Public aggravation over wolves was further augmented by the gross distortions that circulated among the general population regarding the size of the state's wolf populations (perhaps partly explained by the lack of concern of a portion of the public to differentiate between coyotes, or "brush wolves," and timber wolves), little under-standing of (and no concern for) basic principles that govern and limit population increases in wolves, and a lack of knowledge of wolves' consumption rates of deer.

At a Save Wisconsin's Deer Committee meeting at Minocqua in late May 1944, Mercer businessman M. E. Brandt was incensed by the department's stance that the timber wolf was nearing extinction, and very pointedly demonstrated that Madison policymaker (chairman of the Wisconsin Conservation Commission), W. J. P. Aberg's claims of 12 timber wolves in the whole state directly contradicted a response he had received from Iron County warden Stanley Apel (see 6.6), a field man who figured there were at least 20 timber wolves in that county alone (Apel was probably right).[71]*

The meeting was covered by the *Lakeland Times*. Brandt went on to say, "With a normal increase . . . the pack should now number around fifty. Considering that it is believed a wolf kills two deer a week [information he extracted from Apel], . . . it would now take around five thousand deer to feed the present pack of wolves in Iron County for one year."[73]

The action and statements of several wardens further incensed the public's opinions of wolves, as in the case of Apel and Brandt. Rhinelander warden Harley McKeague performed an autopsy before 52 area sportsmen on a 63-pound timber wolf trapped near Willow Lake in late October 1944. The *Rhinelander Daily News* carried an article on the warden's public autopsy entitled "Deer Hair Found in Wolf's Innards."[74]

Articles frequently hit the papers about wolves, and some exaggerated the numbers of wolves in the various packs and the size of the state's population. For instance, in the October 1944 article appearing in the *Rhinelander Daily News* a wolf trapper claimed that two packs, numbering 28 and 35–40 animals, were roaming the Willow region of Oneida County, killing many deer.[75] By coincidence, on that very same day, deer biologist R. A. Schmidt witnessed the power of local gossip when he happened to overhear talk at Bert's Garage in nearby Hazelhurst regarding the sensationalized Rhinelander article. True to form the locals had embellished the original version even more and had added to the pot the notion that the county (Oneida) had 300 or 400 wolves in it. Schmidt was obviously dismayed at how out-of-hand the wolf issue had gotten, and that evening he recorded in his state diary the remarks he had heard, adding the note, "(How can even a trapper tell such lies)."[76]

To be sure, selfish motives were behind some of the wolf rumors that made it to print. In other cases the media were the object of light-hearted

*Aberg undoubtedly borrowed the figure from Leopold's 1943 article published in the *Wisconsin Conservation Bulletin*.[72] (See table 6.1.)

6.6. Iron County warden Stanley Apel inspecting a wolf-killed deer. His comments on wolves and deer were distorted and sparked considerable debate at a Save Wisconsin's Deer Committee meeting in 1944. (Photograph courtesy of Bernie Bradle.)

Table 6.1.   Variations and fluctuations in official "guesstimates" of the Wisconsin timber wolf population appearing in print, 1940–55

Date	State estimate	Authority
1942	150–200[a]	W. E. Scott, WCD
1943	12[b]	A. Leopold
March 31, 1944	<100[c]	Superintendent, Game Management, W. F. Grimmer, WCD
March 31, 1944	<75[d]	Wisconsin Conservation Commissioner W. Aberg
May 5–November 22, 1944	314[e]	Superintendent, Game Management, W. F. Grimmer, WCD
March 20, 1945	<50[f]	A. Leopold
April 26, 1945	<30[g]	W. Feeney, WCD
November 25, 1950	50[h]	WCD
March 16, 1952	≅ 100[i]	Mel Ellis *Milwaukee Journal*
January 31, 1954	30–50[j]	WCD
November 1955	20–50[k]	J. Keener

Note: WCD = Wisconsin Conservation Department.
Sources:
  [a]A. Schorger, "Extinct and Endangered Mammals."
  [b]A. Leopold, "Deer Irruptions."
  [c]*Superior Evening Telegram*, "Wolves Not Serious Problem, Aberg Says."
  [d]*Superior Evening Telegram*, "Wolf Problem Investigation to Be Launched."
  [e]SHSW, Game Management Division materials.
  [f]SHSW, ser. 271, box 26, folder 1.
  [g]*Lake Mills Leader*, "Passing of the Wolf."
  [h]*Merrill Daily Herald*, "He Captured a Prize."
  [i]*Milwaukee Journal*, "Old Lobo, the Timber Wolf, Makes a Comeback in Northern Wisconsin."
  [j]*Milwaukee Journal*, "Few Timber Wolves Left."
  [k]J. Keener, "The Case for the Timber Wolf."

humor and mischief. A letter to the editor appeared in the April 6, 1945, issue of the *Lakeland Times* (Minocqua) from Willow-area resident Herman Witt. He related that Swamsauger Lake resident Ed Norton had told him a good yarn, and he decided, in wry humor, to pass the story on to the newspaper's readers. It seems that one day in January 1945 Norton had decided to check some traps and discovered the lake covered with timber wolf tracks leading south.

"There were twenty-eight separate tracks and they ran abreast of each other. Next day I followed the tracks south, and found that the pack passed southeast of Tripoli, then into Lincoln County.

"The wolves were all strangers, as I know the whereabouts of the local wolves. . . . The wolves had apparently come from the north out of Iron and Ashland Counties or north of these counties. They never came back all winter to the disappointment of a number of trappers.

". . . . Now, where did these wolves come from and where did they go? Perhaps they had heard of the Bounty Bill and this was a delegation sent to Madison to lobby for more Red Points, appealing their case directly to Governor Goodland. I am sorry I cannot answer these stories definitely."[77]

Given the public atmosphere, the many and varied wolf stories that were flourishing throughout the state at this time elevated public misconceptions of the deer-wolf situation. Sadly enough, people who were affiliated with the Conservation Department, such as Aldo Leopold, could not even counter these wild claims with factual information, because very little scientific information was available on timber wolves. Seemingly unknown to anyone in the administration (including Bill Feeney's supervisor, Walter Scott, who was on leave in military service at the time),[78] Feeney and his deer project crew were conducting a formal study of the timber wolf in Wisconsin (see chapter 7).

Feeney was probably the only person armed with hard facts concerning the lack of impact timber wolves had on the deer herd, but he was powerless to fight the sentiments of the administration, the state capital, and the public. In a letter to Leopold on December 18, 1944, one can sense Feeney's exasperation over the deer versus wolf bounty issue:

It is no secret, of course, that the timber wolf is a deer predator and that they are able to and do kill deer. But the timber wolf has been exterminated from the greater part of its range in Wisconsin and the proof is lacking that it is generally as destructive as supposed. Judging from the findings to date, we do not interpret the depredations of the timber wolf as harmful to the deer herd. For example, one of the main last stands of the timber wolf in Wisconsin is in Forest County where they have "always" been. The large area in which the timber wolf runs, except for heavy poaching, has not been hunted for several years and supposedly the wolf population in this area has not been checked except for a few which were taken occasionally under the supervision of wardens. Yet the wolves have not been numerous enough to keep the deer herd in check. The deer population in the past several years has grown in this area to the point where almost all palatable food has been eaten out. In a cruise of this area this week we noted the palatable foods were being heavily browsed so that together with the retarded growth resulting from previous browsing, there is very little deer food left. . . . I mention this example of Forest County area for no purpose except to show how badly the wolf-deer relationship is misunderstood. . . ."[79]

Owing perhaps to the public mood, Feeney felt a sense of urgency in further stating:

> I hope that there will be no bounty on timber wolves. As far as wildlife is concerned, I do not see how there can be any justification for bounty on coyotes except for one thing: that there is more or less public demand for it. For this reason a moderate bounty on coyotes, if properly explained, may be a good temporary public relations procedure until better educational material, based on facts, has been presented to the people.[80]

Independent of Leopold's or Feeney's influence, a committee of Wisconsin professors appointed by the governor to investigate livestock depredations in the northern part of Wisconsin recommended that no attempt be made to "reduce or exterminate" timber wolves. The report was dated December 18, 1944.[81]

Public pressure was, to say the least, very much in support of reenacting the bounty. Intense, emotionally based, wartime propaganda slogans equating wolves with the German Nazis and the Japanese* were circulated, such as the statement released by Washburn County's Trego Rod and Gun Club:

> The wolf is the Nazi of the forest. He takes the deer and some small fry. The fox is the sly Jap who takes the choice morsels of game and the songbirds. Can Professor Leopold justify their existence because deer meant for human consumption should be fed to the Nazi because we must have that protection for the trees? Can he justify the Jap or Nazi because he eats a rabbit or a grouse which are meant for human food, or the songbird on its nest, which are meant by the Lord for our pleasure . . . ?[82]

During the early 1940s when Leopold was campaigning to gain support for removal of the bounty, very few "official estimates" of the timber wolf population were available, and to bring about the bounty repeal, he successfully used the fact that the wolf was nearing extinction (which indeed it was; see chapter 8). But the poor deer season of 1944 was by coincidence during the bounty-free period, and protests claiming that predators, among other things, were to blame for the imagined decline in the deer herd were leveled against officials. Thus, hard-pressed individual administrators were frequently asked to justify their reasons for not reinstating the wolf bounty. A flurry of wide-ranging "guesstimates" of the timber wolf population were

*The U.S. government even capitalized on the evil connotations of wolves in fairy tales, utilizing the wolf as a subliminal object in promoting U.S. Savings Bonds in the postwar years (see 6.7).

Wolf Poison !

There's one 100-proof way to guard your door against this fellow's visit.

There's wolf poison in every U. S. Savings Bond you buy. There's sweet security. too—for your home, your family and yourself.

U. S. Savings Bonds are 100% guaranteed by Uncle Sam. They pay you $4 for every $3 you put in, after 10 years.

Think of this profitable saving in terms of future comforts and luxuries. Think of the advantages it will mean for your children as they grow up.

Think. THINK. THINK.

Then start saving right away—today! Start saving *automatically* this sure, convenient way. If you work for wages or salary, enroll in the Payroll Savings Plan — the *only* installment buying plan.

If you're not eligible for this plan—if you're in business but not on a payroll—ask your bank about the equally practical Bond-A-Month Plan.

REMEMBER—U. S. Savings Bonds are poison to wolves!

Automatic saving is sure saving— U.S. Savings Bonds.

Contributed by this magazine in co-operation with the Magazine Publishers of America as a public service.

6.7. The Playbill U.S. Savings Bond poster advertisement. (Courtesy State Historical Society of Wisconsin.)

made in a short time period by various officials for the public's scrutiny. The confusion amongst administrators, who could not even agree amongst themselves just how many timber wolves there really were (see table 6-1, especially 1943–45), visibly weakened any arguments that might have existed regarding the precarious nature of the state's wolf population. This flaw must have been easily perceived by the public, at least that segment which was especially vocal, as demonstrated by the following statement made by Waldo Rhinehard to Commissioner William Aberg: "One expert [Leopold] says to me in his letter, from what the field men tell me there are perhaps 12 or 24 timber wolves in the state. If he does not know of his own knowledge whether there are 12 or 12 hundred timber wolves in the state how much of an expert is he??"[83]

The coup de grace came in late 1945, when the Conservation Department released the figures it had compiled from trappers' responses to the annual voluntary questionnaire about their harvest of furbearers, showing that 155 "wolves" and 260 "coyotes" had been taken. With regard to wolves and coyotes, the mail questionnaire response was subject to gross inaccuracies, in part because some trappers failed to distinguish between coyotes and wolves and others claimed the catch of a wolf because they were more prestigious. Regardless, the department's own survey revealed that trappers took many more wolves than officials claimed were available in the state. The *Badger Sportsman*, a Wisconsin hunters' organization newsletter, swiftly responded to this error. Their sharp criticism was picked up by many Wisconsin newspapers, including Minocqua's *Lakeland Times*, which carried the article behind the bold headline: "Bounty Report Blasts Leopold Wolf Statements."

> . . . the only one dozen wolves in Wisconsin statement will go down in history with the crack made by the Japs that "Peace would be signed at the White House."

> mature wolves 104
> cub wolves 51
> mature coyotes 180
> cub coyotes 80

> It is expected that the contention will be that the count shown as "mature wolves" were not really timber wolves and that many of them were coyotes or possibly "dyed police dogs." We point out, however, that this list is prepared by the Conservation Department themselves.[84]

Publicly disemboweled, the few department administrators that still opposed reinstatement of the bounty out of a fear that timber wolves might be exterminated must have felt conquered.

Meanwhile a rift had been developing amongst members of the department's administration as to whether timber wolves were truly endangered. In early December 1944, backed by the Wisconsin Conservation Commission,

> . . . Conservation Director, E. J. Vanderwall reported to Governor Goodland at a budget hearing that the wolf population had "unquestionably increased in the last two years.". . . . Goodland, who vetoed a bill for the restoration of the bounties last January after it passed in the final minutes of the extra legislative session, questioned if the number of wolves increased since the bounties were removed. Vanderwall replied that there was no explanation for the rising wolf population and it was now considered "unfortunate that bounties were discontinued at a time when more wolves started to appear."[85]

Vanderwall requested that $60,000 of the Wisconsin Conservation Department's 1945–47 budget of $600,276 be appropriated to pay the $20 adult–$10 young wolf and coyote and $5 wildcat bounties.

On December 19, 1944, following a light deer harvest, Commissioner Aldo Leopold wrote to citizen Waldo Rhinehard, with whom he had exchanged several letters on deer predators, admitting that "the predators responded to excess deer more quickly that I thought they had." Leopold now believed that there were too many wolves and coyotes and was now in favor of a bounty.[86] This was indeed a startling turn of events. Leopold, more than any single person, had provided the impetus to remove the wolf bounty only a year and a half earlier. As Flader put it, "This was an extraordinary admission for Leopold to make, and there is no satisfactory explanation for it, except he was making a judgment about field conditions that he had not personally seen, under pressure of intense public outcry about the shortage of deer and the superabundance of predators."[87]

There may indeed have been, however, an explanation for Leopold's actions. He expressed his support of the bounty in an article printed in the April 1945 issue of the *Wisconsin Conservation Bulletin*. It was probably written prior to the reinstatement of the wolf bounty in early 1945. He reasoned:

> I now favor restoring the bounty because the increase in coyotes make it necessary, there is a probability that timber wolves have increased, and it is impracticable to distinguish between the two species in paying bounties.
>
> The present increase in coyotes, and perhaps wolves, began in my opinion, before the bounty was discontinued a year ago, and therefore could not have been caused solely by that discontinuance. No one can be sure of its cause, but it is reasonable to suppose that the abundant venison available during the starvation winter 1942–43 and the "split season" of 1943–44 had something to do with it. . . .[88]

His logic perhaps would have been flawless given the circumstances had it not been for the inaccurate information he received describing an increased timber wolf population. Why he did not heed the pleas of Bill Feeney,[89] the one man who knew more than any other about the plight of the wolf, remains unknown.

Meanwhile, a report to the governor on predatory animals in Wisconsin stated:

> The Department and Conservation Commission highly recommended that the status of the timber wolf be fully reviewed prior to the convening of the 1947 legislature [when bounty appropriations would next come up for review]. If it should appear from the field surveys that there is an indication that the species is endangered some means of essential control other than bounty payments should be considered. It is possible that necessary control could be assigned to specially trained trappers.[90]

This recommendation didn't have any teeth, especially following the change in governors.

In early January 1945 the "woodchoppers," an alliance of northern legislators, introduced a bill to reinstate the bounty which passed in the state assembly unanimously on February 15th. By early March the bill was forwarded to the governor's desk, awaiting his signature, but once again he refused to sign it. He issued a proclamation that laws cannot change the course of nature and regretted that they

> . . . must expend vast sums of money to gratify demands of this kind, when it is apparent that it is a question of time until repeal measures will follow.
>
> It is high time that in this state we resort to sounder and more basic approaches to problems of this kind. They should be studied on a long time basis, and should be decided upon their merits alone, as determined by men equipped to make such studies. . . .

In further justifying his actions, Governor Goodland stated, "The fox is killed for sport and for its fur, and we now propose to subsidize both the trapper and the sportsman. . . ."[91]

But Governor Goodland stood alone in his stance against the bounty. Such influential men as Director Vanderwall of the Conservation Department and Commissioner Leopold had fallen from the ranks and instead lent their support to the bounty bill. On March 11, 1945, Chapter 5 of the Wisconsin Statutes became law over the governor's veto.[92]

Almost immediately Leopold had misgivings about the reinstated bounty. In a speech on March 20, 1945, Leopold stated, "For example, Wisconsin has now reenacted a wolf bounty despite the fact that there are probably less than fifty timber wolves left in the state." Perhaps realizing that his role in reenacting the 1945 bounty was a grave mistake, Leopold once again began a crusade to abolish the bounty on timber wolves, fearing the bounty would hasten their extinction, but an untimely death (April 21, 1948) prevented him from realizing that goal.[93]

During the late 1940s quite a few university-educated wildlife biologists, many having served terms in the PR W-4-R Deer Research crew, were hired on as regional game biologists under the Game Management Division. They brought with them a more enlightened, ecological approach to the field of game management. Moreover, because most had obtained experience with the Deer Research Project, they also were cognizant of the precarious status of the timber wolf. No longer were Conservation Department officials willing to react so quickly to complaints of wolves killing deer, as is reflected in the following memo:

> John Borkenhagen informed me this morning that Mr. Ed Woody has reported a case of timber wolves running deer in Iron County, and that he would like to have something done about it. . . .
>
> Mr. Borkenhagen wondered if we should inform a bunch of wolf hunters from Colby who are currently working Ashland Co. I said that I didn't believe we should encourage the killing of what timber wolves are left in the state, but that I would inform you of the matter.

A postscript penciled in at the bottom of the memo reflected the change in attitude: "Cliff: My own personal feelings—so what? —Art"[94]

Land Use Patterns That Enhanced Wolf Survival into the 1950s

Certain land use patterns were effective in unintentionally providing sanctuary for the timber wolves from the persecution of humans during the 1930s and 1940s. It was in those few sanctuaries that the last remaining wolves were found by 1950. Land use policies that enhanced wolf survival in the 1920s, 1930s, and 1940s fell by the wayside in the early and middle 1950s. Surprisingly, land use of benefit to wolves varied from range to range. A closer examination of each unique condition is warranted.

By 1950 the few wolf packs remaining in the state were restricted to several widely separated remote areas on county, state, and federal forest lands in extreme north-central and northeastern Wisconsin (see map 8.1 on page 160). Some land parcels within these areas were closed to all hunting and trapping because of their special deer refuge status. The deer refuge management concept that prospered in the 1930s was no longer believed to be beneficial to deer. The refuges had been established to provide herds some protection from hunters. But the herds gradually increased to the point where they were destroying all browse, and death by starvation (rather than the sights of guns) had become chronic. Thus by 1950 the deer refuge program was being dismantled.

Camp Scott Lake Pack

The 72-square-mile Argonne Deer Refuge in the Nicolet National Forest of Forest County was one of the refuges to be dismantled. Game manager Bernie Bradle, who had studied the wolves in the Argonne under Feeney between 1944 and 1947, was visibly upset over the prospect of opening up the area to hunting and trapping.[95] Bradle's fears were not unfounded. Following the dismantling of the Argonne refuge in 1950, he stated, "This total opening of the old refuge appeared to further decimate the remnant . . . timber wolves" (see 6.8).[96] In an effort to prevent further deterioration of

6.8. The Argonne Deer Refuge in Forest County inadvertently protected the Scott Lake wolf pack from bounty trappers. Three wolves were bountied within six months after the refuge was dismantled, including this one held by Bernie Bradle. (Photograph courtesy of Bernie Bradle.)

the wolf population, the old deer refuge was made into a timber wolf refuge in 1951–52. Though now open to deer hunting, trapping was restricted: "For practical enforcement of the regulation, it was necessary to close the entire area to any trapping other than for beaver and otter. It further defined one of the few areas of wolf range and publicized it as such. This is obviously undesirable when trying to protect a few animals—that is, by calling attention to where they may be found."[97]

Once again the Conservation Department was placed in the position of implementing and enacting a dual role regarding wolves: It was mandated by the state legislature to manage and appropriate the finances for the bounty system at the same time that it created a sanctuary where wolves were protected from those who sought to collect the bounty on them. The inconsistency of such a policy was questioned: ". . . the conservation department has set up a refuge in which timber wolves are protected . . . while just outside of the refuge area the state is paying $20 for mature wolves. It just doesn't make sense."[98]

In attempting to rectify the problem and save the wolf from extinction, wildlife managers were faced with two alternatives. The first was to abolish the timber wolf refuge and eliminate the inconsistency. The other option was to remove the bounty. None of the managers, however, possessed the leadership qualities or the power of persuasion that characterized Aldo Leopold in his fight to abolish the bounty almost 10 years earlier.

In their concerns the wildlife managers who wished to prevent the wolf's extermination lacked organization and a clear appraisal of the options available. Knowing that even a concerted effort to remove the bounty would take precious years to accomplish, the only effective alternative, one that would buy time, would be to maintain the timber wolf refuge. Managers at the time, however, were ripe with the reminder that the deer refuge system was antiquated and a death trap for the species it was intended to protect. Having had difficulty convincing the public of the shortfalls of the refuge concept in regard to deer and perhaps tripped up by their own shortsighted logic, many apparently felt they would be opening up another can of worms by supporting the already controversial timber wolf refuge. The timber wolf refuge was probably dismantled in 1952.

Yet it is difficult to accept that the supposed unpopularity of the refuge concept alone led to the dismantling of the timber wolf refuge. In late 1955 fishers transplanted from New York were released in the former Argonne Deer Refuge, and the special Fisher Wildlife Management Area, closed to dry land trapping, was established in a 40,000-acre area (later expanded to 120,000 acres)[99] in the very heart of the timber wolf refuge four years after it had been dismantled. Within that four-year period the wolves had apparently been eliminated, for Bradle, commenting in a "Northeast Game News Release," stated: "I have not seen any timber wolf sign at all in the past two years. Forest County has been one of its last strongholds."[100]

Pleasant Lake and Willow Packs

Another important Conservation Department management program that was dismantled in the 1950s and unintentionally benefited the remnant wolf population involved the locked-gate fire lane policy of the Forest Protection Division (see 6.9). Dan Thompson, who noted this, commented:

> The state-controlled fire lanes have for the most part been closed to public travel since it would have been impossible for the state forest-protection division to maintain the large mileage of fire lanes as public thoroughfares without a considerable increase in manpower and equipment. This administrative contingency had worked to the advantage of the timber wolf by preventing easy access by trappers and wolf hunters into the heart of much of the remaining wolf habitat in Wisconsin.[101]

6.9. The locked-gate fire lanes were an inadvertent aid in preserving wolf habitat in the 1940s and early 1950s. (Photograph courtesy of Daniel Q. Thompson.)

The locked-gate fire lane policy was instituted by Conservation Commission order number M-39 on October 16, 1934, to prevent damage to the lanes by minimizing public vehicular travel on them. The Forest Protection Division simply did not have sufficient funds to maintain their extensive fire lane network. The fire lanes, constructed by state and federal public work crews or converted from old railroad grades and logging roads, were established to provide "a line where fires could be checked . . . and to afford means for transportation into areas otherwise heretofore inaccessible."[102] Fire lane easements were obtained from the owners of the land and the administrators of the county forests through which the lanes ran. A double-locked gate was erected at the entrance to each fire lane, and both the landowner(s) and appropriate state officials held the keys that operated the locks.

During the late 1940s and early 1950s Thompson noted that there was "continued pressure on town government officials to declare sections of the fire lanes as town roads."[103] Forest Protection director Neil LeMay considered that the majority of fire lanes, when deemed useless and abandoned by the Forest Protection Division, were converted to town or county forest roads.[104] These, of course, were open to public travel, an idea that didn't settle well with Thompson:

> In the timber wolf range, the opening of each new section of closed fire lane area to public travel has jeopardized the existence of the wolves. Trappers then drive into an area with a carload of traps where formerly they had to hike in with only as many traps as they could carry in a packsack. . . . If this trend continues, the timber wolf will eventually be extirpated from Wisconsin.[105]

This must have been fairly obvious, because Thompson encountered wolf trappers using vehicles on the federal lanes open to the public in the Chequamegon National Forest in Price County and no trappers in vehicles on gated forest fire lanes in Oneida County.[106]

Thompson studied the Pleasant Lake pack of Iron County and the Willow pack of Oneida-Price counties. At the time (1946–48) both existed in areas made partly inaccessible because of the locked-gate fire lane policy. He felt that the policy was crucial to the survival of the wolf, and discussed the hopes of maintaining the policy to save the wolf with H. T. J. Cramer, assistant director of the Conservation Department. Thompson even persuaded the Wisconsin Society for Ornithology's Bird Conservation Committee to commend the Conservation Department for maintaining its locked-gate fire lane policy. Most of the state's fire lanes, however, were opened sometime between 1950 and 1955.[107]

Virgin Lake and Cisco Lake Packs

In the lake country bordering the Upper Peninsula of Michigan, several lumber companies had large landholdings in the 1930s and 1940s. After the merchantable wood products had been removed, the lands were bought up by wealthy businessmen from downstate (e. g., the Fromm brothers of Wausau) and in Chicago, by universities (Notre Dame), and by hunting clubs (Rainbo Lodge). The estates, with their large landholdings, persisted and the limited access onto these properties enhanced wolf survival. However, immediately to the south and to the north lay the Northern Highlands State Forest and Ottawa National Forest, respectively, with their intricate fire lane networks that were largely opened to public travel. The refuge provided by the estates simply wasn't vast enough, and the wolves' vulnerability while in the vicinity of the fire lanes eventually led to their demise by the late 1950s.

Removal of the Wolf and Lynx Bounty

Between 1953 and 1955 game manager John M. Keener worked in north-central Wisconsin, including the area of the former Argonne Deer Refuge in the Nicolet National Forest. While in the area he occasionally encountered the family group of timber wolves that fellow game manager Bernie Bradle had studied six years earlier. He also noted the lack of timber wolf sign in areas where the animals had existed only 10 years earlier. Concerned that the timber wolf was dangerously nearing extinction in the state, Keener published an article that appeared in the November 1955 issue of the *Wisconsin Conservation Bulletin.* In the opening line of "The Case for the Timber Wolf" the reader is confronted with stark reality: "To be or not to be is the question presently facing the timber wolf in Wisconsin. . . ." Keener became the first and only person to publish an article in a widely circulated, popular magazine disseminating the cold facts on how endangered the state's wolf population was:

> In Wisconsin, timber wolves are now found in only four or five localities of the northernmost counties. . . .
> . . . the breeding range of the timber wolf in Wisconsin indicates a remaining area of about 1,000 square miles. This represents less than 10% of the land area of the northern 12 counties.[108]

The article was then picked up and reprinted by the state's newspapers. A year later, in November 1956 game biologist Harold Jordahl published an article on the Canada lynx in the *Wisconsin Conservation Bulletin*, arguing that the species was for all practical purposes extirpated. He pointedly illustrated the senselessness of maintaining a bounty on the doomed animal:

> Human behavior is difficult to understand in light of our knowledge concerning the lynx. . . . Still, paradoxically and perhaps unthinkingly, we continue to pay $5 for the . . . carcass entire with hide attached . . . for a lynx now virtually extinct in Wisconsin and other northern states.[109]

On October 6, 1956, the Citizens Natural Resources Association adopted the following resolutions:

> According to the information furnished by the State Conservation Department, and from other reliable sources, it is established that the Timber Wolf and the Canada Lynx as wildlife species are in danger of being exterminated. It further appears that the continuation of such species on the bounty list will hasten the time of their complete extinction in Wisconsin.
>
> This association, therefore, strongly urges the removal of the Timber Wolf and the Canada Lynx from the bounty list as an important step to preserve the species in Wisconsin.[110]

This and other petitions were probably circulated and, combined with the Keener and Jordahl articles, influenced state assemblyman Norman C. Anderson, Democrat from Madison, to introduce bill 363A, which would modify the existing Wisconsin State Statute 29.60 pertaining to state-financed bounties by striking the words *wolf* and *lynx*.[111] The bill, introduced on March 6, 1957, was approved and sent to the Senate on April 17, where Senate Conservation Committee member LaFave added amendment 1S, which would have restored the word *wolf* and added "except timber wolf" to the statute narrative. Fortunately the Senate Conservation Committee and floor did not approve of the proposed ambiguous wording (*coyote* and *wildcat* were to remain; therefore retaining the word *wolf* was senseless) and rejected amendment 1S on May 10. The bill was approved by both houses and sent to the governor on May 27 and signed on May 31st. On June 6th the bill was published in Chapter 157 and became law.[112]

The very thing that Leopold and his peers had fought so long and dearly for 14 years earlier, had won at cost, and then lost again, was now easily made into law. Why the lack of resistance? ". . . the bill did not attract a great deal of public attention at the time. Since there were . . . so few wolves and Canada lynx left in Wisconsin . . . removal of the bounty would not have much interest for those persons who are interested in collecting bounties."[113] At the same time the Conservation Department placed the timber wolf and Canada lynx on the list of species protected at all times (Administrative Code 10.02[1]). By then, however, the breeding population of timber wolves had disappeared. Removal of the bounty and place-ment of the wolf and lynx on the protected list, though profound, were moot points.

It would seem that this chapter had come to a close, because by the time the bounty was repealed, the wolf had become extirpated within Wisconsin. But a bounty movement was still alive. In fact, while Anderson's bounty repeal bill was still being reviewed, Assemblyman Riehle introduced a fully restored bounty bill, 780A (including wolf and lynx), on May 21 which was referred to the Joint Committee on Finance. The bill was indefinitely postponed, however, on May 29,[114] and apparently didn't resurface during that legislative session.

State-financed bounties (coyote, fox, wildcat) did not appear in the 1957 statutes (24th ed.: 502, see 29.60), possibly because Assembly Bill 77A, the general fund budget bill, failed to appropriate money to finance them. For the next 10 years, proposed bounty bills including the words *wolf* and *lynx* occasionally resurfaced within the legislature, but each time the Anderson modifications were upheld. The latest attempt to restore the timber wolf bounty was introduced in 1967 by Assemblyman Lawrence Kafta of Denmark and Ervin Conradt of Shiocton, but it was killed while in committee. State-financed coyote and fox bounties were implemented in 1959, but have not appeared in the books since.[115]

Although the state didn't finance bounties in 1957–58, and when reinstituted in 1959 and 1961 the words *wolf* and *lynx* were stricken from 29.60, under 29.61 the state gave local governments the authority to impose bounties on, among other things, wolf and lynx. The wording of statute 29.61 remained essentially the same in all the biannually published statutes through 1975. Thus, under the Administrative Code a person who killed a timber wolf in Wisconsin between 1957 and 1974 could be penalized, but at the same time could collect a local bounty under the provisions of 29.61. As if this enigma weren't enough, the 1973 statutes providing for the newly endangered species protected under 29.415 didn't list the timber wolf; it didn't qualify, because it was listed by the Department of Natural Resources Endangered Species Committee as extirpated, and there were no statutory protective provisions for extirpated species. However, the timber wolf was listed by the federal government as endangered in Wisconsin at the same time that statute 29.61 with its bounty listing for wolf and lynx remained on the books. What a legal nightmare.

If there had been a few wolves in the state during the period 1957–74, and evidence suggests there were on occasion,[116] sufficient legal loopholes and entanglements existed so as to render their protection ineffective despite charges that could have been brought against an individual hunting or trapping them.

In 1975 the wolf was placed on the state's Endangered Species List under 29.415, and at the same time the words *wolf* and *lynx* were stricken from 29.61.

Perceptions and attitudes of Wisconsin's citizens towards deer and wolves have changed markedly over the past 100 years. Deer, once used for food and clothing, were viewed in utilitarian terms and were typically overexploited. Somehow in the early decades of the twentieth century the notion of conservation came into vogue, fortuitously in time to save the deer. But that "conservation" theme was merely a masked version of the same old utilitarian use of nature, and it applied only to those creatures that held some societal value—in this case as objects of sport enthusiasts. In its infancy, "game management" was all too self-serving—a form of utilitarianism that exercised control over the *level* of exploitation and advocated the elimination of natural competitors of the species being managed. The transition of most conservation agencies from *game* management to *wildlife* management policies in the 1970s reflected acceptance of a more ecological approach to management and broadened responsibilities of conserving nongame species as well.

As this history reveals, wolves existed outside the realm of conservation and game management in Wisconsin. In fact wolves were the antagonists of conservation, because they were viewed as the destroyers of wild game—the true object of conservation. Therefore it was logical that wars were waged on Wisconsin's wolves right up to and beyond the bitter end of their existence within our state.

Reflecting back upon these past 100 years, society's actions are understandable. The society of Wisconsin's past was naive, ignorant, and incapable of concerns about environmental matters. Game management and the so-called conservation movement were infantile growing notions and products of their time. Ideas, values, and perspectives, when given sufficient time, evolve in societies that are truly progressive. One may speculate whether Bernie Bradle's beloved Forest County pack would have survived had the chimes of time been moved forward 10 or 15 years. Forest County would certainly be a different place had they survived. Unfortunately for the wolves—and succeeding generations of Wisconsinites—their time ran out.

History can provide something very important to society: the knowledge of which actions to avoid in the future. While the biopolitical actions that led to the demise of Wisconsin's timber wolves are understandable, they are far from excuseable.

7

Wisconsin's Secret Wolf Study

Bill Feeney had had a rough winter. The public was still reeling from the effects of the November deer season—the first doe season in Wisconsin's short history of regulated deer seasons. As project leader of the Wisconsin Conservation Department's Deer Research Project, Feeney took his share of insults and cheap shots from those who voiced indignation over the slaughter of 1943.[1]

Bill had responsibility for surveying every known deer yard area in the state. This was a formidable task, but he and a handful of men went about their duties each winter, usually working alone (see the biographical sketches in appendix C). The crew was nearing the conclusion of the 1943–44 winter season, and Feeney had called together some of his men to review and discuss the season's findings.

The meeting was scheduled to run from Wednesday, April 5, to Saturday, April 8. This year he chose an unlikely spot to sequester his men—a cabin belonging to Herbert Hurd, northwest of the Turtle-Flambeau Flowage in the wilds of Iron County. It was a favorite retreat of Feeney's. Hurd was an acquaintance of Feeney, and he graciously offered the use of his cabin for Deer Research crew use.

Crew member Les Berner came up with Bernie Bradle and Felix Hartmeister from Ladysmith, meeting Clarence Searles, a Wisconsin Conservation Congress* member and Deer Research crew volunteer, at the cabin. The weather had turned warm, making the old Roddis Line logging railroad grade, recently turned fire lane, a quagmire that made the last leg of their journey especially grueling. Despite a few hours' delay in negotiating the fire lane with the old state car, the party arrived safely at Hurd's cabin.

A few days prior to their arrival a wolf had walked down the fire lane south and east past Pleasant Lake (see 7.1). The sun had worked over the track, rotting it out. Upon seeing the track in front of the cabin some of the

*The Wisconsin Conservation Congress is a legislatively sanctioned advisory body to the Wisconsin Conservation Commission. It is composed of a delegation of concerned sportsmen elected from each of Wisconsin's 72 counties. It provides a democratic forum for public advice on proposed rule/regulation changes.

7.1. The abandoned Wisconsin Conservation Corps camp no. 15 in the Pleasant Lake country of Iron County around 1941. (Photograph courtesy Wisconsin Department of Natural Resources Photo Archives.)

fellows joked that it was as big as a horse's track. The track also caught the eye of Feeney when he arrived.

Feeney had decided the crew would combine their discussions with a little fieldwork. As all the crew members knew, Feeney believed in making hay while the sun shone. It was so warm during the day that snowshoeing was next to impossible, because the rawhide lacing became water soaked and sagged. But the fellows were expected to work. Discussions could wait until the idle moments of the evening, when the group gathered around the cabin's wood stove.

Bernie Bradle snowshoed a total of 10 miles in the swamps surrounding Pleasant Lake on the first day. He had been wearing wool long-johns and chafed the skin on his legs so badly that he could no longer walk, much less snowshoe. That night Bradle lay on his bunk nursing his injured legs while the others sat at the table (see 7.2). Feeney asked each to summarize the timber wolf activity they had seen while cruising isolated deer yards across the northern reaches of the state that winter. Eventually the conversation turned to the wolf track outside the door stoop. Curious about what the wolf was up to, Feeney decided the crew would have a little fun and find out.

Since Bradle had demonstrated the folly of working on snowshoes during the warmer daytime temperatures, Feeney determined they were going to

7.2. Bernie Bradle in camp for the night. (Photograph courtesy Wisconsin Department of Natural Resources Photo Archives.)

work at night. After all, the weather was perfect. The plan was to wait until the evening temperatures plummeted enough to firm up the snow so the men could snowshoe with less effort. Then the group would begin its field-work, searching and following timber wolf tracks beneath a full moon through the forests of Iron County.

It was towards nightfall on Thursday, the 6th of April, when Feeney began briefing his men on the fire lane next to the cabin. Feeney said, "Look, this animal is heading south. Bradle, you can't travel anyhow, so you go on and get in the car and you go down the fire lane. Berner and Hartmeister, you take this fire lane to the west of here, and then you come down. Searles and I will follow this track. We'll all go on down six miles, meet at the car, and Bradle will take us back."

After further discussion Feeney added, "You know, no one has ever determined how far the human voice will carry. Let's now synchronize our time-pieces and at midnight I will call to the fellows to the west [a distance of about three miles], and then I will try to call Bradle to the east, and we'll see if we can communicate. It's a nice still night—full moon."

Clarence Searles recalled the incident years later:

So that was the plan. We started out I suppose 8:30 or 9 o'clock when it got crusty enough so the shoes would work fairly well. Feeney and I took the track and headed on down the fire lane while the other boys headed on over the other way. It got along pretty much towards midnight and we were down in a swampy depression, the track still following the firelane. I said, "Bill, wouldn't it be well for us to try to get up onto a rise so that our voice will carry better?" He said, "Sure, let's hurry up through here."

About that time the track left the fire lane. We continued on down, got up on a ridge, watching carefully. Amongst a couple of stumps that lined the east side of the fire lane was a small pine tree about 20 feet high with a limb about 12 feet up. Without taking off our snowshoes we straddled the stumps and ate our sandwiches. Bill said, "Gosh, you know what I'm going to do is call as a wolf." So he cupped his hands, faced west, and let out a beller . . . listened for Berner and Hartmeister, didn't get an answer, and he let out another beller.

I think it was about the third time that he gave voice—as though it were yesterday I can still remember my reaction to it—there was a reply and it was a *fire engine*. I couldn't imagine a fire engine out there, but that's what it was. Rrrrrrrrooooooooooouuuuuuuuuuuuuu. Bill looked at me and I looked at him; we both knew what it was. But the first reaction was that a siren has to be a fire engine—that's all.

Bill shinnied up the pine tree after taking off his shoes and he said, "Well look, Searles, I'm up here and there's room enough for you." And I said, "Well, if it gets any closer, don't worry, I'll be up there too." But as it was I stayed on the ground and I said, "Go ahead, call again." We spoke in subdued voices of course.

On the second or third emission by this animal, as he started on up the scale, another voice came in at a higher pitch—Uuuuuuuuuaaaaahhhh—came down to the point of the first one, and dropped down to bass. There was a pair of them; no question about it. Though it was very sparse cover—small maple about an inch and a half in diameter—we never caught a glimpse of the animals. Every time that Bill called, why, we had an answer. This lasted for a half hour or more.

About that time the animals apparently started moving to the south—west of the fire lane we were on. We decided there was no need of our going any further. We found what we wanted—we'd located the wolves. And it was still quite some distance down to the lane that led east to where Bradle waited for us. Desiring to come back in daylight to show the whole crew and to find out for ourselves what had happened here, we decided to abort our earlier plans, and so we turned and headed back to the north towards the cabin.

The wolves, by that time, had apparently crossed away to the south and cut east. By this time coyotes were coming into the picture too. Every time Bill would call, the wolf would answer and then the coyotes would chime in. Gosh, there was really quite a musical out there. As we came north, the wolves followed us back from along our east side, as I remember, for about two miles. They quit giving voice just about the time we reached the cabin.

Meanwhile Hartmeister and Berner were following south on the fire lane about three miles to our west, but they hadn't seen any tracks. Finally, two tracks cut across the lane heading northeast, and they decided that since these tracks were reasonably fresh they would follow them out. After following them some distance the tracks led out onto Duck Lake, crossing to the northeast shore, where they re-entered the forest. After some time the fellow in the lead exclaimed, "I don't know where the tracks went. I can't find them." In searching around the area they discovered a big hollow log right ahead of them. One of the animals walked on top of the log and the other went into the log and came out the opening at the other end.[2]

Les Berner's field notes reflected the discovery: "(3:45 A.M. of April 7) We discovered a den that may be used by T. wolves about ½ mile N of Duck Lake. We (Hartmeister and I) didn't have nerve enough to crawl in with only matches for light."[3]

Searles continued:

> Feeney and I hadn't been back at the cabin more than half—three-quarters of an hour, just making a pot of coffee, when Berner and Hartmeister came in. Poor Bradle waited for us a long time in my car at the appointed meeting place when finally he decided to return. He didn't get in 'til five o'clock in the morning and he didn't hear the wolves, didn't hear us, he didn't hear anything— and he didn't see any tracks. That was the night the den was found by Berner and Hartmeister.[4]

Bernie Bradle didn't need to stand long next to the potbelly stove to thaw out—the excitement of Hartmeister and Berner's discovery was electrifying. A few of the men wanted to go right back out and see the den, but after a bit more talk Feeney convinced everyone that it was best not to disturb the area, get some rest, and go back out on Saturday night to investigate the events that took place only hours ago.[5]

The following evening the fellow returned to the spot where Feeney and Searles had had their experience, and they discovered that the two wolves had been within 50 yards of them when Feeney had begun "bellering." They also determined that these were the same two wolves that Hartmeister and Berner had followed to the den only a half mile from the pine tree that Feeney had scurried up.

The group heard howling on the second night too, but nothing as spectacular as the first night. Between 11:00 P.M. and 3:00 A.M. they once again elicited howls from a pair of wolves that apparently was on the move, and occasionally a pair of coyotes chimed in.

At 5:00 A.M., when they were turning in for the evening, a single timber wolf howled from somewhere to the east of the cabin. The next day the researchers broke camp, leaving the Duck Lake country and bringing with them memories that would last a lifetime.[6]

Interest in a Timber Wolf Project

When Feeney got back to his office at Ladysmith, he found a letter from Aldo Leopold. As chairman of the Wisconsin Academy of Science, Arts and Letters Natural Resources Committee, Leopold thought that an investigation into the ecology of timber wolves in the state was needed. Leopold wanted to know Feeney's thoughts on formulating such a committee, and asked if Feeney would consent to serve as its chairman.

On April 10th Feeney responded: "Your recent note found me very receptive to the suggestion of further study of the ecology of the wolf in Wisconsin. We had just come back from a wolf survey on which we had some very unusual experiences."[7]

In fact, during the meeting at Hurd's cabin up in the Pleasant and Duck lakes area of Iron County, Feeney had laid out the ground work for a timber wolf study. The men were to gather information on the sex and age of wolf-killed deer, and they were expected to inspect or collect timber wolf droppings to tell what the wolves' diet was. In addition, the crew was to follow wolf trails when encountered, obtain counts of the number of wolves in study packs, determine their circuits, and generally learn what the wolves were up to.

This work assignment was not on the list of objectives for the Pittman-Robertson–funded Deer Research Project and would be a dangerously volatile issue should the public catch wind of it. For these reasons the men decided that, though the work would be done, their initial investigations should be kept secret. As it was, Leopold's suggestion would provide perfect cover for Feeney's men to carry on with their occasional reconnaissance of the state's wolf population.

Professor Leopold hadn't been idle in awaiting a response from Feeney. Throughout the early months of 1944 he had been promoting the creation of a wolf study through various scholarly channels. His suggestion of establishing a Wisconsin Academy of Science, Arts and Letters committee to study wolves materialized in July 1944. At Leopold's request, Bill Feeney was placed in charge of the Ecology of the Wolf in Wisconsin committee. Other members included the deputy director of the Conservation Department, Ernie Swift, the secretary of the Wisconsin Conservation Congress, Clarence Searles, and woodsman and trapper George Ruegger.[8]

Problems began to surface between Leopold and Feeney. Leopold, an astute politician and immaculate scientist, felt it was important to collect bountied timber wolves and coyotes to determine sex ratios, age patterns, and fecundity rates. Feeney, however, was already a battle-scarred veteran of the deer war dilemma, and he despised bounty trappers and the pro-bounty advocates. Feeney refused to have anything to do with trappers.[9]

Leopold pursued other avenues to obtain this valuable information. In January of 1945 he drafted a proposal to study wolf and coyote populations in Wisconsin. Because of budgetary problems due to the war, he suggested the study should be limited to the collection of carcasses, which would be shipped to the university for necropsy work. There an assistant would examine stomach contents to determine food habits, obtain information on reproduction by examining placental scarring and fetuses, and study sex-age ratios, parasites, and the taxonomy of carcasses submitted.

He believed this work would be a companion piece to the work Feeney's field crew was doing. He proposed that the Conservation Department and the university share equally the $1,000 research request, adding that "financial participation by the University will support the impartiality of the research . . . important in so controversial a question." Unfortunately, Hans Thomsen, the student Leopold had in mind for the job, was drafted, and both the university and the Conservation Department failed to appropriate any funds for the project. [10]

Feeney's secret wolf study, the academy's wolf ecology study, and Leopold's continuing initiatives weren't the only inquiries into wolf ecology circulating about the state. At the insistence of the Conservation Department, a predator abundance survey was also initiated to obtain information on animals such as wolves, and it relied on observers accurately reporting tracks they encountered. For the first time since the Deer Research Project had begun, a large number of wardens, forest rangers, and citizen volunteers were to be made a part of the 1944–45 winter deer yard survey work force, and personnel attended a training program headed by Feeney.

This new predator appraisal program was probably instituted at the suggestion of Ernie Swift, despite misgivings by Feeney, who seriously questioned the veracity of the participants. The track survey was designed to show the public just how abundant (or rare) various predators were. Results of the track survey weren't widely circulated amongst the public, but they did reveal that wolves weren't all that common. Most significantly the track survey gave legitimacy to the efforts of Feeney's men, who were more actively pursuing wolf sign.

Working on the Deer Research Project

The Deer Research Project was under the supervision of Walter Scott, with Feeney serving as the principle investigator. Many of the biologists assigned to Feeney's work crews were college trained, having studied under Aldo Leopold. The majority of men served short terms with the Deer Research Project, [11] and most of them were referrals from Scott. Occasionally

Feeney enlisted the aid of trustworthy volunteers, such as Clarence Searles.

Walter Scott, an administrator who started with the Wisconsin Conservation Department as a warden, was in charge of the administrative tangles. He had a keen interest in wildlife and a rare appreciation of the values of research. Scott provided the vehicles, gasoline, and equipment necessary to conduct such extensive fieldwork. During the height of World War II many commodities were in short supply. For instance, gasoline and meat were rationed, but Feeney recalled that the project was assigned more than enough to get the work done. The work crews even had a prototype snow-machine, which they called a snow toboggan (see 7.3).

All men assigned to the project spent a lot of time away from their homes. Many areas were so remote that arrangements were sometimes made to stay in logging camps or hunting cabins. Feeney basically relied on his men to search out such opportunities for lodging. Bernie Bradle took advantage of the Goodman Lumber Company camps when he worked in the Robago Lake area of Florence County. It seems that co-worker Ralph Hovind's brother Jim was the forester for Marinette and Florence counties, and he made the connections enabling Bradle and others to use the camp facilities. "We paid $1 for our room and about 75¢ for our meals and we ate like kings."

7.3. Early prototype snow machines used by the Deer Research Project crew in Iron County during the mid-1940s. (Photograph courtesy of Bernie Bradle.)

Frequently crew members would stay in a cabin near Gobler Lake while working in the Willow area. Felix Hartmeister knew the people who owned the cabin, and they allowed crew members to use it provided they kept it clean.[12]

One of the Deer Research Project assistants was an acquaintance of Dr. Benjamin Dike from Owen. Dr. Dike and his wife, Hazel, purchased land and a cabin near Duck Lake in Iron County from the Roddis Lumber Company in June of 1940. Dr. Dike allowed Feeney's men the use of their cabin. The crew also used Herbert Hurd and Fred Piltz' cabin near the Pleasant Lake fire tower just four miles north of Dike's cabin. The crew had been staying at the Hurd and Piltz cabin the night they found the timber wolf den.

The men were given an allowance for food. Employees and some volunteers, such as Clarence Searles, were also given an allowance for gas, because they frequently used their own cars. Some samples of Searles' daily expenses follow:

March 7, 1945:		
Breakfast	.50	
Dinner	.75	
Total	1.25	
Gas—5 gal.	1.18	
Oil	.30	
Miles—173	Total—$2.73	
March 8, 1945:		
Breakfast	.50	
Dinner	.35	
Supper	.85	
Total	1.70	
Gas—10 gal.	2.28	
Oil	.38	
Miles—96	Total—$4.33[13]	

Feeney demanded a lot out of his men. Their average work day did not begin at the office shop at 8:00 A.M. with a bull session over a cup or two of coffee. At 8:00 A.M. his men were already in the field working. But Feeney was sufficiently lenient to grant them enough time to get back to their cars by dark! Then at night the crews had field notes to catch up on. The men were also expected to be available 24 hours a day, seven days a week, and the work crews frequently worked weekends. The men often worked alone, come rain, shine, snow, or subzero weather, from sunup to sundown.

Many of the project employees had to endure extended periods away from home; this, of course, involved their families. During Bradle's first winter (1942–43) he was assigned to work primarily in the northwest part of

7.4. Bill Feeney took this photograph of warden Bill Curran, apparently while putting him to the test. (Photograph courtesy Wisconsin Department of Natural Resources Photo Archives.)

the state. Not having a car made it difficult to get home to Crandon to visit his wife and children on those occasions when he had a few days off.

Feeney ran a tight ship and frequently tested his men's faith and dedication to the job, but it seems he took special pleasure in breaking in new recruits. Bradle summed it up curtly: "Bill was thin and wiry and he could throw a pair of snowshoes around. On their first day on the job he took Bruce Stollberg and Harry Strobe out and walked the asses off of them, and he took me along with him to walk the asses off of them"[14] (see 7.4). Searles also made it a point to mention Feeney's knack at snowshoeing. "That darned Bill Feeney only weighed 140 pounds. At the time, I weighed 210. And I wore [snow] shoes, but boy I'm telling you he'd kill me on snowshoes."[15]

The climate and some of the people in the area also often presented challenges to the Deer Research crew. In March 1945, Searles and Armin Schwengel were virtually snowed in at Hurd's cabin. Every night, storms would blow in off Lake Superior and dump up to six inches of snow. One particular morning when Searles got up, the thermometer read −38°. Anxious to do something to avert cabin fever, he waited until it warmed up a bit and then hauled the "snow toboggan" out of the cabin ("They were devils to start when cold!"). Jumping on it, he took off south on the fire lane, intending to make the circuit around Duck Lake and back to the cabin, looking for wolf tracks.

By the time he got down to Dr. Dike's cabin he was just about frozen, so he decided to go in, brew himself a cup of coffee, and warm up. He scooped some snow into the pot and began melting it down. When the water began to boil he went to the cupboard, pulled down a cup, and reached for the pot to pour a cup of coffee. "When I poured it in that cup it just fell apart." Feeling terrible for making such a silly mistake, Searles left Dr. Dike a note explaining the incident, and a dollar to replace the cup.[16]

Once, Feeney and Searles decided to check out some wolf tracks reported on the north end of the Willow Flowage in Oneida County. Accompanied by the local warden, Bill Curran, and cruiser Forrest Spahr, the group got out to the flowage in midafternoon on January 23, 1945. Because of the lateness of the day and the distance involved, they split into two groups. Searles and Feeney struck out from Doberstein's Resort over the flowage ice, heading northwest into a brisk wind, but the wind obliterated all traces of tracks, including their own.

To make matters worse the power company had recently drawn down the flowage, making the channel ice unsafe. The two men carefully retraced their way as best they could but missed Doberstein's landing. They were forced to leave the flowage and walk through an extensive young pine plantation to avoid a large marsh, but they finally made it to Doberstein's Road at 9:30 P.M. They didn't get back to their hotel in Tomahawk until 12:30 A.M. Two days later a fever and bad cold forced Feeney to return home to Ladysmith.[17]

On another occasion Dan Thompson was conducting a browse survey in the Argonne Deer Refuge in Forest County when he encountered an illegal wolf trap. The trap was a number five reinforced with number two springs. As Bradle recalled, "Danny ran into some traps set for timber wolves in the refuge, and boy, Danny hated anybody that had one bad word to say about timber wolves. He took the trap and hid it, and he never got the chance to show me where the damned thing was. We'd o' hauled it outta there."[18]

Feeney and his men had some unpleasant duties too, such as apprising citizens of their deer investigations at local town halls throughout the north. Quite typically there was a lot of name calling, shouting, dirty accusations, and irrational outbursts from those attending. On the evening of May 21, 1944, Deer Research crew worker Ralph Schmidt took notes, incognito, at a Save Wisconsin's Deer meeting at Minocqua, attended by more than 400 people. Although no one from the Conservation Department was officially present at this particular meeting, the dialogue was quite typical of the meetings that *were* officially attended by Feeney and others.

The speakers even featured several state senators and assemblymen as well as respected citizens of the community. At issue were Conservation Department recommendations that hunting license fees be raised and an antlerless deer season be established the following fall. The group noted the absence of Conservation Department representatives and Senator Heddeen from Price County alertly pointed out that troubles are caused when the government, in this case the Conservation Department, is not answerable to the will of the people—which is the law of the land.

Another person identifying himself as Bert Claflin, a sports writer, jumped up and lambasted Aldo Leopold, whom he called "the king of Wisconsin." Claflin first met Leopold in a saloon in one Happy Noye's basement in Milwaukee. He claimed that Leopold, who was then, as he put it, "down and out," got a job making a survey through Noye's influence, and then slid into a position as wildlife professor at the university. "Today he tells Aberg [fellow Wisconsin Conservation commissioner] what to do about the deer. No deer hunter needs advice from Leopold. . . . The King says deer must be shot to avoid annihilation. Money from tourists go to everyone while that from the deer license sales go to the King for politics!"[19]

The discussion eventually turned to wolves. Following a brief discourse on the deadly impact of wolves on the deer herd, the group unanimously recommended restoration of the recently rescinded bounty.[20]

Feeney and his men took such public "roasts" in stride. "They were ignorant on the subject and we knew what to expect—it was no surprise." Feeney added that he knew his recommendations to reduce the deer herd to a point where browse reproduction throughout the state's deer range could survive were appropriate. Surveys in all the deer yards indicated that many prime browse species were being seriously depleted. For most species no recruitment was occurring, because deer were clipping the reproduction off as soon as it sprouted. Only on the Menominee Indian reservation did they note normal recruitment, primarily because the Indians kept the deer herd within the limits of the vegetation needed to support them. Feeney felt that even poaching was a beneficial practice, because it acted to suppress deer numbers.[21] However, he kept this opinion to himself, because to express support for poaching would have earned him a rope necktie and reservations for the most convenient limb on the nearest tree.

Discoveries from Feeney's Wolf Study

Despite several initiatives to study Wisconsin's timber wolves, Feeney's "unofficial" project was the only one that progressed beyond the planning stage and yielded information of substance. The cadre of biologists assigned to Feeney's "secret wolf study" improved their understanding of the role wolves played in the debate over the deer conservation issue. This information had utility beyond Wisconsin's borders in Michigan's Upper Peninsula and northern Minnesota, where citizen concerns about deer and wolves were similar to those in Wisconsin.

Feeney's study was only the third serious investigation ever conducted on wolves. The first objective look at wolves had been concluded a decade earlier by pioneer wildlife biologist Sigurd Olson, in the Superior National Forest in northeastern Minnesota. Olson's work provided nothing more valuable than tidbits of the wolf's life history, but it also provided a fresh perspective of this predator that differed from popular views.

Another work was in the process of being published when Feeney and his men sequestered themselves in the Iron County wilderness in April of 1944. National Park Service wildlife biologist Adolf Murie had recently completed his epic fieldwork on the wolves of Mount McKinley, Alaska. This study was the first comprehensive field study of wolf biology, and revealed previously undescribed aspects of the wolf's behavior, impacts on prey populations, and life history.

Whereas Sigurd Olson and Adolf Murie had worked alone, Feeney's wolf project was the first collaborative effort of a number of biologists in an attempt to document wolf biology. In order to maintain continuity in their observations, Feeney had drilled each of his men in the art of recording information. Each day the biologists carried with them small notebooks and pencils into the field. They were expected to scribble down *everything* they saw. When the men encountered wolf sign they recorded information on the number of tracks observed, the trails used by the wolves, the distance the biologists followed wolves, and anything else they noted while on the trail of this elusive species.

Bradle was given control over studies of wolves in the Argonne area of Forest County, and Hartmeister was assigned to keep tabs on the Willow wolves in western Oneida County. The Iron County wolf range was to be left under the direction of Feeney and Clarence Searles. All the biologists summarized their progress in the wolf study at infrequent meetings held by Feeney.

Movements and Pack Territory Size

In those days it was very difficult to follow the daily travels of wolves and to determine the home range of wolf packs. The wolves were simply more mobile than the scientists who attempted to follow them. These difficulties wouldn't be overcome until the advent of radio telemetry in the mid-1960s.

As a consequence, Bill Feeney and his biologists were rarely able to determine how far their study wolves traveled in a single day. Problems with access confounded their attempts to trail the wolves very far. Nonetheless the crew recorded minimum daily movements of from 4 to 12 miles from the wolves they followed. This probably represented more the limitations of the biologists than the wolves.

Trailing wolves often entailed a considerable amount of detective work, as Deer Research Project biologist Felix Hartmeister found out when he became momentarily confused by patterns in the snow. He was impressed when he finally unraveled the following scenario: "February 21, 1945 Town of Sherman—Iron Co. . . . [In] many places [the two wolves] walked on logs just like [bob]cats over and under brush to avoid deep snow. The logs were not always large but tact in walking on them was good."[22]

The biologists had some interesting experiences while trailing the wolves. On the 13th and 14th of February in 1946 biologists Felix Hartmeister, Ralph Hovind, and Cliff Bakkom trailed members of the Willow wolf pack along the border between Price and Oneida counties southwest of Willow Lake. They encountered the tracks of two animals in the afternoon of the 13th, but weren't sure if the tracks were of wolves or dogs. One track looked queer: "The two side toes were way out."[23] They were looking at the tracks of Old Two Toes of the Willow pack. One of the biologists quickly scribbled a summary of the day's event in his notebook: ". . . Followed [the wolves] by foot and car to . . . where they left road again at logging shack. Crossed road on S. end of loop going south—got dark."[24] The next morning the boys resumed tracking:

Weather: Snowing at 0700 ½" and flurries thru day. Temp. from 0 at 0700 to −10 at 1900 Wind NW 20 [mph] gusty.
Wind blowing with snow falling at times. Followed tracks of yesterday which I thought could be dogs but am inclined to believe they are TW [timber wolves]. We followed them into Oneida [County] and until they discovered us they were easy to follow. . . . found where they had bedded down. This must be where they got up in the morning, but [they] didn't seem to be frightened till when they . . . came to within 10 feet of our snowshoe tracks.[25]

Another biologist recorded:

In sect[ion] 5 we found where they made a loop to go to an old carcass and then back on their previous trail. The animals must have sensed that we were following them about this time because the tracks led onto a logging road which they followed a short way until a worn glove in the road turned them back about 25 yds. where they again hit the brush. In the alders we found a dropping frozen only on the outside. The tracks circled back to the north . . . until they came to our tracks made only 15–30 minutes before. . . . the animals retraced their steps a short way and then headed straight west to [an] open swamp where the wind covered their tracks.[26]

A few weeks later Hartmeister and others had another interesting experience in the Willow country:

Feb. 20, 1946: Oneida Co. Clear 0, NW wind 10 mph. last snow Feb. 18. Followed track that first thought could be a dog but was a T.W. [timber wolf] with a trap on his foot. Noticed one place where he bedded down, & then moved again when the trapper followed him. The trapper did not follow [more than] a mile. Crossed West and Muskellunge Lake firelane.

Feb. 21, 1946: Oneida Co. Resumed trail north of firelane. The TW was down wind from us & kept going back & forth till he crossed Lamer Springs road and west crossing Co. T going west. One place where he bedded down for the night on top of semi open slope the blood was in quantity. . . . Followed tracks of the trapped timber wolf for about 10 mi.[27]

They picked up the trapped wolf's tracks briefly on February 23rd, but weren't able to learn the fate of this creature because the weather and other work duties prevented them from following it farther. However, on April 9th one of the crew found tracks of two or three wolves in the sand of a nearby fire lane and jotted down the following observation: "The one with all the toes missing [Old Two Toes] was in the group. He has a new track of only one toe."[28] Although it will never be known, perhaps the wolf Hartmeister and others followed that winter survived after all.

Feeney and his crew were extremely limited in obtaining information on the size of the territories of their study packs. Despite the obstacles, they faithfully plotted pack movements on maps. Meaningful information was patiently accumulated only after several winters of monitoring the wolves.

Eventually they were able to estimate home range sizes for the Pleasant Lake, Camp Scott Lake, Michigan Creek, and Willow wolf packs. These territories ranged from 91 to 310 square miles and were large in comparison with those for which telemetry information has been obtained in recent times (table 7.1). Since the early 1900s Wisconsin's wolf population was subjected to intense persecution, and the size of the pack territories observed by Feeney's men may have been a reflection of how poorly the wolves fared in the state by the 1940s.

It is also possible that the crew may have overestimated the size of their pack territories, because wolf movements were collected over several years. Occasional shifts in wolf activity within the large, remote wolf ranges could have gone unnoticed.

Range estimates varied from year to year. One of the most studied groups of wolves was Oneida County's Willow wolf pack (map 7.1). During the winter of 1936–37 state control trapper Jake Jakoubek reported that a single pack of wolves ranged 216 square miles in a six-township area. Wolf crew

Table 7.1.   Size and population densities within northern Wisconsin and Upper Michigan timber wolf ranges, 1940–56

Wolf range	Study period	Range size (in square miles)	Wolf density (number of square miles per wolf)
Wisconsin			
Pleasant Lake	1940s	186	26–93
Camp Scott Lake	1940s	225	32
Willow Pack	1941–49	300	75
	1944–46	124	31–42
	1946–48	150	42–50
Michigan Creek	1941–50	90	45
Twin Lakes	1944–46	86	—
Average		166	49
Michigan			
Cusino	1938	260	65
Cusino	1950	75	25
Hulbert[a]	1950	48	8
Hulbert	1950	335	56
Average		179	39

Sources: Wisconsin Conservation Department Pittman-Robertson Deer Research Project materials; Stebler, "The Ecology of Michigan Coyotes and Wolves."

[a]These data pertain to a limited winter range when the pack, the biologist, or both were confined to a small area because of deep snows (with concomitant high deer densities).

members Felix Hartmeister and Bernie Bradle recorded wolf activity in a 125-square-mile area between 1944 and 1946. Biologist Dan Thompson documented wolf activity in a 150-square-mile area between 1946 and 1948 in the same region of western Oneida County.[29]

The pack boundaries described by Hartmeister, Bradle, and Thompson were very similar (Map 7.1). Records left by other biologists between 1941 and 1949 indicate that wolf activity was encountered in a 300-square-mile area, twice the area reported by Bradle, Hartmeister, and Thompson, who intensively studied the Willow wolf pack. Did more than one group occupy this larger area, or were the Willow wolves accustomed to shifting activity from one area to another periodically?

Feeney's crew didn't have the benefit of the hindsight the reader has in attempting to evaluate what they were observing. Their assessment of Wisconsin wolf pack territory sizes was similar to what Adolf Stebler would

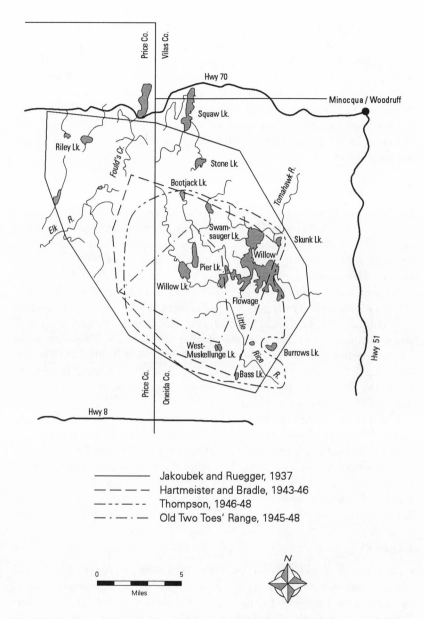

Map 7.1. Boundary estimates of the Willow timber wolf range, Oneida and Price counties, 1937–48

observe in Upper Michigan in 1950 (table 7.1). With the Wisconsin and Michigan data combined, the average wolf pack territory was 171 square miles. This was considerably larger than the 74 square miles that Milton Stenlund would report from his northern Minnesota wolf study during the early 1950s, using the same laborious ground tracking techniques.[30] The difference in sizes of wolf territories between Wisconsin and Michigan on the one hand and Minnesota on the other may be explained by the fact that Minnesota's wolf population was much larger and more stable than Wisconsin and Michigan's.

The Range of a Crippled Wolf

The movement of one particular wolf of the Willow pack was recorded periodically by the Wisconsin Conservation Department biologists. It was a male and was easily identified by its tracks, because it had lost toes in encounters with traps (see 7.5). This wolf had been dubbed Old Two Toes by local woodsmen and the biologists.

Trapper Walt Rosenlaf considered Old Two Toes the pack's alpha male. He was identifiable by his peculiar tracks from at least 1945 to 1949, when he was finally trapped and killed. During that time he ranged an area of about 44 square miles, considerably smaller than the 125–150-square-mile range reported for the rest of the pack by Hartmeister, Bradle, and Thompson (map 7.1). Although tracks of Old Two Toes were frequently encountered, the biologists rarely plotted his movements, so the range of this wolf may have been underestimated.

Dan Thompson felt the old wolf was unable to keep up with his packmates. "He was evidently handicapped under these particular snow conditions for his maimed pads would frequently break through the light crust. The three wolves accompanying him trotted along easily on the surface of the snow."[31] The old two-toed wolf's area of activity may have been confined to the core of the Willow wolf pack's range (map 7.1), especially during the winter months, when most observations of his tracks were made.

Densities

Once territory sizes had been determined, Feeney and his crew were able to figure out wolf densities. This was accomplished by dividing the size of the pack home ranges by the number of wolves they counted each winter.

Feeney and the others knew there were few timber wolves remaining in Wisconsin in the 1940s. Pack ranges were extraordinarily large, and they knew wolf densities would be low. Thompson, for instance, estimated a density of one wolf per 50 square miles in the Willow wolf pack. Northern Wisconsin's wolf densities were similar to the one wolf per 65 square mile

7.5. Tracks of the old two-toed wolf of the Willow wolf pack in western Oneida County. Photo taken in February 1947. (Photograph courtesy of Daniel Q. Thompson.)

figures that Adolf Stebler observed in Upper Michigan between 1935 and the 1950s. Wolf densities in the Wisconsin and Michigan wolf ranges were much lower than the estimated one wolf per 17 square miles then existing in northeastern Minnesota.[32] This also reflected the poor condition of the wolf population clinging to existence south of Lake Superior.

Relations with Other Predators

Feeney's wolf crew also observed aspects of wolf behavior that had rarely been recorded. Predators like bear, bobcat, fox, and coyote roamed the forested tracts as would-be competitors of the wolves. It was the bears and coyotes that posed the most serious competition for the wolves.

Wolves came into occasional contact with bears during the winter hibernation period, which Bernie Bradle was able to attest to through first-hand experience. On December 11, 1944, Bradle had an unusual encounter while trailing the Scott Lake wolf pack in Forest County.

> 3:05 P.M. While following timber wolf tracks came upon the working of some animal, bear. The timber wolves had made much sign around area also walked on top of a place where bear was making den. Walked over to uprooted cedar to examine same and was snarled at. Also, the bear thumped his front paw hard on ground when I was about 5 feet from bear. I walked backwards about 40 feet and bear came out and went his way, northeast. It is possible the wolves went through here [earlier that day], no old bear tracks around, only tracks were fresh ones of today.[33]

Undoubtedly the wolves had harassed the lethargic bear at its den shortly before Bradle happened upon it.

Wolf and bear encounters also occurred in spring shortly after bears emerge from their dens. At this time of year bears seek out carrion and occasionally scavenge on wolf kills. Perhaps Feeney learned of the following incident from discussions with Daniel Tyler, who later became a Wisconsin Conservation commissioner. One April in the early 1940s wolves killed a doe near the gate leading to the Tyler family cabin at Foulds Springs in eastern Price County. When discovered, the wolves had eaten the fetus, but upon checking the kill the next day the Tylers discovered a bear had dragged the doe off into the thickets.[34]

This type of interaction was probably not uncommon. On the first of May in 1945 Bernie Bradle and Felix Hartmeister found droppings of one large bear and several timber wolves near the remains of a deer in Forest County.[35]

Coyotes existed within the timber wolf ranges of northern Wisconsin and even Upper Michigan, because there were too few wolves to have any appreciable impact on them. Not surprisingly, Bill Feeney's crew frequently encountered coyote sign within the state's wolf ranges. On March 12, 1942, one deer biologist scribbled into his notebook: "Cruised from Savage to Robago Lake [Florence County]. fresh tracks of timber wolf and coyote all around lake." On August 3, 1944, Bernie Bradle recorded: "Numerous wolf and coyote scats all through. . ." the Stevens Lake area in northeast Forest County.[36]

Trails of coyotes and wolves often were encountered in the same places. Clarence Searles noted the following while working in the Willow Flowage area in January of 1945: "In three places coyote had intersected the wolf tracks and in each case had followed the backtrack a short distance. Never did they go in the direction that the wolves were going."[37]

On the night that Clarence Searles and Bill Feeney experienced the wolf howlings in Iron County, the two actually shared exchanges between a pair of wolves and several coyotes. The following night they again heard the wolves and three or four coyotes chattering to one another.[38]

Coyotes were so bold that they frequently fed from the remains of kills while the wolves were temporarily absent from the site. In one of the Deer Research Project reports this note appeared: "It is possible that the coyotes might have helped the timber wolves prevent, scatter, or thin out excessive localized deer concentrations. Last winter project workers noted where two coyotes had followed a lone hunting timber wolf and helped her dispose of her prey."[39]

Wolves undoubtedly killed coyotes whenever they caught them, but there were too few wolves to have a cleansing effect on local coyote numbers. Biologist Felix Hartmeister and warden George Curran probably found evidence of a coyote that was killed by wolves. On January 26, 1945, they were led to the carcass of a coyote while trailing the Willow wolf pack near the northwest corner of the Willow Flowage in Oneida County. "A dead coyote was found by Curran and it had been dead a long time since there was quite an odor. There were wounds on the abdomen on the right side. The timber wolves discovered it . . . dug it up . . . but did not touch it."[40]

Wolf Predation and Its Impacts on the Deer Herd

The single most important factor that fueled the public's condemnation of wolves was the fact that they preyed on deer, Wisconsin's prized big game animal. Nearly 40 years after the Deer Research Project, Bill Feeney reflected with amusement, "We didn't have to convince people that timber wolves were killing deer."[41]

Feeney and his Deer Research Project biologists nonetheless recorded such details as the length and duration of chases, the age and health charac-

7.6. Bernie Bradle inspecting the remains of a wolf-killed deer in Iron County. (Photograph courtesy of Bernie Bradle.)

teristics of wolf-killed deer, and impacts of predation on the overall welfare of the deer herd (see 7.6). "We would be out in the deer yards and find wolf kills and [we would] try and decide how many wolves we had and what they were doing."[42]

The research crew's descriptions of wolf-killed deer were based on remains and sign left in the snow. Sometimes they had a lot of evidence to work with; other times they were left with very little:

March 25, 1943, Ashland County Spider-Mineral Lakes Deer Yard.
Buck fawn found by Bradle at 10:15 one hind leg had been badly cut by timber wolf. Killed deer and dressed it out because it was decided that death would inevitably occur anyways. . . . Back was bitten by wolves. Lungs, liver and heart appeared in perfect condition.

March 13, 1942, Florence County Savage and Robago Lakes.
Found where wolf had killed a yearling buck (spike), carcass still warm and fresh. Throat cut, guts opened up, hams and rump torn open. . . . Deer was very thin with razor back, no fat on hide. Marrow on femur completely jellied. Deer was weakened from malnutrition before taken by wolf.

November 20, 1944, Forest County in the vicinity of the South Branch of the Pine River.
Ravens circling carcass called my attention to kill (canada jays also feeding on carcass). Examined kill, found wolf tracks all around area, some snow had fallen since kill dusting out older tracks[.] yet fresher ones showed two wolves, could have been three. Examining carcass which was about two/thirds eaten found that left hind foot of the doe was broke before killed because around this area it was bloody. . . . the bone marrow above the break was creamy, opaque. . . . at break looked like bloodshot . . . pussy, thin or watery. . . .[43]

Most successful chases encountered by the crews were apparently made over short distances.

December 28, 1945, Oneida/Forest County border, vicinity of Scott Lake.
Checked the tracks leading up to the kill and found where there had been one or two trails and two or three places where the deer had come down before the final kill. The entire struggle took place in about 40 yards.[44]

There were exceptions, however:

March 23, 1944, Iron County. Swamp Creek north of Forest Wonder Lodge.
Mature Doe kill steaming when examined. . . . Pulled down in a chase of 300 yards. —Bernard Bradle[45]

Although wolves didn't rigorously direct their attacks at any specific area of a deer's body, the throat, back, or legs were often targeted. Wolves also appeared to be catholic in their taste preferences, with first choices ranging from the loins to the heart and hams. Usually kills were entirely eaten by the time the wolves abandoned them. And although an occasional carcass was vacated before being thoroughly cleaned up, the wolves seldom forgot its location.

Bernie Bradle found the remains of 13 wolf-killed deer during three successive winters between 1944 and 1947. In 11 instances the wolves eventually returned to their old kills. On March 23, 1944, Bradle discovered the remains of an old doe killed within the past seven hours near Pleasant Lake in Iron County. A wolf visited the carcass on March 28th and again on April 6th, the day he chafed his legs so badly. He even recorded a visit to the carcass of the doe with the broken hind leg 51 days after it had been killed by the Scott Lake pack. Nothing except some bleaching bones and patches of hide remained, but the wolves did sent-mark them.[46]

Altogether the Deer Research Project biologists found the remains of at least 32 deer killed by wolves between 1942 and 1953. Twenty-seven of these deer were aged in much the same way that horses are aged: by looking at the wear on the animal's teeth.[47] A majority of these were fawns (30 percent) and adult deer between two and five years of age (52 percent). In comparison to the ages of deer taken by hunters, who took mostly yearlings and two-year-old deer, it was evident that wolves were preying more on the inexperienced and older deer.

The biologists reported the sex of 22 wolf kills. Gender was rarely established for fawns, because the wolves usually ate the entire carcass, including the skull. However, they were able to identify three buck fawns, one doe fawn, and one yearling buck and doe. Among the adults there were 3 bucks and 12 does, or a ratio of 1:4. This was a lower ratio than the biologists estimated at large in the deer herd.

Often skeletal and soft body tissues had been consumed, and only scattered fragments of the carcass were available for the biologists to examine to determine the health of the deer before being taken by wolves. If found, the biologists inspected the bone marrow by cracking the deer's long leg bones. Fat made the marrow a pinkish white color in contrast with the oozy blood-red color of fat-depleted marrow in deer that were nutritionally stressed.

Of 21 kills where sufficient body parts remained, half showed signs of health problems. They found seven deer with depleted marrow fat, three deer with heavy infestations of parasitic nose botfly larvae, and one deer for each of the following problems: jaw abnormalities, pneumonia, and a broken leg prior to being killed by wolves.

Feeney and the Deer Research Project crew concluded that wolves had no impact on the deer herd, *even in the few areas of the state where wolves remained*. Reflecting back on those years, Feeney commented that the wolves

> . . . weren't doing much because there weren't enough of them. Roughly speaking, five times as many deer were dying of starvation as what the wolves were eating. The hunters couldn't cover the territory up in that country, and the wolves weren't cleaning up what was being lost from starvation. So we figured, if anything, wolves were beneficial, but there weren't enough of them to be really beneficial.[48]

7.7. A buck fawn and a doe fawn found dead from starvation in Vilas County's Star Lake yard. The first fawn was discovered dead on March 13, 1943, and upon returning five days later, Bernie Bradle discovered the second curled up beside the first. (Photograph courtesy of Bernie Bradle.)

Starvation was a persistent problem—one that none but the biologists seemed to recognize (see 7.7). Diligently the biologists gathered information from the state's northern deer yards. Typical of their findings was the report of biologist Ralph Schmidt, who found the remains of 39 deer between the 13th and 19th of May 1943 in Forest County's Wildcat Creek deer yard. He did as thorough a job in autopsying the decaying bodies as could be expected, and he determined that 27 (70 percent) died from starvation, 6 (15 percent) were killed by humans (4 illegally), and 3 had died of disease. Two bodies were too far gone to ascertain the cause of death. This deer yard was located within the territory of the Scott Lake wolf pack, yet Schmidt's analysis indicated the wolves hadn't touched any of the remains, much less killed any of the deer.

Dan Thompson used a different approach to learn whether wolves were having an impact on the deer herd. He compared deer census records between 1935 and 1940 from the area inhabited by Oneida County's Willow wolf pack with those of an adjacent wolf-free area. He found no differences in the deer densities within these two areas.[49]

Many hunters of that era believed wolves were a menace to the deer herd and cut into the take otherwise available for human hunters. Despite these opinions, deer harvest records from that time period do not bear this out. In fact, deer harvests did not differ appreciably between counties within and outside of wolf range. By the 1930s and 1940s wolves probably no longer had *any* impact on deer numbers. The information Bill Feeney and his fellow biologists assembled demonstrated that there were simply too few wolves in Wisconsin to "do their job."[50]

Food Habits

Feeney's crew knew the wolves had no impact on Wisconsin's deer herd, but they were interested in just how important deer were to the wolves. To answer this question, Bernie Bradle, Felix Hartmeister, and Clarence Searles began collecting timber wolf droppings, or scats, and shipped them to the Poynette Game Farm pathology lab for analysis.* Field notes from Deer Research Project personnel recorded food items in 48 wolf scats found between November 1942 and June 1946. They found that wolves relied to a great degree on deer. Deer remains were found in 90 percent of the scats, and 7 percent consisted of rabbits and snowshoe hares. Bradle even found one summer scat packed full of berry seeds.[51]

The most thorough study conducted on wolf food habits was completed at this time in Wisconsin, but it wasn't conducted by Feeney's circle of wolf biologists. Dan Thompson had worked briefly with the Wisconsin Deer Research Project before the war interrupted his employment. In 1946 he returned to the state and hired on with the project for a short while. Thompson was impressed with ". . . timber wolf travel [that] was particularly heavy on a stretch of fire lane in Oneida County. . . . this looked like a promising opportunity for a wolf food habits study. . . ."[52] Dan returned to Madison and chose this topic for his thesis work as one of Aldo Leopold's graduate students at the University of Wisconsin.

Thompson's food habits study focused on the Willow wolf pack and Iron County's Pleasant Lake pack. Between 1946 and 1948 he collected 435 scats from area fire lanes (see 7.8) and trails. Back at the lab he carefully teased each scat apart and painstakingly identified the bone fragments and masses

---

*Unfortunately, the results of this survey were never published, and the analysis has since become lost.

7.8. Collecting a timber wolf scat. Note the wolf tracks in the center of the fire lane. (Photograph courtesy of Bernie Bradle.)

of hair found within. Thompson methodically tabulated the number of scats in which a particular type of food item was found and compared these with the total number of scats collected to obtain the frequency with which each food item appeared in the collection of droppings.

White-tailed deer were by far the most prevalent food item, occurring in 97 percent of the scats. Snowshoe hare were found in 5 percent, and other small mammals such as cottontails, voles, and chipmunks appeared in 5 percent of the scats. Deer predominated in all four seasons, and snowshoe hare was encountered more often in spring and summer scats.[53]

Thompson also set out to determine to what extent the two wolf packs relied on white-tailed fawns during the summer months. Fortunately he was able to distinguish a difference between the hairs of adult deer and fawns in most cases. He found the remains of fawns in 45 percent and adults in 50 percent of the 141 scats he collected during summer months. Although he did not take into account a bias towards fawns,[54] wolves undoubtedly killed more fawns than adults, because fawns composed about a third of the summer deer population in a normal year.

Thompson also wondered whether wolves preyed on fawns when they became more active around a month and a half following birth. The proportion of fawns changed from about 40 percent to 60 percent after they became more active in July.[55] Wolves more efficiently preyed on fawns following this change in their development.

These food habits studies basically verified the wolves' reliance on deer. No detectable seasonal changes in the prevalence of deer was found. During the summer months wolves capitalized on the inexperienced, vulnerable, and more numerous fawns, whereas in winter they relied heavily on fawns and aged adult deer.

Deer weren't the only source of food for wolves. Hares and rabbits were occasionally captured by wolves, but aside from scat work the biologists rarely observed evidence of predation on these small mammals. In 1937 state wolf trapper Jake Jakoubek witnessed an incident while trailing the Willow wolf pack: "For the first time I have found where timber wolves have killed a rabbit which I really believe was for the fun of it, although they devoured it."[56] In January of 1945 several Deer Research Project biologists were trailing some wolves in the general vicinity where Jakoubek had earlier made his observation, and Clarence Searles wrote: "West of the Willow Springs campground the [wolves] caught a cottontail rabbit bringing it out on the lane. All that was left was the skin which appeared to have been carefully removed."[57] Surprisingly, a red squirrel was eating the rabbit's hide.

Beaver and porcupine were not found in the scats of wolves. Thompson considered beavers scarce and porcupines common in the western Oneida County Willow wolf pack territory.[58]

Had Feeney and his crew collected carcasses, perhaps they would have found some evidence of wolves utilizing beaver and porcupine. In 1945 Reino Herlevi trapped a pair of wolves in central Iron County, most likely within the Pleasant Lake wolf pack's range. ". . . when I skinned them I found that they both had many porcupine quills in the hide around the jaws and neck[.] one had a quill near its eye."[59] Minnesota biologist Milt Stenlund mentioned that the lips, nostrils, and nose of a 64-pound male wolf contained at least a dozen quills embedded an eighth inch into its skin.[60] On December 20, 1945, Bernie Bradle was trailing the Scott Lake wolf pack in the vicinity of the Hiles Flowage in Forest County. He mentioned that the wolves "inspected . . . every home of a porcupine (two)."[61] These observations indicate that wolves displayed at least an occasional curiosity for these spiny creatures.

In the 1930s and 1940s beavers were fairly uncommon in the upper Great Lakes. Still, it was odd that this large aquatic rodent did not show up in the diet of the wolf, because recent studies have shown it to be a fairly important component of the wolf's diet. During this same period in neighboring Minnesota, beavers were not recorded in the diet of those wolves either.[62]

Despite the lack of evidence that beaver served as a food item, wolves evidently showed some interest in beaver activity where they encountered it. On March 10, 1945, Clarence Searles followed several wolves along Swamp Creek in Iron County. "Fresh [wolf] tracks went up the creek[.] at one place a beaver had come out and cut a few branches. The wolves followed his trail but without luck."[63]

Beavers were important to wolves in other ways. For instance: "2 different males [wolves] used beaver house as scent post" in the old sinkhole swamp area within Forest County's Scott Lake pack territory on December 19, 1946.[64]

It wasn't until the early 1950s that beaver showed up in the wolves' diet. Although Bernie Bradle had transferred to other job duties within the Wisconsin Conservation Department, his interest in wolves continued. One summer in the early 1950s he collected a timber wolf scat in Forest County that was composed entirely of beaver hair.

The Status of Wolves

In the course of their travels throughout the northern forests of the state, the Deer Research biologists obtained fairly accurate appraisals of timber wolf numbers and distribution. Yet determining the status of Wisconsin's timber wolf population presented difficulties. Wolves were highly mobile and, because of the remote regions they inhabited, it was hard to find sign and keep up with the packs.

The research crews also experienced problems in distinguishing dog and wolf sign. And then there was the matter of convincing Feeney that they had actually observed timber wolf sign: "A labrador [retriever] and a timber wolf track—well you've gotta look close."[65]

Feeney's insistence on being absolutely sure about the identification of tracks didn't help some of his biologists build confidence in their abilities. Large canid tracks also were sometimes observed outside the core wolf ranges in Iron, Price, Oneida, Forest, and Florence counties. For instance, biologist Felix Hartmeister was hesitant to identify the tracks that he observed on the old Hines Railroad grade in southeastern Sawyer County:

> January 22, 1945. Light snow on road where it had been newly plowed. Tracks follow the road for about a half mile. They were clear, longer than width of my hand and wide as the length of my longest finger. There was much urinating on the snow banks. There seemed to be three, but two possitively [*sic*]. *Don't think they are timbers* [emphasis added].[66]

The consistent size of the tracks, the number of individuals, and the urinations indicated these animals were indeed wolves. Yet Hartmeister was reluctant to call them what they were.

That summer Hartmeister found tracks a few miles to the south in northeastern Rusk County. Once again he expressed hesitancy:

> The tracks I took pictures of are either dogs or TW [timber wolves]. I am still with doubt if they are the latter, because of the great difference in the tracks of the 1 large one and two smaller ones. [This was] The only time of their appearance there in many times having cruised in that area; the running [i.e., pattern of the tracks] was very good tho, the hind feet placed in tracks of front feet.[67]

He may have been looking at tracks of an adult with several pup wolves.

Part of Hartmeister's difficulty was that this area lay outside the core wolf areas of the state. Feeney was especially critical of track identification in areas where wolves were not regularly encountered. He seems to have discounted the presence of wolves in the Mason Lake–Price Creek area of southeastern Sawyer, northeastern Rusk, and southwestern Price counties, where Hartmeister encountered these tracks (the Price Creek wolf pack ranged in that area until 1954; see chapter 8).

Between 1943–44 and 1947–48 Feeney and his crew identified five to seven active wolf ranges scattered across north-central and northeastern

Wisconsin in Iron, Price, Oneida, Vilas, Forest, and Florence counties. Even within the wolf ranges familiar to the crew, doubts sometimes surfaced regarding the number of packs roaming each range. For instance, within the Willow region of western Oneida County, Felix Hartmeister wrote in his summary report for 1945–46: "There may be a possibility that there may be two groups since there is not a possitive [sic] identification of all animals."[68]

Despite the difficulties, the wolf crew obtained fairly accurate figures on wolf numbers. But the numbers they kept coming up with were lower than those envisioned by Wisconsin Conservation Department administrators, and far lower than those in the public's perceptions. Feeney and the tight circle of biologists working on the wolf project felt frustrated that the administration did not see how seriously close to extinction the wolf was.

During the winter of 1944–45 they counted 24 wolves in six packs. In 1945–46 they estimated 22 wolves in five packs. The average pack size in 1944–45 was 4 wolves; in 1945–46 it was 4.3 wolves. Bernie Bradle obtained the most meaningful counts on yearly pack changes from Forest County's Scott Lake pack, which ranged from five to eight individuals in the four winters studied between 1943–44 and 1946–47 (figure 7-1). In 1945 Feeney estimated that fewer than 30 wolves remained in Wisconsin.[69]

The wolf packs Feeney's crews studied were undoubtedly in the best shape of those that remained in the state, which wasn't saying much. Packs like the Price Creek group, whose sign Hartmeister dubiously encountered and whose existence Feeney was prone to discount, were close to collapsing. Blinded by his reluctance to accept wolf track observations from his crew beyond ranges familiar to him, Feeney underestimated the number of timber wolves Wisconsin harbored in the mid-1940s. However, his estimate was far closer to the truth than other figures that were circulating at the time (see chapters 6 and 8).

Wolf Vulnerability

Bill Feeney and his crew recognized that the state's timber wolf population was in imminent danger of extinction. They realized state-supported bounty trapping threatened to extirpate the wolf.

On numerous occasions the crew noted trapping activity, and they witnessed the impacts of bounty trapping in removing wolves from the study area. Oneida County's Willow wolf pack provided a good example of the pressures being brought to bear on the small family groups that remained in Wisconsin. Felix Hartmeister and Clarence Searles made the following entry in their notebooks: "April 6, 1945 Oneida Co. Note. Talked to Warden

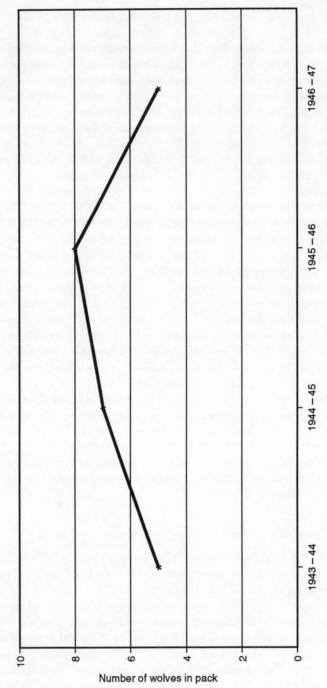

Figure 7.1. Midwinter count of the number of wolves in Scott Lake pack, Forest County, 1943–44 to 1946–47

Number of wolves in pack

McKeague at Rhinelander about two TW [timber wolves] trapped NE of Flowage. There were three in the pack and . . . [trapper Herman Witt] got two. . . . Both were males and one weighed 72 pounds; the other weighed 76 pounds."[70]

Dan Thompson paid particular attention to the activities of area trappers. On January 9, 1947, he noted: "Two trappers are working this area. One has several sets along the Iron Gate road. . . . he comes in from the north on skies [sic]. A second trapper has sets near Muskellunge lake."[71] On February third he recorded the following:

NOTE: A trapper is working this area by car. He stopped to examine tracks in several places. An active snow set was discovered on firelane shoulder. A coyote track led into the set—the snow around the set was greatly disturbed. . . . Car and man tracks indicated the trapper had stopped—killed coyote. . . . The wolves passed down the center of the road past this set without stopping—They passed before trapper arrived—probably before the coyote was caught.[72]

Dan Thompson gained a description of the demise of the Willow pack's old two-toed wolf in January of 1949 when he interviewed Walt Rosenlaf, one of the trappers whose activities Thompson had noted. The old wolf had pulled free of Rosenlaf's sets on at least three occasions, leaving behind several toes each time. In late December of 1948 one of the pack's female pups was caught firmly in a trap.

Rosenlaf reported that the cripple had apparently remained in the vicinity of the set which held the young female. . . . Several snow beds indicated that he spent more than a day in the vicinity. The trapper put out a second series of sets in this vicinity and found upon return that the cripple had come back to the site and stepped into one of the new sets.[73]

Feeney and his crew were truly disturbed by what they witnessed. With unregulated bounty trapping the few remaining timber wolf packs were facing extermination. But as biologists they could only make recommendations. The fate of Wisconsin's wolf population lay with decision makers—the public, the state legislature, and the Conservation Department administrators (see chapters 6 and 8).

Night Howling Surveys

Not only did Feeney's secret wolf project build up the meager biological information available on the wolf's ecological role in the upper Great Lakes region at that time, but also his crew developed a technique useful in censusing timber wolves. The "howling technique" was used to locate and count wolves in the rugged, forested tracts of northern Wisconsin, where foliage and distance obscures visual contacts.*

Feeney was raised in coyote country in the western part of South Dakota. He learned as a kid how to howl to coyotes to elicit their replies. It was Feeney who had elicited responses the night Berner and Hartmeister discovered the timber wolf den in Iron County. Some of the others were more self-conscious about howling to the wolves. On at least two occasions Bradle and Hartmeister spent the night wrapped up in sleeping bags along the Sinkhole Road in Forest County, listening for wolves, though neither of them howled on those occasions.[74]

However, on another occasion, an October night in 1946, when Bernie Bradle was spot-lighting deer as part of a population survey in the Argonne area of Forest County, he had an ideal opportunity to try out his howling skills. His wife, Marge, frequently accompanied him on these surveys and recorded the sex-age information of deer they encountered on their 80–100 mile nightly journeys along the national forest fire lanes. She was along this night too.

They were heading east along the Pine River Campground road beyond Haystack Corners. When they rounded a bend, Bernie's eye caught a black spot in the road. He thought his eyes were playing tricks on him, because he swore it was steaming. Checking it he discovered a fresh timber wolf dropping. An eighth of a mile farther on they encountered another soft, black splotch. Could he still be imagining steam coming off it? He stopped the car, let out a wolf howl, and got an answer right away. It seems the wolves (there were five in the group) had been chased off the fire lane by the approach of Bradle's car. They were not too far off the road in the brush. Bernie got them to howl several more times before silence reclaimed the night. Jumping back into the car, he realized Marge was chuckling. She exclaimed, "That proves it, that proves it. You're a wolf!"[75]

The Wolf Project—A Well-Kept Secret

Sitting in his office back in Ladysmith following that eventful evening when the crew discovered the timber wolf den in the wilds of Pleasant Lake in Iron County, Bill Feeney contemplated his response to Aldo Leopold's sug-

*The late professor Douglas Pimlott and George Kolenosky are credited with devising this technique for use in Algonquin Provincial Park, Ontario, during the late 1950s. Principally used during summer, when foliage precludes the ability to obtain visual counts, the technique consists of imitating wolf howls at certain intervals along prescribed routes at night when sounds carry better. The purpose is to record the number of individual wolves that respond and thus obtain a minimum count of wolves in the pack and in a population.

7.9. Bill Feeney inspecting the remains of a starved deer in Bayfield County. (Photo courtesy Wisconsin Department of Natural Resources Photo Archives.)

gestion of a Wisconsin Academy investigation of timber wolves in the state. His crew's own wolf project was really an outgrowth of the Deer Research Project. Feeney saw it as a facet of deer ecology and felt justified in investigating wolves from that standpoint; he also noted that the public made it an issue, because they ignorantly thought wolves were a serious threat to the deer herd (see 7.9).[76]

Of course Feeney thought an academy study a worthy topic of investigation. If nothing else it would cover his crew's activities. He was, perhaps, even flattered that Leopold had suggested he chair the investigative committee. After thoughtful consideration Feeney replied in agreement. Prophetically he mentioned, "With such a study some publication would seem essential even though its final appearance should embarrass us either by unpopularity or by too closely preluding the last rights of an exterminated species."[77] No doubt Leopold was immensely pleased to read of Bill's willingness to commit any accomplishments to paper.

In the spring of 1945 a presentation, probably summarizing the findings of the committee and crew's wolf project, was given by Clarence Searles before the Wisconsin Academy convention.[78] Catastrophic events abroad overshadowed the academy committee's contribution to knowledge about wolves and rendered it almost meaningless. Unfortunately the war disrupted many things, including record keeping and academy publications. A copy of that talk was not preserved.

As fate would have it, only one work would ever see print, but it wasn't the results of the Wisconsin Academy's committee or Feeney's Deer Research Project timber wolf investigation. Few within or outside the Wisconsin Conservation Department would know that several of Feeney's men were investigating the ecology of wolves as an adjunct to their deer project work. This subterfuge was largely Feeney's doing.

By 1946 the nightmarish public debates over deer management were having an impact on Feeney. He had difficulty focusing attention on the objectives of the Deer Research Project and effectively supervising his people. And he wasn't known to be a particularly sympathetic supervisor. In light of the abusive poundings Feeney and the others had repeatedly taken during the on-going public "deer wars" debacle, it was no surprise that Deer Research Project personnel were suffering from low morale.

Feeney began coveting any and all information the Deer Research Project crew had accumulated on timber wolves. "Bill forbade his project members from discussing timber wolves with the public or any of the WCD's [Wisconsin Conservation Department's] forest protection or law enforcement divisions." He even forbade his own staff from entering the Iron County wolf range that he personally chose to study—home to the largest concentration of timber wolves remaining in the state.[79]

Despite the painstaking effort of the dedicated biologists who helped conduct pioneering wolf work, Feeney's control over his employees was so complete that no information was ever made public.*

So it turned out that the only work ever published on Wisconsin's timber wolves was Dan Thompson's food habits study. After returning from the war in 1946, Thompson decided to focus on timber wolf food habits as the topic of his graduate thesis under the guidance of Professor

---

*As examples of its secrecy, Feeney's supervisor, Walter Scott, though on military duty at the time, found out about the wolf work only when he reviewed a draft of this chapter in November 1982. Conservation Department director E. J. Vanderwall, responding to a formal University of Wisconsin proposal to study wolves, suggested that the work be connected with Feeney's Deer Research Project. At that time Feeney's men had already been studying wolves for six months.[80]

Aldo Leopold at the University of Wisconsin. Feeney apparently didn't share their enthusiasm.

Feeney's position and his absolute paranoia presented an obstacle, and only after delicate negotiations was Thompson given the go-ahead to proceed with his food habits work on the Willow wolf pack in western Oneida County. He completed the study in 1948, and his thesis was approved two years later. His thorough investigation would be a model for future wolf food habits studies across the continent for the next 25 years. In 1952 his article, entitled *Travel, Range and Food Habits of Timber Wolves in Wisconsin*, was published in a professional publication, the *Journal of Mammalogy*. It is the first and only scientific treatise to have been published on Wisconsin's wolves.

Sadly, the times, circumstances, and perhaps personalities kept a pioneering wolf study from public view. The results of years of collective effort and dedicated labors, of information on the status and ecology of wolves, and a wolf-howling census technique that could have been put to use years before Ontario biologist Doug Pimlott discovered its usefulness, were lost among the file drawers in a half dozen Wisconsin Conservation Department offices. Tragically, some of this information may have helped combat public perceptions about deer predation in time to save the wolf from annihilation in Wisconsin.

8

The Annihilation of the Wolf
South of Lake Superior

Wolves once roamed throughout Wisconsin and Michigan. Some naturalists speculate that Wisconsin alone was home to perhaps as many as 25,000.[1] But this figure is a gross exaggeration according to present-day knowledge of wolf densities and the species' dependence on big game. Wildlife biologists were not present in settlement-era Wisconsin, and any estimates of the numbers of wolves present in presettlement Wisconsin would be nothing more than worthless wild guesses.

Wolves were undoubtedly more abundant in the southern portions of the state, where they were at home with the roving bands of elk, bison, and deer. By contrast, northern Wisconsin's and Upper Michigan's vast expanses of old-age virgin forest probably did not support much more than an occasional moose and perhaps some caribou. The wolves that were present probably hung tightly to areas of disturbance, such as wind-throws or recently burned areas, where there was likely to be a plentiful supply of deer and elk.

Settlement proceeded from the southern and eastern parts of Wisconsin northward. In Upper Michigan, the Keweenaw Peninsula and Lake Superior mining centers and, in Wisconsin, the Lake Michigan shoreline at the head of Green Bay were settled at an early date. The last wolves disappeared from the southern portion of Wisconsin by the early 1880s (and from the entire Lower Peninsula of Michigan around the same time), and the last one was taken from central Wisconsin in Waushara County in 1914.[2] A few wolves haunted the cutover lands from Washburn, Rusk, and Taylor over to Langlade and Oconto counties up until the 1920s.

By the 1920s the timber wolf population had been reduced to a mere vestige of its former numbers, and the species clung to existence in isolated portions of northern Wisconsin and the adjacent Upper Peninsula of Michigan. Most of the fragmentary information on the wolf's population status and distribution during the period from 1920 to the late 1950s comes in part from studies conducted by Wisconsin Conservation Department personnel under the direction of Bill Feeney and Dan Thompson, and by Adolf Stebler, Dave Arnold, and others in Michigan.

158

Wolf Distribution in Wisconsin and Upper Michigan
—1920s through the 1950s

Around the turn of the century, wolf distribution in the upper Great Lakes states was limited to the northern third of Wisconsin, the Upper Peninsula of Michigan, and north-central Minnesota. By the close of World War I wolves were nearing extermination in west-central Minnesota and north-western Wisconsin. Henry Schrader, who settled in the town of Bruno in eastern Pine County, Minnesota, about eight miles west of the Wisconsin line, stated that timber wolves were present when he first arrived there in 1918, but disappeared shortly thereafter.[3] Noted wildlife historian Arlie Schorger likewise mentioned that timber wolves were "found occasionally in Pine County [Minnesota] as late as 1918."[4] The elimination of wolves in this region sealed the fate of the species south of Lake Superior. The timber wolves of northern Wisconsin and Upper Michigan were "virtually isolated."[5] Without constant recruitment from the substantial and stable reservoir populations of northern Minnesota and adjacent regions of Canada, this estranged population could not maintain itself indefinitely, especially with a bounty system that constantly whittled away at its ranks. And with a vehemence wolves continued to be bountied, ultimately bringing to an end the era of the wolf in Wisconsin and Upper Michigan.

In the mid-1940s biologist Dan Thompson wrote that wolves were "largely confined to the north-central and northeastern portions of the state." The Bayfield and Ashland county line defined the western limit of their breeding range.[6] This was, surprisingly, their limit in the early 1930s.

Wisconsin's wolf ranges were clustered in three fairly distinct areas after 1930 (map 8.1) (see appendix D for details on these wolf ranges). The north-western region included several active wolf ranges west of Highway 13 in Bayfield, Sawyer, Ashland, and Price counties. Notable among these were the Upper Ghost Lake, Spider Lake, Moose River, and Price Creek wolf ranges. The best wolf ranges remaining in the state of Wisconsin were located in the north-central tier of counties. The Iron-Ashland county block in particular was a stronghold and included the Pleasant Lake and Flambeau groups of wolves. Ranges of the Virgin Lake and Cisco Lake groups lay along the border with Michigan's Upper Peninsula. A large wolf range stretched across eastern Price and western Oneida counties. This was the famous Willow wolf range, the southernmost breeding range then remaining in Wisconsin. In the northeast several very active wolf ranges, including the Scott Lake, Michigan Creek, and Woods Creek ranges, existed in extreme eastern Vilas County and in the Forest-Florence county areas.

Wolves were similarly concentrated in several regions of the Upper Peninsula of Michigan. Several ranges occurred along the common border with

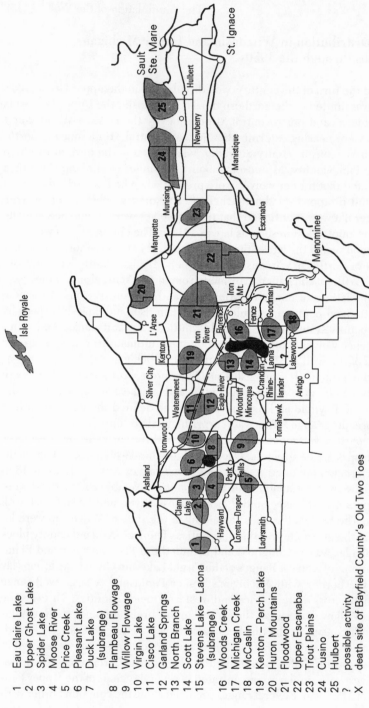

1   Eau Claire Lake
2   Upper Ghost Lake
3   Spider Lake
4   Moose River
5   Price Creek
6   Pleasant Lake
7   Duck Lake
      (subrange)
8   Flambeau Flowage
9   Willow Flowage
10 Virgin Lake
11 Cisco Lake
12 Garland Springs
13 North Branch
14 Scott Lake
15 Stevens Lake – Laona
      (subrange)
16 Woods Creek
17 Michigan Creek
18 McCaslin
19 Kenton – Perch Lake
20 Huron Mountains
21 Floodwood
22 Upper Escanaba
23 Trout Plains
24 Cusino
25 Hulbert
?   possible activity
X   death site of Bayfield County's Old Two Toes

Map 8.1. Timber wolf ranges in northern Wisconsin and Upper Michigan after 1930

Wisconsin, from Iron River to Ironwood in Gogebic, Ontonagon, Iron, and Dickinson counties. Wolf activity was particularly heavy near Perch Lake and the Bond Falls Flowage, Chaney Lake, and the Cisco chain. Another major range lay to the east of the Keweenaw Peninsula along the rugged Lake Superior coast in Marquette, Luce, Alger, and Chippewa counties. The big wolves persisted in their greatest numbers in the Hulbert range within the Tahquamenon River basin. It was here that Michigan's wolves made their last stand. Wolves were occasionally reported outside these breeding ranges. However they did not persist long within these temporary refuges.

Timber Wolf Harvest Methods, 1930–60

A wide variety of methods were used in killing wolves to collect government-sponsored bounties. Early methods included trapping, poisoning, and shooting. The primary manner in which wolves were taken in Wisconsin and Michigan between 1930 and 1960 was through trapping. Among 88 Wisconsin wolves for which the manner of death was recorded, 68 percent were taken through trapping, followed by shooting (23 percent) and den digging (9 percent) (table 8.1). The fall months of September through November accounted for nearly 60 percent of the annual kill, and a smaller, secondary peak occurred between March and May. Trapping deaths were greatest in October, and shootings were highest in November, coincidental with deer hunting.

Michigan Conservation Department records taken from 85 wolves bountied between 1954 and 1958 show many similarities to the Wisconsin mortalities. Seventy-one percent of the wolves were trapped, and 29 percent were shot. Fifty-five percent of the wolves were bountied between September and November.[7]

Trapping

The majority of wolves killed during the twentieth century in northern Wisconsin and Upper Michigan were trapped. Most trappers probably were pursuing the more abundant coyotes and only occasionally snagged a timber wolf (see 8.1). Lifetime captures of as few as two or three wolves and as many as several hundred were reported.

Some went after both species, like Toivo Haapala, who bountied 36 coyotes and 5 wolves in Alger County, Michigan, in 1955. A few prided themselves as timber wolf trappers. Walt Rosenlaf's claim of trapping three or four wolves annually translates to between 55 and 72 wolves over the 18-

Table 8.1.   Percentage and numerical distributions of 88 Wisconsin timber wolves taken between 1930 and 1960, by season and method of harvest

	Season				
	Winter (Dec.–Feb.)	Spring (Mar.–May)	Summer (June–Aug.)	Fall (Sept.–Nov.)	Total
Number	10	23	3	52	88
Percent	11	26	3	59	99

Month	Trapped	Shot	Dug from den	Other	Total	Percent
Jan.	2	3	0	0	5	6
Feb.	3	0	0	0	3	3
Mar.	2	3	0	0	5	6
Apr.	6	0	0	0	6	7
May	5	0	7	0	12	14
June	1	0	0	0	1	1
July	0	0	0	0	0	0
Aug.	2	0	0	0	2	2
Sept.	12	2	0	0	14	16
Oct.	21	0	0	1	22	25
Nov.	4	12	0	0	16	18
Dec.	2	0	0	0	2	2
Total	60	20	7	1	88	100
Percent	68	23	9	1	101	

Source: Data obtained from newspaper accounts and written documents of the Wisconsin Conservation Department.

year period he was active. Trapper Frank Tomaier kept a bounty diary during the 1940s. He trapped 18 wolves in six years—an average of 3 wolves yearly.[8]

The techniques employed by trappers varied, but the majority of trappers concocted their own scents as attractants. A few used dirt-hole sets with bait, and a number also used blind or trail sets to capture wolves. The trapping operation consisted of three stages: trap preparation, site selection and setting, and checking trap sets.

Because wolves are intelligent and can readily detect human scent, care had to be taken to remove human smells where possible (where not, they had to be masked). Traps were boiled in water to which hemlock, maple, or tag alder bark had been added. Traps were often waxed by dipping them into melted wax to assure they would work in cold, snowy conditions. All trapping paraphernalia, including gloves, boots, canvas pan covers, canvas tarps, picks, sifters, and backpacks, were left out in the open air away from human contact or were buried for weeks before trapping began.

Wolf travel-ways were often the best locations to set traps, although some

8.1. A trapper's catch showing one timber wolf amongst coyotes. These animals were caught in Ashland County near Mellen by Russ Olson. (Photograph courtesy of Russ Olson.)

trappers set along stretches of fire lanes or abandoned railways used by wolves. During autumn in the late 1920s one Clearwater Lake (Oneida County) trapper actually sat at night wrapped up in a blanket in his car, listening for the Scott Lake pack wolves to howl. He noted the directions, which greatly aided him in selecting sites to set traps and catch them.

In the snow-free months the trap, chain, and drag were concealed about a half inch beneath the soil surface. The trapper selected a site, set his trap, and kneeling down on his tarp, excavated a hole in which to place the set, taking care to arrange all the dirt "spoil" on the tarp. The drag, chain, and finally the trap were placed on top of one another in the hole and dirt was tamped in to fill any spaces outside the trap jaws. Next, a canvas cloth was gently placed over the trap pan, and the spoil was placed in a sifter and sifted over the whole set until it was almost flush with the surrounding ground. Dry surface dirt was collected and sprinkled on top of the site to give it a natural, even appearance. Excess dirt in the tarp was removed from the location and discarded.

Sometimes trappers placed small sticks or stones roughly along the edges of the concealed trap jaws to help "guide" the wolf's paw into the trap. Any bait or scent was placed 9–14 inches behind the trap. Gloves were worn while setting the traps but never while applying the scent, because the scent would persist on the gloves and foul up subsequent sets.

The same basic procedures were applied when trapping in the snow. Sometimes traps were even put in paper bags and placed beneath the snow, thus preventing snow from filtering beneath the pan, which would in turn prevent the trap from firing. Knowing that wolves usually step in each other's tracks when trailing through deep snow, some ingenious trappers selectively "lifted" a wolf track out of snow trails, placed a trap beneath, carefully replaced the print, and touched up the set by dusting the area with some loosened snow.

Timber wolf trappers used Newhouse 4, 4½, 114, and 5 traps exclusively, with a double-hook drag attached to a chain about six feet long. The trap, chain, and drag were usually welded together with rings. Newhouse traps were the strongest made, and the only types that would detain a wolf for any length of time.

The importance of the toggle (hooked drag) and chain was not to be under-estimated, as trapper Russ Olson attested. One winter he discovered wolf sign while trapping beaver along the Torch River in Sawyer County. He immediately decided to switch one of his beaver sets to a wolf set. His traps didn't have long chains or drags, so he decided to improvise by carefully attaching a cedar log to the trap by wiring it with "at least ten strands of stove-pipe wire." Shortly thereafter, he caught a wolf, but the wolf lunged so forcefully that it succeeded in breaking the wire and escaped with the trap. Luck was on Olson's side, for the next day he found the wolf under the exposed roots of a wind-thrown cedar. The chain had become wrapped around the roots and had frozen into the mire the wolf created in its at-tempts to extricate itself.[9]

Wolves are immensely powerful animals for their size, so it is little won-der that they could and did on occasion damage or destroy trap chains and/or drags. Nearly every trapper with any experience caught wolves that broke traps. Along Swamp Creek in Iron County, Wisconsin, Orvid Donner caught a large wolf that broke off the drag and escaped down the creek. He later found the animal after the chain had become tangled up in some alders, causing the wolf to drown. Frank Tomaier caught a wolf near the Brunet (River) fire tower in Sawyer County; the wolf had lunged with such force that it completely broke off one of the prongs on the drag and nearly straightened out the other one. The mutilated drag had become temporarily wedged between a log and a snag when Tomaier happened upon the wolf, and he quickly shot it to prevent it from escaping.[10]

Occasionally trappers employed the use of dogs to run down wolves that had carried off broken traps. In spite of the odds and tremendous physical exertion, wolves usually eluded dogs and hunters for days while encumbered with a steel trap.[11]

Wolves that succeeded in breaking sets apart were just as often not found. In late February of 1946 Walt Rosenlaf trapped a wolf just north of Bass Lake in western Oneida County, but the wolf broke the drag. Rosenlaf followed its trail for about a mile before he lost it in a deer yard. Coincidentally, on the 20th of that month Conservation Department deer biologists Felix Hartmeister and Bruce Stollberg picked up its trail and the trail of Rosenlaf and followed the wolf north and west from Bass Lake, continuing to trail it for three days. The wolf crossed West and Muskellunge lakes, continued up through the Lamer Springs country, and went west across the Willow Road. The biologists estimated the wolf traveled about 10 miles in one 24-hour period. They noticed considerable blood loss at bed sites and mentioned on the 23rd of February that the wolf was using deer trails where possible.[12]

Wolves were sometimes successful in their frantic struggles to escape from traps, but they usually sustained injuries—such as the loss of toes, paws, or portions of legs, or broken limbs—if left in the trap for any length of time (>24 hours). A few of these maimed survivors received nicknames because of their peculiar tracks.

The most notorious crippled wolf in Wisconsin was Old Two Toes of the Willow wolf pack. Deer biologists first positively noted his presence on March 23, 1945, and recorded his tracks on 12 subsequent occasions by November 1946. During that time Old Two Toes lost some additional toes in an encounter with a trap. On April 9, 1946, Felix Hartmeister made a notation in his field book that Old Two Toes had left a "new" track with only one toe on one of his paws. Biologist Dan Thompson observed the tracks of Old Two Toes among the trail of four wolves one day in February of 1947, and saw that the wolf was having more difficulty than his pack-mates staying on top of a light crust. (see photo 7.5).[13]

More than once Old Two Toes stumbled into traps set by Walt Rosenlaf, and each time he managed to pull free, leaving one or two toes behind. On one occasion about two weeks after the wolf ran off with a trap attached to its hind foot, Rosenlaf encountered fresh sign and began pursuing it. He eventually got a peek at the wolf and took a shot with his 30-30, but the bullet missed its mark. The shocked wolf ran headlong into a poplar tree so forcefully that the trap and two of his toes broke off, and the wolf vanished from sight. When Rosenlaf finally captured and killed Old Two Toes in early January of 1949, Dan Thompson noticed that two central toes from each hind foot were missing, and an inner toe from its right front foot was also missing.[14]

Wolves rarely had as many toes missing as this notorious Willow wolf.

Biologist Bernie Bradle noticed a toe missing from the hind foot of a wolf in the Scott Lake pack in 1945, and Dan Thompson also identified a wolf that was missing a toe from a hind foot in the Willow pack in 1946.[15]

Another locally famous wolf was the Old Two Toes of northern Bayfield County, who was so identified in his range between 1954 and 1958 because he had two toes missing from his right front foot. A three-legged wolf dubbed Old Three Legs roamed the same region of Bayfield County until November of 1947, when he was killed by a deer hunter.[16]

Ray Smith captured a club-footed female wolf during the mid-1940s west of Long Lake in Forest County. From the eastern Upper Peninsula of Michigan, a Hulbert pack wolf, locally known as Clubfoot, lost its left front foot in a trap. In the Porcupine Mountains of Michigan, Clarence Allen trapped a wolf that managed to pull free. Allen was staying that fall in the towerman's shack near Government Peak, and one day when he went down to the spring to fetch up some water he brushed up a wolf. The wolf was hobbling slowly, so Allen decided to chase it. Being unarmed he picked up a couple of sizable rocks, and when he got close enough he threw one at the wolf, hitting it on the head and killing it. Upon examination he found that the wolf's leg had been broken in two places and infection had set in.[17]

Trapped wolves usually bite and level all brush in reach when the drag becomes hooked on some object, and sometimes a stick becomes firmly wedged across their palates between the upper molars. The wolf that drowned itself in Swamp Creek after breaking Orvid Donner's trap drag had a stick lodged in its mouth from a previous trap encounter. The wolf's flesh had grown around the stick and a groove was worn in its tongue. This was not an isolated incident. A coyote trapped in Florence County in the fall of 1954 had a stick wedged long enough in its mouth to destroy some teeth and put a groove in its skull.[18]

Wire snares were placed along wolf trails or in areas wolves were likely to travel. When set properly the wolf would get caught around the neck. In struggling to free itself it would pull against the wire, which was anchored down, causing the wolf to suffocate. Snares were outlawed in Wisconsin by the 1930s, primarily because too many deer were caught and accidentally killed, but in spite of this snares were sometimes used illegally. In 1930, government trapper Charlie Walker snared a timber wolf in the Argonne Deer Refuge in Forest County, but the wolf managed to break free. Walker found it dead nearby. The snare had cut into the wolf's neck, severing the animal's jugular vein, causing it to bleed to death. In 1937 in the Sailor Lake country of eastern Price County, George Ruegger and Jake Jakoubek live-captured a male wolf that had a snare wire embedded in its neck. The wolf's nose was functionless because of a hole cut into the windpipe by the snare.[19]

Shooting

Most of the wolves that were shot were taken incidentally to other forms of hunting. Sixty percent of the wolves shot in Wisconsin were killed during the November deer seasons (see 8.2 and 8.3). Bona fide wolf hunters employed the use of dogs. This was a winter sport. Hunters dropped their dog pack on any fresh trail encountered and then attempted to predict where the chase would lead in order to post hunters in likely locations. Needless to say few hunts were successful owing to the inaccessible conditions in most of the wolf ranges and the vast mobility of the species. Even wolves with traps were able to elude both dogs and hunters for days on end. Dogs often lost their nerve when closing in on wolves and, not infrequently, their lives.

Warden-sponsored wolf hunts using dogs took place in the Boulder Junction area of Vilas County and the Argonne Deer Refuge in Forest County. A local wolf hunting group also existed in the 1940s in the Willow area of western Oneida County.

Many shootings were the result of opportunistic encounters, including the majority of those wolves taken during deer seasons. Around 1927 Russ Olson and another fellow wintered out in a shack on Spider Lake in Ashland County. One day Olson went in to Mellen with the intention of returning that same day, but he ended up staying the night. The next day, thinking his partner would be mad, he coaxed Jim Conley into taking him back out on Conley's motorcycle, but it was suppertime before they left. Olson was dropped off near Mineral Lake and began the four-mile walk back up the creek to Spider Lake. In his words:

> I had a packsack full of grub and a gunny sack loaded with eight loaves of bread. When I was close to where the west creek comes in between the two lakes, I stuck my head up a little bit higher to see right where the two creeks met. There was a curve that led to Spider Lake.
>
> I seen something coming out of the west creek—it was a timber wolf. He went right around the curve staying right on the ice. I had a pistol and got that out. There was an old dead stump there, and I thought when he gets in line with it I'll shoot. I did. One shot, boy, and he took off. I checked in the snow the next morning and found that I shot right under him.[20]

A most unusual form of "hunting" was sometimes employed by the Billers north of their Fence (Florence County) homestead.[21] Bert had been picking gensing with his sister near the headwaters of Cody Creek when around noon he heard a pack of timber wolves howling from across the marsh.

8.2. A 90-pound timber wolf shot by Lawrence Babl near Tower Lake, Vilas County, during the 1945 deer season. (Courtesy of Wisconsin Department of Natural Resources Photo Archives.)

8.3. A large male timber wolf shot by Harold Ruprecht near Roach Lake, Vilas County, during the 1950 deer season. (Photograph courtesy of Harold Ruprecht.)

169

I knew about the existence of an old beaver house about in the center of the marsh, which would make a good place to hide. When I crawled into the house I began to imitate the wolves, howling like they were. It worked and they started to come towards me. They would howl and I would answer them. About 15 minutes later I saw them coming out of the tamarack swamp, eight full grown ones. They headed right for my little island. I was laying on my stomach and they came up within 75 feet of me. I drew a bead on one and he dropped in the grass and began to kick in his death struggle. The rest of them gathered around in a circle and watched the one I'd shot. I emptied the gun, wounding two more, and that was enough for the rest. They bounded back into the swamp and out of sight.[22]

Den Digging

Occasionally people stumbled into wolf dens while otherwise occupied in the woods. For instance, a pair of fishermen found a wolf den along Deadman Creek in Ontonagon County, Michigan, in 1950. The Petts brothers found an active wolf den along the north branch of the Pine River in Forest County in either 1923 or 1924 by listening to the howling of the wolves during evening hours. For several nights they noted that one remained stationary, and they placed two stakes in the ground lined up in the direction from which the wolves howled. A careful search in that direction revealed the den's location.[23]

The majority of dens found by woodsmen were located by taking advantage of April snowfalls. Wolf tracks encountered on fresh April snows usually led to or from dens, and by following the trails the dens were sometimes found. Once located the pups were usually dug out. Sometimes they would be dragged out by a person bold enough to crawl into the den hole. In the case of pine logs, the pups were usually dragged or pried out.

Vehicle Collisions

Occasionally wolves were struck by cars. Some of these collisions were purely accidental. In some situations, however, the drivers took advantage of an unusual means to bounty a wolf.

One day in February of 1948 as timber cruiser Keith Jesse rounded a bend in the fire lane south of Iron County's Duck Lake, he spied a wolf standing in the road. It appeared reluctant to leave the lane because of the steep snowbanks, so Jesse sped up and struck the wolf, which managed to escape into the brush. The wolf apparently died, because biologist Dan Thompson, who had heard of the incident, was able to find tracks of only two wolves in the same area, where earlier that winter there had been three.[24]

The Twilight Years of the Wolf in Wisconsin and Upper Michigan

Wolves were on their way out for a long time in Wisconsin and Upper Michigan. The forces that act upon any population of animals are many and varied. The two principal components are *recruitment* through birth and immigration and *attrition* through death and emigration. When these two major factors are in balance the population is considered stable. Fluctuations or imbalances in either will cause increases or decreases in the population.

The population dynamics of Wisconsin's and Upper Michigan's wolves in the twentieth century are largely a history of decline. Little was known of their birth rates, and records of numbers killed by humans for bounty were poor, but this collective knowledge far exceeded the knowledge of natural deaths and rates of immigration and emigration by dispersers. The latter effects were of little consequence after 1920, when the south shore wolves became isolated from the U.S. and Canadian wolf population north of Lake Superior.

News of epidemics would likely have surfaced if large numbers of sickly wolves and coyotes had been encountered either in the woods or when they were turned in for bounty. Diseases were probably present though not prevalent, and in earlier times may have precipitated occasional outbreaks. An observation made by Art Winslow in the area surrounding Wabeno in Forest County during the winter of 1886 was related to warden R. A. Keeney in 1936. Winslow had told Keeney that "the timber wolves were in this country by the hundreds and that the following winter they all seemed to disappear . . . at the time that the Indians that were here seemed to think that they all contracted some sort of venereal disease that killed them off."[25]

Natural deaths, although present, probably did not play a significant role in the mortality rates of the wolf population in the last few decades of their existence. Accidents occurred infrequently. Wisconsin biologists Bernie Bradle and John Keener once snowshoed to the abandoned site of Camp 11 of the Civilian Conservation Corps southeast of Forest County's Luna Lake to investigate a report that a timber wolf had fallen into an old well covered by boards and snow. Their recollections differ: Keener claimed they found tracks leading up to the hole, and Bradle claims they found nothing.[26]

The Wisconsin wolf population was estimated by pooling the testimonies of numerous woodsmen, trappers, and biologists (see the subsection "Personal Communication" in the references), field notes from the Wisconsin Conservation Department's Deer Research workers and Michigan Conser-

Table 8.2.   Number of timber wolves bountied in Wisconsin, Michigan, and Minnesota, 1935–60

	Wisconsin[a]	Michigan	Minnesota[a]	Regional Total
1935	—	27	—	27
1936	—	22	—	22
1937	—	37	—	37
1938	—	49	—	49
1939	—	35	—	35
1940	—	30	—	30
1941	—	42	—	42
1942	—	43	—	43
1943	—	35	—	35
1944	—	44	—	44
1945	—	27	—	27
1946	—	23	—	23
1947	46	24	—	70
1948	27	28	—	55
1949	—	40	—	40
1950	—	28	—	28
1951	34	27	—	51
1952	26	27	252	305
1953	7	27	181	215
1954	22	23	185	230
1955	13	24	199	236
1956	1	30	198	229
1957		7	186	193
1958		7	122	129
1959		1	177	178
1960			171	171
Total	176	707	1,842	1,886

Sources: Wisconsin Conservation Department Pittman-Robertson Deer Research Project materials; Michigan Department of Natural Resources, Wolf and Predator Bounty files; Minnesota Department of Natural Resources, various files.

[a]Wolves began to be separated from coyotes in Wisconsin in 1947–48 and in Minnesota in 1952–53.

vation Department officials, and the few bounty records that are available (appendix E). Memories and written records did not precede 1920 by much, but became increasingly available through the decades into the 1950s, when the wolves ultimately disappeared. Unfortunately, bounty records for Wisconsin wolves extend back only to 1947–48 (table 8.2). Prior to that time the records did not distinguish between wolves and coyotes.

By 1920 the big wolves were confined to 12 of Wisconsin's northernmost counties and to Michigan's Upper Peninsula (map 8.1). At least 12 wolf ranges, containing perhaps as many as 18 packs, were identified by old-time trappers and early-day wildlife officials in Wisconsin during the early portion of the twentieth century. Similarly, at least nine wolf ranges were known to the old settlers in the Upper Peninsula. Unfortunately it was not possible to obtain counts on the number of packs in Upper Michigan wolf ranges.

An estimated 200 wolves existed in northern Wisconsin's cutover country prior to 1925 (figure 8.1; appendix D). Pack size averaged over eight wolves per pack (considered fairly healthy on the basis of recent studies of deer-dependant wolf packs in Minnesota and Ontario).[27] Between 1920 and the mid-1930s average pack size slipped quickly from about nine to fewer than five wolves per pack. The population fell sharply from around 200 to 115 wolves in those 15 years; yet there was no notable decline in the number of active packs.

By 1940, about the time Wisconsin's Deer Research Project began under the direction of Bill Feeney, the average pack size hovered just above four wolves and the population declined further to under 100 animals. The coup de grace was delivered during the late 1940s and early 1950s. Pack by pack, the wolves were being annihilated from the hinterlands south of Lake Superior.

On several occasions biologists witnessed first-hand the devastating impact overtrapping had on individual families of wolves. Dan Thompson's meticulous study of the Willow wolf pack provides a picture of the demise of each of the small family groups that remained in Wisconsin at that time.[28]

Walt Rosenlaf usually took three or four wolves per year from this pack. In addition to his exploits, other area trappers caught wolves there. Trapping activity really intensified in the mid- to late 1940s. During the fall of 1944 Charles Gustafson reportedly trapped five wolves in the Willow area. Despite this the Wisconsin Conservation Department's Deer Research crews were encountering sign of three or four wolves throughout the winter of 1944–45. On April 2, 1945, local resident Herman Witt trapped two adult male wolves near the north shore of the flowage in some coyote sets. Somehow a few pack members managed to survive; sign found in sandy stretches of fire lanes during the summer months indicated three wolves were still present, including the famed Old Two Toes.[29]

However, three years later the existence of this small family group was once again threatened by overtrapping. In the spring of 1948 Dan Thompson reported sign of three wolves, one of which was Old Two Toes. "On the evening of June 26, at least two adult wolves howled intermittently from 8:30 to 11:00 P.M. Their voices came from the suspected denning area. At 11:20 they gave voice to a brief interval of short, excited howls . . . of wolf

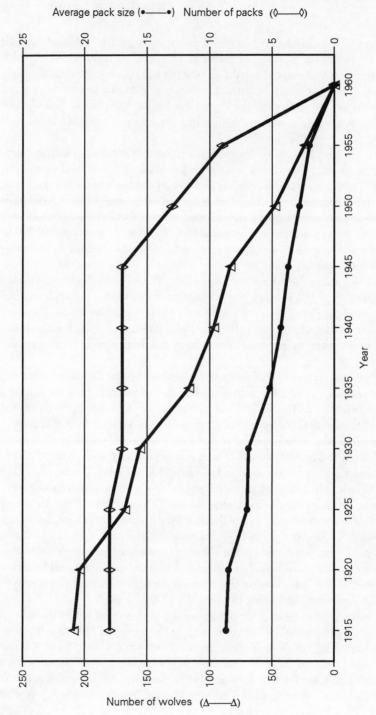

Average pack size (●———●) Number of packs (◊———◊)

Figure 8.1. Decline to extinction—the Wisconsin timber wolf population, 1920–60

Number of wolves (△———△)

pups."[30] In late September a local hound hunter reported "tracks of two adult and four young wolves on a tote road south of Willow flowage."[31]

Thompson heard that a trapper caught a wolf near the flowage in October. Alfred Denzine may have been the man, because he reported trapping a wolf there in 1948. Thompson stated that Rosenlaf began trapping in December and "took two adult male and two young female wolves in thirty days. . . . Rosenlaf reported tracks of one adult and one juvenile when he lifted his traps in January." Old Two Toes was among the wolves taken by Rosenlaf.[32]

Thompson was concerned about the heavy mortality that bounty hunters inflicted on his study pack. He wrote:

> The history of this small family group which successfully raised a litter of four young and then lost more than this increase in numbers to trapping mortality indicates the precarious position of the wolves on this range. However, Rosenlaf recalls taking from three to four wolves annually from this area over the past decade. Considering that additional numbers were probably taken by other trappers during this same time period, it would seem unlikely that a family group could maintain itself in the face of such trapping pressure. Recruitment or drifters from adjacent range would perhaps account for this rather high annual take.[33]

Occasional observations of wolf sign were made up until the mid-1950s, but the Willow wolf pack showed no sign of breeding after 1948.

By the late 1940s fewer than 60 wolves remained in Wisconsin. The average number of wolves present in each pack plummeted to fewer than three animals by around 1950. But worst of all, the number of active wolf packs dwindled to fewer than 10. Those packs that remained were foundering, prevented by the trapping pressure from being able to replenish their ranks through reproduction.

The pressure didn't let up much either. Many of the most expert timber wolf trappers turned their attention to the wildest blocks of land after the more accessible wolf packs had disappeared. At least six fellows were active within Wisconsin's Willow and Scott Lake wolf ranges, and seven trapped the Moose River and Pleasant Lake ranges. In earlier times these ranges may have provided the dispersers that other packs depended on for recruitment, as Dan Thompson suggested. But by the late 1940s, when the trappers overran these last reservoirs, Wisconsin's original wolf population began its final slide toward extinction.

Wisconsin Conservation Department biologist Bernie Bradle felt that efforts to save the wolf—had any come into effect—would have been too late by the 1950s to be of good (see photo 6.8). At that very time, prominent outdoor journalists, like the *Milwaukee Journal*'s Mel Ellis, wrote glowing articles on just how well off "Old Lobo" seemed to be faring according to stories heard from trappers and woodsmen who were perhaps most interested in keeping bounty money available.[34]

In its final seven years Wisconsin's wolf bounty accounted for an average mortality rate of 37 percent of the state's estimated wolf population per year, ranging from a low of 15 percent to a high of 47 percent. These mortality rates, which do not include deaths by natural causes, are considered high enough by modern-day wolf biologists to result in population declines among wolves.

By 1955 only the ranges remaining in central and northeastern Iron County and the northern Forest and western Florence county region (map 8.1) showed any signs of breeding. Average pack size was now fewer than two (the minimum necessary to breed, assuming each was of a different sex and both were physically mature). But even in these remote expanses of forest the wolves found no sanctuary. At least 15 wolves were bountied in Forest County in the eight years between 1947 and 1956, and 28 wolves were taken out of Iron County during the same period. By decade's end all would witness the passing of the wolf from the Wisconsin scene.

The same held true in neighboring Michigan. The last two wolf ranges in that state lay along the rugged Lake Superior shoreline from the town of Munising eastward to Whitefish Bay and contained perhaps three families of timber wolves. The Cusino range spread out over the eastern portions of Alger and Schoolcraft counties, spilling into western Luce County. The Hulbert wolf range sprawled through the wild lands of eastern Luce and western Chippewa counties.

Adolf Stebler was afforded a glimpse of the work of bounty hunters in Michigan's Hulbert wolf pack. In 1950 he reported the loss of nine wolves, representing a 64 percent mortality rate for that single pack. What was particularly distressing was the fact that eight of the nine wolves were pups, and the remaining wolf was the pup's mother. Stebler expressed concern about the far-reaching impacts of removing one or both breeding adults in a stressed population where most packs were small and consisted primarily of the breeding pair and a few surviving offspring.

An average of seven wolves was taken in this four-county area between 1950 and 1953—a loss small enough to be easily absorbed by the several family groups of wolves inhabiting these two ranges. However, the annual take increased to 19 wolves by 1956 and averaged 16 per year during the three years between 1954 and 1956. In the last two years combined, 1957 and 1958, only eight wolves were bountied. Undoubtedly the removal of 47 wolves between 1954 and 1956 seriously disrupted the fragile pack structure, causing the demise of the last of Michigan's wolf packs.

So thorough was the work of the bounty trappers and hunters that most

Wisconsin and Michigan wolf packs were completely wiped out. However, in some cases individuals left when their packs disintegrated. In other situations lone survivors remained in the area their packs once roamed. These animals were considered loners, remnants of packs that had been eliminated. Curiously, most of these loners were males. A few managed to elude their pursuers; of those, nothing is known of their ultimate fate. Others eventually succumbed to those who sought the bounty.

Carl Heizler caught a 98-pound male wolf in April of 1954 that he claimed was the sole remnant of Wisconsin's Price Creek pack, which roamed the Price-Sawyer county line west of Phillips. Russ Olson recalled seeing occasional tracks of a lone wolf that roamed the Coffee Lake country of southwestern Bayfield County for years in the late 1940s and early 1950s. Harold Ruprecht shot a large male timber wolf near Roach Lake in Vilas County during the November 1950 deer season (see 8.3).[35] Was it a remnant loner from the Cisco wolf range or a disperser coming out of the Virgin Lake area?

Some never settled down and lived out their lives, but instead wandered about in search of others. These loners sometimes showed up in areas where resident packs had disappeared decades earlier. A 98-pound wolf was shot at a Hannibal (Taylor County) farm in 1951, and a 75-pound male wolf was hunted down in the Birchwood Hills on the Washburn-Sawyer county line in January of 1952.[36]

Despite the odds, a few wolves managed to outlive the bounty era. One such wolf was the Old Two Toes of northern Bayfield County. He had been a loner since at least 1954. His fate finally caught up with him one snowy night in early January of 1958, seven months after the state removed the wolf bounty (photo 8.4). Banker Willard Ogren recalled:

I was driving my vehicle, which I believe was a 1956 Buick four-door, at about 65 miles an hour and crested a small knoll on County Trunk C between Bayfield and Cornucopia. The road was generally snow covered; therefore, upon seeing the wolf, which I thought was a dog, I did not have much choice but to allow the vehicle [to] continue on at the same speed we were traveling. The wolf ran in an exact straight line in the direction we were going and, that being, right down the middle of the road. It was about 12:00 in the evening, and as I recall, there was light snow falling. As we ran over the wolf, the car was lifted up. We did not run him over with the tires. The wolf was standing in the middle of the road when we first saw him looking over his shoulder.

It took at least a city block to stop and we backed up only to find the wolf struggling off the road dragging its hindquarters. It was obvious to us that its back was broken, and with that, Wallace Chamberlain jumped out of the vehicle and grabbed the wolf by the tail and dragged it back on the road. Much to our surprise, the wolf was not growling or snarling at us, as it obviously was very stunned. Thinking the only humane thing to do was to kill this animal and

8.4. Printed on the back of this photograph in the family album of retired forest ranger George Gillette is this notation: "Me and Georgia holding a timber wolf (maybe the last one in Wis.)." The photograph was taken shortly after Bayfield County's Old Two Toes was struck by a car in January 1958 on the county's peninsula. (Photograph courtesy of George Gillette.)

put it out of its misery, we proceeded to look through the vehicle for a knife or something to end its life. The best thing we came up [with] was a tire iron, and with the tire iron, we hit it over the head thinking we were going to knock out the animal. There was a surprising number of blows before he appeared to be unconscious. His skull at that time was pretty much mush. Still thinking that this was just an ordinary wolf [that is, a coyote], we threw the animal on top of the trunk of my '56 Buick, and as you recall that vehicle, it had a very horizontal trunk lid that was at least three feet wide. The animal layed on that trunk for approximately 15 miles or 15 minutes, appearing to be dead.

As we came into Cornucopia and under the street lights, we could see the silhouette of the wolf through our back frosted window. At that time, he was standing on his front paws looking around trying to determine where he was and what was going on. At the intersections of County C and 13 in Cornucopia, a car was behind us and we could see the silhouette of the wolf still sitting on our trunk. We continued driving down the road at 65 to 70 miles and hour and after approximately five miles, the wolf dragged himself off of the trunk and rolled down the road, and one would expect that he would have been killed after that incident. He still seemed to be [as] much alive as he was when we tried to render him unconscious immediately after the collision with the car.

He again got the tire iron treatment which appeared to render him unconscious again. We put him back on the trunk and proceeded on to Herbster where Grandish's Restaurant was open. We acquired a hunting knife and proceeded to slit the throat of the wolf, and it was surprising yet how much blood came out of the wolf before there appeared to be one final death groan or sigh and it was all over.[37]*

*The hide and skeleton of Old Two Toes of Bayfield County repose within the University of Wisconsin Zoology Museum's mammal collection (UWZ-15213). The crushed vertebrae, bashed in skull, and slit throat are there, testifying to the manner in which the last verified specimen of the original Wisconsin timber wolf population was killed.

9

Epilogue: A Future
for the Wolf?

Timber wolves are creatures of the wilderness. Under protection, will they prosper—or succumb to an encroaching civilization? Time alone holds the answer. Meantime, better not wager much on the wolves.

So read the back cover of the January 1959 issue of the Wisconsin Conservation Department's official publication, the *Wisconsin Conservation Bulletin,* in response to the death of the Old Two Toes of Bayfield County (see 9.1). Despite the removal of the bounty, Old Two Toes died at the hands of man. Protection seemed to offer little hope that the wolves could stage a comeback.

Old Two Toes died in his Bayfield County haunts in January of 1958. Another wolf, said to be a subadult female, was reportedly taken by a hunter near the Woods Flowage in Florence County in November of that year. In the winter of 1959 Gerald Wick said he trapped a "small timber wolf" near Moose Lake in central Iron County.[1] These three dead wolves closed the decade of the 1950s. To a few individuals—biologists and the bounty trappers who pursued wolves—the wolf had ceased to exist in Wisconsin. Although officials acknowledged rare sightings of lone wolves or their sign within the state, these occurrences were ascribed to the occasional stray from the Upper Peninsula that wandered across the border into Wisconsin.[2] In the meantime of course, Michigan officials were attributing infrequent sightings on the western flank of the Upper Peninsula to drifters moving in from Wisconsin.

A few wolves lingered on in the most remote forested tracts in both states. In the spring of 1960 game manager Cliff Wiita found the tracks of a single wolf in the Hay Creek drainage northeast of Park Falls, Wisconsin. In 1963 game biologist Bert Dahlberg encountered tracks of one lone timber wolf on the Iron-Ashland county line. He and his crew trailed the animal until it went east into Iron County.[3] In neighboring Michigan several dead

9.1. Bayfield County's Old Two Toes. Photograph from "What's Going On?", *Wisconsin Conservation Bulletin* 24, no. 1 (1959):40.

wolves were brought to the attention of wildlife officials. In each case the death was attributed to humans.[4]

By the mid-1960s the few veteran game biologists and managers in both states who had witnessed the decline of timber wolves agreed that they had all but vanished from the area south of Lake Superior. None held out any hope for their return.

Meanwhile, the state of Minnesota removed its bounty in 1965. In 1973, under provisions of the federal Endangered Species Act, passed in 1967, the timber wolf was given endangered species status in the lower 48 states. Hunting and trapping pressure slackened in Minnesota.

By then wolves had already begun reappearing in areas outside their northeast Minnesota stronghold in the Superior National Forest. In the winter of 1974–75 the Minnesota Department of Natural Resources notified its Wisconsin counterpart that a wolf pack was discovered in the Nemadji State Forest along the Minnesota border within Douglas County, Wisconsin.

On August 3, 1975, a motorist called the Wisconsin Department of Natural Resources, claiming that he had accidently struck a wolf along Highway

35 about 25 miles south of the city of Superior. The discovery of the yearling female timber wolf surprised Wisconsin DNR officials. This Douglas County animal was the first wolf kill they were able to inspect and thus confirm for science since the death of Bayfield County's Old Two Toes some 17 years earlier. That same August, after reviewing documentation from a university survey of sign left by at least one wolf in the northern Nicolet National Forest, the DNR switched its classification of the wolf from extirpated to endangered, which permitted access to state funds for studies.[5]

At first wildlife officials dismissed the car-kill incident, claiming the creature had wandered out of Minnesota's wolf range. But, by 1979 four more dead wolves had been recovered from Douglas County, and two packs were known to be living and breeding within the remote Douglas County forest lands.[6]

The next shockwave hit on July 9, 1979. Another yearling female wolf was struck by a truck on a dusty fire lane. This time the incident occurred in western Lincoln County's forest lands, a full 120 miles southeast of the Douglas County wolf packs. A quick survey of the area by wildlife officials revealed the presence of an entire pack of wolves. All doubts vanished that November when another yearling wolf was shot illegally by a young deer hunter.[7]

By the late 1970s officials hesitatingly recognized that the wolf had returned to Wisconsin. Most didn't hold high hopes, and some still doubted that the events of the late 1970s were anything more than a passing occurrence.

Finally in 1979 the Wisconsin DNR's Bureau of Endangered Resources initiated a three-year survey in cooperation with the U.S. Fish and Wildlife Service to determine precisely where the timber wolves could be found and what their population status was. Initial winter ground-tracking surveys indicated that close to 30 wolves in four or five packs roamed portions of Douglas and Lincoln counties. In 1980 a radio telemetry program was begun to complement the annual winter track surveys.

In the next few years other small family groups of wolves were found. A few more loners continued to turn up. One large, lone male was eventually captured and radio-collared in the wilds of the Woods Creek drainage of western Florence County—one of the species' last strongholds in the 1950s. In another of the wolf's old stamping grounds, the Bootjack Lake country northwest of the Willow Flowage, a pack was discovered in 1982. History seemed to be repeating itself.[8]

During the next 10 years over 50 wolves were collared. Many things were found to be plaguing the wolves. Canine parvovirus and Lyme disease, two newly introduced diseases, were taking their toll, especially on pups. People, too, continued to kill wolves. According to autopsies performed on 25 wolves, over 40 percent of the deaths were caused by gunshot alone. Between the period of 1979 and 1986, two hunters and a backwoods resident were fined for killing wolves. Annual mortality averaged about 35 percent, a rate considered critically high by wolf authorities.[9]

The fragile population plummeted to 15 by 1985–86, largely as a consequence of the abysmally low recruitment of pups and excessive death rates that humans caused among yearlings and adults. At about the same time an aggressive public information program started by the department in the early 1980s began having an effect by increasing public awareness and reforming popular opinion. A slow rebound in the number of wolves was evident. Luckily disease problems also abated somewhat, and in the winter of 1987 pups were again seen in packs. In 1990 over 35 wolves in 10 packs were counted in Wisconsin's northern forest region.[10]

In 1986 the Wisconsin Department of Natural Resources inaugurated a three-year effort to develop a state wolf recovery program. The recovery team confronted many issues, worked with Wisconsin citizens to resolve conflicts, and moved forward in developing an assertive and realistic management plan that was adopted in 1989 as the first state-oriented wolf recovery plan in the nation.

In neighboring Upper Michigan, biologists have recently found sign of wolves, and the future for wolves has some promise there, too.[11] The Upper Peninsula has more remote forested tracts than Wisconsin. This remote quality is considered a habitat necessity for wolves today, because they need "quiet space" to avoid contacts with humans.[12]

Wisconsin, Michigan, and the nation are being afforded a second chance by this resurgence of wolves. Presently the upper Great lakes states of Michigan, Wisconsin, and Minnesota harbor the largest concentration of timber wolves in the states immediately south of Canada. In the 1990s an estimated 1,650 wolves are present in Minnesota, 45 have been counted in Wisconsin, an estimated 20 wolves roam Michigan's Upper Peninsula, and an additional 12 wander throughout Isle Royale National Park.[13]

But the future of the wolf outside Minnesota is still uncertain. The return of the wolf to the forests south of Lake Superior in recent years demands that we acknowledge the shortcomings of our past while working in the present with an eye to our future.

In the preceding chapters we have journeyed into that past and witnessed a society with dominionistic and utilitarian views towards nature and the wolves. Our founding fathers worked tirelessly to conquer the wilderness. Early-day conservationists jealously coveted their precious game animals and worked fervently to eliminate any would-be competitors. Almost no one then questioned whether these actions would be scrutinized or looked upon with disdain by future generations.

Men like Aldo Leopold, Bill Feeney, Bernie Bradle, Dan Thompson, Lee Smits, and others were disadvantaged in their appeals to save the big wolves. Today the conservation of wolves is supported by a more favorable societal view of predators, laws, and an evolving ecologistic policy of governmental conservation agencies. Still, places like Wisconsin and Michigan (and likewise Montana, Wyoming, Washington, Idaho, New Mexico, and Arizona) face a very great conservation challenge: Can today's citizens secure a future for their newly returned wolves?

The future will bring more people, more access, an unending explosion of developments, and quite probably fewer tax dollars with which to carry out conservation efforts. This will strain our remaining wild lands and place incredible and unrealistic political demands on a conservation system already rupturing from the stress which burdens it.

The agonizing death of Bayfield County's Old Two Toes is more than moving. It is stunningly symbolic of the collision between man and nature, civilization and wilderness. What passed with this wolf was much more than an individual life. It was a way of life, a life-stream of organisms, one more bit of Wisconsin's vanishing natural heritage, and a part of humanity.

Those Wisconsinites who cherish this state's history, its abundance of natural resources, and its leading role in environmental awareness must not allow the timber wolf to vanish a second time, because this state may never get another chance.

The epitaph written about Old Two Toes' death in 1959 is still fitting. *Time alone holds the answer.* Instead of hedging our bets on the wolf's survival, dare we wager confidently on society's conviction to preserve such a fundamental part of the wild as the timber wolf?

Appendices

Notes

References

Index

Appendix A. Specimens of
Wisconsin Timber Wolves

Despite a seemingly unlimited opportunity to amass quite a number of specimens of wolves destroyed through the bounty, only 13 specimens were collected and preserved in science museums. The following table and list show Wisconsin timber wolf specimens taken before 1960 and where they are located. The table contains museum specimens; the list contains specimens in private hands.

Specimens of Wisconsin Timber Wolves in Museum Collections

Museum catalogue number[a]	Location of specimen collection		Date of specimen collection	Sex, age	Current disposition
	County	Tnshp./range/sec.			
MPM-938	Oconto	—	6/13/03	M, juv.	—
MPM-731	Ashland	near Marsh	12/19/03	—	—
NMNH-150421	Vilas	near Eagle River	3/20/07	F, —	skull
NMNH-156838	Taylor	Perkinstown	1/10/08	—	skull
MPM-1435	Oneida	near Three Lakes	2/26/08	F, —	disposed
MPM-1441	Oneida	near Rhinelander	4/18/08	—	disposed
MPM-1204	—	—	3/01/10	—	—
NMNH-225395	Price	—	5/19/17	—, juv.	scalp
FMNH-51772	Vilas	near Michigan line	2/19/41	M, adult	—
UWZ-13029	Forest	town of Hiles	11/19/45	M, adult	skin and skull
UWZ-13509	Oneida	T37NR5E, Sec. 31	1/10/49	F, juv.	skin and skull[b]
UWZ-15213	Bayfield	T49NR5W, Sec. 18	1/18/58	M, adult	skin and skeleton[c]
FMNH-21208	Langlade	White Deer Lake	—	—	—

[a]MPM = Milwaukee Public Museum; NMNH = National Museum of Natural History; FMNH = Field Museum of Natural History, Chicago; UWZ = University of Wisconsin Zoology Museum, Madison.

[b]This wolf was the juvenile that was captured by Walt Rosenlaf at the same time he captured "Old Two Toes" of the Willow wolf pack.

[c]Here rest the bones of Bayfield County's "Old Two Toes."

Specimens of Wisconsin Timber Wolves in Private Collections

1 & 2) Two adult male wolves trapped by Herman Witt northeast of the Willow Flowage in Oneida County on April 2, 1945. These specimens were sold to Joe Mercedes, Chicago, for mounting at the "Wildlife Museum—Rhinelander." However, no museum exists there, and the specimens are presumed lost.

3) An aged adult female wolf shot northeast of the Willow Flowage in Oneida County in January of 1947 while "courting" a farm dog (see chapters 3 and 6). The skull was given to Doberstein's Resort on the east side of the flowage. Its present disposition is unknown.

4) Old Two Toes, the Willow wolf pack's alpha male, trapped by Walt Rosenlaf in January of 1949. This wolf was reportedly missing two central toes from both hind feet and the inner toe of its right front foot. The hide is in the possession of Walt Rosenlaf, Brantwood, Wisconsin.

5) Age and sex of wolf unknown and no definite date of death, but probably trapped in the 1940s by Walt Rosenlaf from the Willow wolf pack in Oneida County. Walt Rosenlaf possesses a throw rug.

6) Age and sex of wolf unknown and no definite date of death, but probably taken during the 1940s by Walt Rosenlaf from the Willow wolf pack in Oneida County. This specimen is mounted and displayed at Talbot's Resort on Willow Lake in Oneida County.

7) "The Thing," a large male wolf shot by a farmer near Hannibal (Taylor County), Wisconsin, in 1950. A mount of the wolf is displayed at the Hungry Hollow Tavern east of Gilman.

8) A large timber wolf shot by Harold Ruprecht near Roach Lake in Vilas County during the November 1950 dear season. Reportedly it was mounted and displayed at "Shrimp's Museum" near Boulder Junction, but with no one currently knowing of such a place, the specimen's present disposition is unknown.

9) A 94-pound male wolf shot by David Christie of Milwaukee in Florence County along the Popple River southeast of Long Lake during the November 1955 deer season. Christie possesses a throw rug and the skull.

Appendix B. The Wolf and Its Relatives

Three species in the genus *Canis* existed in Wisconsin at the time of settlement: dogs, wolves, and coyotes. These three creatures are closely related and often confused by casual wildlife observers. From a historical viewpoint, they have coinhabited Wisconsin for thousands of years.

Early visitors to Wisconsin recorded the dog's presence: "A vast number of lean and wolfish-looking dogs were prowling about the [Winnebago's] lodges. . . ."[1] These dogs could have been more than "wolfish-looking"; they could actually have been wolves. Famed fur trader Alexander Henry observed Indian dogs mating with wolves in the vicinity of the Red River on the present-day Minnesota–North Dakota border in January of 1801.[2]

It is commonly believed that coyotes are more recent arrivals to Wisconsin, being an artifact of habitat changes brought on during the settlement period.* In fact, fossil evidence of their presence in the state extends back some 7,000 years from an archeological site unearthed in Sauk County.[5]

Coyotes (*Canis latrans*) were familiar sights on southern Wisconsin prairies. In that locale they were called prairie wolves. Juliette Kinzie, wife of the Winnebago Indian agent at Fort Winnebago (present-day Portage, Wisconsin), observed a "gaunt prairie-wolf" on several occasions near the Blue Mounds in March of 1831 while she was en route to Fort Dearborn (Chicago).[6] In 1834 Charles Rodolf complained that Grant County's "prairies were full of prairie wolves,"[7] and in 1836, prairie wolves were common in Walworth County.[8] Others reported them in Dane County, Kenosha County in the 1830s, and as late as 1865 "another prairie wolf has been caught within the city limits of Milwaukee."[9] One was collected from Racine in 1852 and placed in the collection of the Natural History Association at Madison, but that collection has long since disappeared.[10]

Although coyotes were commonly encountered in southern Wisconsin, they were probably absent in the northern forested region until the loggers opened up the country. They were first recorded along the south shore of Lake Superior near Ashland in 1904.[11] Soon after their appearance in the north, local folk began referring to them as brush wolves, a name that sticks with them in certain circles to this day.

*Noted mammalogist Hartley Jackson incorrectly interpreted the meaning of historic Prairie du Chien as a label given to that locality by French traders "on account of the coyotes in that region."[3] Hope Ryden undoubtedly perpetuated Jackson's mistake. Robert Gard and L. G. Sorden state that it was named after a Fox Indian chief whose village was located on that site. He was known as Dog.[4]

Some old-timers insist that the brush wolf is a distinct species, different from the coyote or timber wolf. "We have a wolf in this area that comes near being called a timber wolf. In 1945 I trapped two of these animals. . . . [They] were not coyotes. But they didn't seem to quite measure up to timber wolves."[12] No scientific evidence exists to support contentions that a third species exists. However, coyotes, wolves, and dogs can interbreed. So it is possible that wild hybrid coyote-wolf mixes have existed.

Appendix C. Biographies of Wisconsin Biologists Influential in Wolf Conservation

Bernard J. Bradle was born on May 22, 1914, at Laona, Wisconsin. He graduated from the White Lake Union Free High School in May 1932. In October 1936, he worked temporarily for warden Royce Dallman, who was stationed at the Argonne Deer Refuge headquarters, north of Crandon. "Some of the first timber wolf sign that I saw up in this area was in 1936, probably in November. He [Dallman] had me follow the Jones [Creek] for illegal trapping, and I got up in there—timber wolf sign!"[1]

Bradle's temporary job with warden Dallman was influential later in landing a job with Feeney's Deer Research Project crew. Feeney hired Bradle on the basis of the advice and recommendation of his supervisor, Walter Scott, himself a former warden. Bradle began in Feeney's employ in February 1943 and transferred to a position in the Game Management Division in the fall of 1947.

Bernie always had a soft spot for wolves. In his youth his family owned a hunting shack east of Blackwell in Forest County, and there still were a few wolves in that area then. His uncles did not believe in condemning an animal on the basis of what it ate, and they left the wolves alone—definitely a rare philosophy among hunters in the 1920s and 1930s. Bradle was always sensitive about policies that affected the wolves. He wasn't happy with the annual warden-sponsored wolf hunts in the Argonne Deer Refuge and was visibly upset when the Wisconsin Conservation Department decided to dismantle the old refuge, thus allowing bounty trappers to follow their deadly pursuits within the 72-square-mile area that was as much a refuge to timber wolves as it was to deer (photo 6.8).

Bernie Bradle retired in 1973, and lived in Crandon until his death on March 28, 1993.

William S. Feeney was born on June 17, 1905, in Chicago, Illinois, and grew up in the vicinity of Belle Fourche, South Dakota. He graduated in biology and geology from the University of Minnesota in June 1931 and pursued additional courses in 1931–32 and 1933–34. During the late 1930s Feeney was employed by the National Park Service in Madison at the university arboretum. During this period Feeney became acquainted with Aldo Leopold.[2]

In 1940 Feeney was hired as the project leader of the Wisconsin Conservation Department's newly created Deer Research Project under the supervision of Wal-

191

ter Scott. The project was funded by the federal government's Pittman-Robertson Act, which generated money through excise taxes on the sale of firearms and ammunition. Feeney organized and supervised the activities of many field men while they systematically surveyed and "cruised" all deer yards in central and northern Wisconsin between 1940 and 1948. Deer Research Project personnel documented deer feeding habits, movements, birth rates, sex ratios, densities, types of mortality, and the productivity and availability of deer browse species within the deer yards.

As a falconer, Feeney was interested in predators and instructed his field men to maintain detailed records of the predator signs they encountered in the course of their activities. He thus accumulated the ammunition necessary to counter claims that Wisconsin Conservation Department mismanagement and predators were decimating the state's deer herd.

Bill Feeney was at times mercilessly demanding of his employees and possessed an abrasive personality, which caused friction with top management. Following a change in administrators, Feeney fell from favor and was forced to resign in 1948 or 1949. He died on May 25, 1982.

Felix A. Hartmeister was born on April 2, 1917, in Altamont, Illinois. He graduated from Valparaiso University in June 1940 and studied biology and ecology at the Universities of Minnesota and Wisconsin, respectively. In September 1943, he began working for Walter Scott and, on the basis of Scott's recommendation, began with Feeney on the Deer Research Project crew in December 1943. He worked in that capacity until 1947. Nothing further is known about Felix Hartmeister.[3]

Aldo Leopold was born in 1886, and raised in Burlington, Iowa. Following his graduation from Yale, Leopold hired on as a forester and administrator with the U.S. Forest Service in New Mexico. During this period Leopold became interested in the management of big game populations on public lands. Believing that the removal of predators would benefit wildlife populations and ultimately hunters, he advocated the extermination of such animals as wolves and mountain lions.[4]

In 1924 he took a position as director of the Forest Productions Laboratory in Madison, and in 1933 he published *Game Management* and thus became the "father of wildlife management." Shortly after, he took a newly created position as professor of wildlife management at the University of Wisconsin at Madison.

About this time Leopold became a prominent figure in the state's deer controversy. He supported deer research as a means of finding a solution to the problems of deer herd management. He was nationally influential in wildlife policy and a dominating figure in the biopolitics of Wisconsin. In 1943 he was appointed to the Wisconsin Conservation Commission, and he devoted a good portion of his energies to resolving the volatile issue of deer politics.

Over the years Leopold's feelings towards predators had changed. The Wisconsin deer wars taught him the important role predators like wolves play in keeping the balance between deer and the range they depend on for food and shelter. By the time of his appointment to the commission, Leopold advocated maintaining a population of timber wolves in Wisconsin. Unfortunately, he died an untimely death in

April 1948, but he blazed a trail through ignorance and greed, and introduced to the world the philosophy of ecological ethics.

Clarence Searles, operator of a cranberry bog near Wisconsin Rapids, served as secretary for the Wisconsin Conservation Congress, which had a vested interest in the deer management dilemma. While serving in this capacity he met and began an association with Aldo Leopold. Occasionally, Leopold would drop by the Peshtigo Preserve, the grounds of an elite hunting and fishing club in southeastern Forest County, of which Searles was a member. "We would go over the deer thing as it pertained to Forest County and also the timber wolves and things of this nature."[5]

Leopold arranged for Searles to work as a volunteer during the winter months with Feeney's Deer Research Project crew. Searles spent most of his time studying the habits of timber wolves.

Clarence Searles operated a cranberry bog in the vicinity of Wisconsin Rapids until the late 1980s, and died on October 31, 1990.

Daniel Q. Thompson was born in Madison on October 3, 1918, and graduated in wildlife management as a student of Aldo Leopold's at the University of Wisconsin in 1942. Following graduation Thompson worked as a field biologist for Feeney until April 1942, when he enlisted in the U.S. Coast Guard. After the war he returned to Wisconsin and worked for the Wisconsin Conservation Department from April 1946 to 1948 while pursuing a master's degree in wildlife management at the University of Wisconsin. His thesis focused on the food habits of Wisconsin's wolves. A condensed version of his thesis appeared in the scientific periodical *Journal of Mammalogy* and was the only professional article published on Wisconsin's original wolf population.[6]

Thompson was deeply concerned about the plight of Wisconsin's wolves. Fellow Deer Research Project worker Bernie Bradle said of him, "Danny hated anybody that had one bad word against the timber wolf."[7] Bradle was correct in his assessment. Almost 40 years later Thompson confided, ". . . I will admit to keeping a can of ripe human urine for my return trips to Oneida County." He used the urine to foul up two popular areas used by wolf trappers. After discovering them, he "always anointed the set with a pint or so of old urine . . . in the interest of wolf preservation. . . ."

Dan's regard for the Willow pack wolves was genuine. "I can still recall the ghoulish shock of driving into Walter's yard and seeing the Oneida wolf pack hanging by wires from the trees. It was as though some of my own family were hanging over the bright snow."[8]

Thompson went on to earn a doctoral degree in wildlife management from the University of Wisconsin in 1955, worked for years in the Cooperative Wildlife Research Unit at Cornell University, and later on the U.S. Fish and Wildlife Service's editorial staff at Fort Collins, Colorado, until his retirement in January 1984. He lives in Fort Collins.

Appendix D. Details of Wisconsin and Upper Michigan Timber Wolf Ranges, 1920–60

After 1920 timber wolves were restricted to about a dozen and a half remote ranges that extended from northwestern Wisconsin's Bayfield County east to Michigan's Chippewa County. It was difficult to determine the exact number of packs that existed within each of these ranges. Usually between one and three packs were believed to occupy each range early in the period; after 1945 most ranges contained only a single pack.

This appendix summarizes wolf activity within each of the timber wolf ranges. It identifies known denning grounds and highlights major pack observations by loggers, trappers, biologists, and woodsmen between roughly 1920 and 1960. The same information was used to construct the wolf population information presented in table 8.2 and appendix E.

Wisconsin Timber Wolf Ranges

Eau Claire Lakes Wolf Range

PHENOLOGY OF DECLINE

Year	Number of wolves	Locale, comments
1944	2	northwest Washburn County
1946	1	Totagatic deer yard
1946	pack	rumored pack activity in the headwaters of the Totagatic drainage

LAST NOTABLE SIGN. January 1946. State control trapper Alvin Jaeger reported seeing a single timber wolf track in the Totagatic deer yard.

SOURCES. SHSW, ser. 271, box 26, folder 1; Wisconsin Conservation Department, miscellaneous materials, in author's possession; Wisconsin Conservation Department Pittman-Robertson Deer Research Project Materials; Wisconsin Conservation Department, "Giant Wolf Dies," *Wis. Conserv. Bull.* 2, no. 11(1937):36.

Upper Ghost Lake Wolf Range

DENNING GROUNDS. McCloud Lake. Warden Fred Minor claimed, "This breeding ground was remote, about three miles from the road."

PHENOLOGY OF DECLINE

Year	Number of wolves	Locale, comments
1927–28	7	center of activity near Upper Ghost Lake
1938	3	Star Lake; one trapped there by Walt Rosenlaf
1938	pack	ranged from McCloud and Upper Ghost lakes to Dells and Chippewa lakes

LAST NOTABLE SIGN. January 11, 1945. Warden Leon Plante reported two timber wolf tracks in the Lake Five deer yard.

Warden Fred Minor said, "They frequented these areas in the 1930s and early 1940s. I cannot give a year time when they became quite scarce, but will state this, that one trapper out of Mellen or Glidden trapped seven or eight of them one fall for bounty, and it is my opinion that this trapping activity at that time put an end to this wolf pack."

SOURCES. SHSW, Game Management Division materials; Wisconsin Conservation Department Pittman-Robertson Deer Research Project materials; Fred Minor, pers. comm., 1970; Stan Plis, pers. comm., 1979; Walter Rosenlaf, pers. comm., 1970.

Spider Lake Wolf Range

DENNING GROUNDS. Near McCarthy Lake, in the early 1940s. An observation of a probable homesite was found in a notebook belonging to Conservation Department biologist Felix Hartmeister. It was dated September 22, 1944: "Ashland Co. While cruising at 7:50 A.M. at Twin Lakes a howel [sic] of a wolf was heard to the NE & E— one started and another chimed in; then there was a great clammer [sic] of howels. It was not the short choppy howel of a dog or coyote, but a long drawn out howel."

PHENOLOGY OF DECLINE

Year	Number of wolves	Locale, comments
1913	12	crossed railroad grade near English Lake
1916–22	pack	sign found at Woodtick and Twin lakes and along Ding-dong Creek
1938	pack	sign found on north end of Mineral Lake
early 1940s	—	Two pups and two unknown aged wolves were trapped one fall between McCarthy Lake and Hwy. 77.

LAST NOTABLE SIGN. This pack probably disappeared by the mid- to late 1940s. After they had more or less vanished, trapper Russ Olson noted occasional sign of a loner in the Coffee Lake area during the late 1940s or early 1950s immediately northwest of the Spider Lake territory.

SOURCES. Wisconsin Conservation Department Pittman-Robertson Deer Research Project materials; Russell Olson, pers. comm., 1979; Bo Popov, pers. comm., 1975; Clarence Schmidt, pers. comm., 1974; Frank Tomaier, pers. comm., 1979, 1980; Corrigan, *Caulked Boots and Cant Hooks.*

Moose River Wolf Range

PHENOLOGY OF DECLINE

Year	Number of wolves	Locale, comments
1930	2	Lawrence Schmidt trapped two along the Hungry Run Creek.
1938	4	Walt Rosenlaf trapped two between Bear and Cub lakes and saw sign of four wolves along the Moose River.
1946	pack	one pup trapped on the west fork of the Chippewa River by Billy Bay and sold to the Poynette Game Farm

LAST NOTABLE SIGN. Warden Robert Markle shot at a timber wolf standing alongside the recently constructed County Highway GG, which was converted from a fire lane in the early 1950s. Warden Pat Burhans found occasional tracks and droppings from wolves near the Torch River, and game biologist John Keener felt that a small pack persisted in the area until about 1955.

SOURCES. SHSW, Game Management Division materials; Wisconsin Conservation Department Pittman-Robertson Deer Research Project Materials; Kenneth Beghin, pers. comm., 1979; Pat Burhans, pers. comm., 1978; Orvid Donner, pers. comm., 1979; John Keener, pers. comm., 1973; Neil LeMay, pers. comm., 1979; Russell Olson, pers. comm., 1979; Walter Rosenlaf, pers. comm., 1970; Sam Reugger, pers. comm., 1974; Clarence Schmidt, pers. comm., 1974; Frank Tomaier, pers. comm., 1979 and 1980; *Glidden Enterprise,* "Funds Asked for Liberal Wolf Bounties," December 8, 1944.

Price Creek Wolf Range

DENNING GROUNDS. Lower stretch of Price Creek.

PHENOLOGY OF DECLINE

Year	Number of wolves	Locale, comments
1943–44	3–5	tracks found in Flambeau State Forest
1944–45	2–6	sign found from Price and Connor creeks to Mason Lake

LAST NOTABLE SIGN. Game biologist John Keener felt that this small family group persisted into the early 1950s. In April of 1954 Carl Heizler trapped a 98-pound timber wolf along Price Creek. He claimed this animal was the last of its pack.

SOURCES. Wisconsin Conservation Department Pittman-Robertson Deer Research Project materials; Bill Feeney, pers. comm., 1979; Carl Heizler, pers. comm., 1984; John Keener, pers. comm., 1973; *Milwaukee Sentinel,* April 18, 1954.

Pleasant Lake Wolf Range

DENNING GROUNDS. Between O'Brien, Island, and Pleasant Lakes.

PHENOLOGY OF DECLINE

Year	Number of wolves	Locale, comments
1908	—	one timber wolf trapped near Island Lake
early 1930s	6–7	sign found in the Lake 15 area
1943	2	Twin Lakes
1943-44	4	Island Lake area
1947–48	3	One of these was struck by a car and disappeared.
1950	3	O'Brien and Pleasant lakes
1951	3	howling heard near Lake One
1952	4	sign at deer kill near Island Lake
1954	3	seen near Island Lake

LAST NOTABLE SIGN. Local woodsman Walter Peltonen saw a lone timber wolf track in this area in 1959. This corroborates an observation made by game biologist Cliff Germain, who recorded seeing tracks of a lone timber wolf along a stretch of fire lane near Little Moose Lake on March 12, 1959. Gerald Wick claims to have trapped a small timber wolf on the Moose Lake fire lane in 1959.

PHOTO. 7.6.

SOURCES. AL, ser. 9/25/10 4, box 1; Wisconsin Conservation Department, miscellaneous materials, in author's possession; George Corrigan, pers. comm., 1979; Bill Feeney, pers. comm., 1979; Reino Herlevi, pers. comm., 1970, 1971; Keith Jesse, pers. comm., 1979; Russell Olson, pers. comm., 1979; Walter Peltonen, pers. comm., 1970; Gerald Wick, pers. comm., 1970; Ellis, "Old Lobo, the Timber Wolf"; Swift, "The Biography of a Self-made Naturalist," part 1.

Duck Lake Subrange

DENNING GROUNDS. Northeast of Duck Lake. A den was found in April 1944 by Bill Feeney's Deer Research personnel in a hollow pine log. Another den was found in the spring of 1950 by warden Ken Beghin northeast of Duck Lake along the Swamp Creek drainage.

PHENOLOGY OF DECLINE

Year	Number of wolves	Locale, comments
1940–41	7	sign found near Forest Wonder Lodge
1944	2	Tracks of a pair led up to a den site.
1945	9	Deer biologists trailed a pack from Forest Wonder Lodge northwest to Duck Lake.

LAST NOTABLE SIGN. Bill Feeney, leader of the Wisconsin Conservation Department's Deer Research Project, felt that the two main packs in the area were the Flambeau group and the Pleasant Lake group. Wolf sign in the country in between—the Duck Lake block—was generally believed to be caused by occasional dispersers from the more stable groups to the north and south that succeeded in raising pups. Trapping was particularly heavy along the Duck Lake fire lane and in the vicinity of Forest Wonder Lodge, and probably kept this group trimmed down. It probably became extirpated shortly before the Pleasant Lake and Flambeau packs did.

SOURCES. Wisconsin Conservation Department Pittman-Robertson Deer Research Project materials; Bill Feeney, pers. comm., 1979; Frank Tomaier, pers. comm., 1979, 1980.

Flambeau (Flowage) Wolf Range

DENNING GROUNDS. Beaver Creek Basin Southwest of the Flowage.

PHENOLOGY OF DECLINE

Year	Number of wolves	Locale, comments
1940–41	pack	Orvid Donner trapped three wolves on the flowage near the carcasses of 13 deer killed by the pack.
1944	2	tracks found near the Springstead tower
1949–50	pack	Two adults and two pups were trapped in the fall along Hay Creek.
1952	pack	sign found in the spring along Hay Creek
1953	—	An adult female was chased into a den along the flowage shoreline near Beaver Creek, and two live pups and one dead were removed.

LAST NOTABLE SIGN. In February of 1955 Deer Research crews reported tracks of three timber wolves near Sardine Lake. In November of that year deer hunter Darrell Tomkins of Elroy shot an 82-pound wolf near the flowage. In the spring of 1960 game manager Cliff Wiita found the track of a single timber wolf within the Hoffman Lake Wildlife Area.

SOURCES. SHSW, Game Management Division materials; N. C. Anderson, pers. comm., 1980; Pat Burhans, pers. comm., 1978; Royce Dallman, pers. comm., 1976; John Keener, pers. comm., 1973; Bo Popov, pers. comm., 1975; *Elroy Leader Tribune*, "Gets Wolf Instead of Deer," November 25, 1955.

Willow Wolf Range

DENNING GROUNDS. South range: The traditional denning ground was centered on the Little Rice River northwest of Gobler Lake. North range: A den was apparently known to locals along the headwaters of Willow Creek west of Bootjack Lake.

PHENOLOGY OF DECLINE

Year	Number of wolves	Locale, comments
1900–05	pack	Willow Lake and Tomahawk River
1930	8	sign abundant from Bass Lake to the flowage
1938–39	15	south of the flowage
1942	8	south of the flowage
1944	5	south of the flowage
1949	2	After winter trapping ceased only one adult and one immature wolf could be accounted for.
1951–52	—	one trapped by a local trapper

LAST NOTABLE SIGN. In 1953 the county forester found tracks of a lone timber wolf near Willow Lake. Trapper Walt Rosenlaf felt that three wolves were present in the area in 1955, but former biologist Dan Thompson briefly visited the usual haunts of the old pack he had studied 10 years earlier and failed to find any evidence of wolf sign in 1957.

PHOTOS. 1.1, 3.1, 4.2, 4.3, 7.5

SOURCES. SHSW, Game Management Division materials; Wisconsin Conservation Department Pittman-Robertson Deer Research Project materials; Kenneth Beghin, pers. comm., 1979; Max Morehouse, pers. comm., 1971; Walter Rosenlaf, pers. comm., 1970, 1972, 1973, 1980; "Pete" Tyler, pers. comm., 1975; Swift, "The Biography of a Self-made Naturalist," part 3; Thompson, "A Preliminary Study of the Timber Wolf."

Virgin Lake Wolf Range

PHENOLOGY OF DECLINE

Year	Number of wolves	Locale, comments
1941–42	7	Five were trapped by Ray Sensenbrenner.
1945	2	Tracks of this pair were trailed up onto Chaney Lake in Michigan by deer biologists Armin Schwengel and Clarence Searles.
1954–56	—	timber wolf sign found near Black Lake by Michigan biologists

LAST NOTABLE SIGN. On January 29, 1959, game biologist Bill Creed saw tracks of a lone timber wolf about a mile west of the headwaters of Black River. Warden Warren Holger remarked, "The last track that I saw and could be positive of was . . . on the south side of Virgin Lake in about 1959."

SOURCES. Wisconsin Conservation Department Pittman-Robertson Deer Research Project materials; Warren Holger, pers. comm., 1969, 1970, 1979; Bo Popov, pers. comm., 1975; Clarence Searles, pers. comm., 1977; Ray Sensenbrenner, pers. comm., 1979; D. Arnold and R. Schofield, "Status of Michigan Timber Wolves, 1954–56," Mich. Dep. Conserv. Game Div. Rep. No. 2097, mimeo.

Garland Springs Wolf Range

Note. This is the southern area (in Vilas County, Wisconsin) of a range that extended across the state border into Michigan. (The northern area is known as the Cisco Lake wolf range, in Gogebic County, Michigan; see the next section, "Upper Michigan's Western Wolf Ranges"). The range division occurred along Highway B just south of the state border. The entire range probably contained several packs in the 1920s and 1930s.

PHENOLOGY OF DECLINE

Year	Number of wolves	Locale, comments
1930	3	trailed from a deer kill near Tenderfoot Lake
1933	2	Star Lake
1936	9	reduced to three following a warden-sponsored hunt from Palmer Lake to Garland Springs
1937	5	—
before 1945	3–6	—
1947	7	Two were trapped and five were shot.

LAST NOTABLE SIGN. Deer hunter Harold Ruprecht shot a large timber wolf in November of 1950 near Roach Lake. No further activity was noted in the Garland Springs wolf range.

PHOTOS. 8.2, 8.3

SOURCE. SHSW, Game Management Division materials; Tom Spurgeon, Sr., pers. comm., 1974; Ellis Wendt, pers. comm., 1980; Pat Wilsie, Sr., pers. comm., 1976; Wisconsin Conservation Department, "Praise Hunters," *Wis. Conserv. Bull.* 1, no. 5(1936):10; Wisconsin Conservation Department, "Timber Wolf," *Wis. Conserv. Bull.* 9, no. 1(1944):24; Wisconsin Conservation Department, "Timber Wolf," *Wis. Conserv. Bull.* 11, no. 1(1946):10.

North Branch Wolf Range

DENNING GROUNDS. North branch of the Pine River.

PHENOLOGY OF DECLINE

Year	Number of wolves	Locale, comments
1923	—	The Petts brothers removed one adult female and her six pups from a hollow log on the north branch of the Pine River.
1930	6	sign found along Alvin Creek
1931	6	tracks found on the Pine River headwaters
1933	—	one adult female and seven pups taken from a den
1936–45	3–4	sign found from the Michigan line south to McDonald Creek
1945	pack	A pup was trapped on the Windsor Dam Road.

LAST NOTABLE SIGN. In March of 1956 game manager Bernie Bradle found tracks of two timber wolves east of Howell Lake near the north branch.

SOURCES. Loren Fishel, pers. comm., 1973; James Huff, pers. comm., 1971; Perry Petts, pers. comm., 1974; Ray Smith, pers. comm., 1976; Pat Wilsie, Sr., pers. comm., 1976; *Forest Republican*, "Houston Stamper Gets $90 Bounty on Eight Wolves," May 18, 1933.

Scott Lake Wolf Range

DENNING GROUNDS. Somewhere along the headwaters of the south branch of the Pine River above the old Civilian Conservation Corps camp off the old Sinkhole Road, a long-abandoned trail that ran north from the junction of present-day U.S. Forest Service roads 2183 and 2184 through the great bog until it met U.S. Forest Service Road 2414.

PHENOLOGY OF DECLINE

Year	Number of wolves	Locale, comments
before 1920	7	sign prevalent in the Fourmile Creek and Julia Lake area
1930	pack	howling heard along headwaters of the South Branch
before 1935	pack	howling common along Kimball Creek
1936	10–12	tracks found on Pine Lake and the Hiles Mill Pond
1938	7	The pack was flushed out by hunters using dogs along the Popple River.
1940	8	sign within the Argonne Deer Refuge

1949	5–6	tracks leading from a scavenged hunter-killed deer near the Double Bend Road
1953	3	tracks at a deer kill near Scott Lake
1954–55	4–6	sign in the area around the old CCC camp
before		
1955	3	trails in the vicinity of Scott Lake

LAST NOTABLE SIGN. U.S. Forest Service employee David Stover last saw sign of timber wolf activity near the Highway 55 Nettleton firetower in 1958. In a 1958 news release by the Wisconsin Conservation Department, game manager Bernie Bradle was quoted as saying, " 'I have not seen any timber wolf sign at all in the past two years.' Forest County had been one of its last strongholds."

PHOTOS. 6.8

FIGURE. 7.1

SOURCES. Wisconsin Conservation Department, miscellaneous materials, in author's possession; Wisconsin Conservation Department Pittman-Robertson Deer Research Project materials; Kennell Elliott, pers. comm., 1979; John Keener, pers. comm., 1973; Bo Popov, pers. comm., 1975; David Stover, pers. comm., 1971.

Stevens Lake–Laona Activity

Note. Pack activity was never fully documented in the area between the Forest County packs and the Woods Creek pack of western Florence County. However, wolf sign was occasionally seen in this large region, possibly the result of local dispersers moving through or temporarily settling within the region.

PHENOLOGY OF DECLINE

Year	Number of wolves	Locale, comments
1941–42	—	Deer biologist Dan Thompson noted wolf sign in the area.
August 1944	—	Bernie Bradle found a number of coyote and timber wolf droppings on the lane going past Stevens Lake.

LAST NOTABLE SIGN. In 1950 and 1951 a lone wolf was followed closely by Laona trapper Joe Novak. It ranged from Kersten to Otter Creek, north and west of Laona. It frequently traveled segments of Highway 139 and County Trunks O and G, scent-marking on the snow banks. He eventually caught the 93-pound wolf near Wabikon Lake.

SOURCE. Wisconsin Conservation Department Pittman-Robertson Deer Research Project materials; Ray Smith, pers. comm., 1976; R. McCabe, "The Mammals of the Pine and Popple River Area," *Trans. Wis. Acad. Sci., Arts and Lett.* 60(1972):275–289.

McCaslin Wolf Range

PHENOLOGY OF DECLINE

Year	Number of wolves	Locale, comments
1933	4	sign reported near Lakewood
1938	—	Two wolves were trapped in the town of Wabeno.
1940	3	sign found near Lakewood
before 1945	—	Sign of a small family group was found in the McCaslin country.
1945	—	One adult and two pups were trapped in the McCaslin Mountain region.

LAST NOTABLE SIGN. On a winter evening in 1950–51, warden Carl Miersch heard a timber wolf howling from the vicinity of McCaslin Springs and Bear Lake and found its tracks the following morning in the snow.

SOURCE. Wisconsin Conservation Department, miscellaneous materials, in author's possession; Bernie Bradle, pers. comm., 1980; Max Morehouse, pers. comm., 1971; Leslie Rugg, pers. comm., 1980; *Forest Republican,* October 20, 1938.

Michigan Creek Wolf Range

PHENOLOGY OF DECLINE

Year	Number of wolves	Locale, comments
1944	pack	scats found near the Burnt Bridge and a single timber wolf seen by Bernie Bradle on a fire lane south of Goodman
1950	—	timber wolf–killed deer found on the Peshtigo River by deer biologists
		Warden Bud Kuhrasch recalls processing a bounty claim on a timber wolf shot by a deer hunter.
1951	—	timber wolf–killed deer found on Otter Creek

LAST NOTABLE SIGN. A single timber wolf, bountied in 1956–57, was taken from Langlade County. A remnant perhaps from Michigan Creek?

SOURCES. Wisconsin Conservation Department, miscellaneous materials, in author's possession; Wisconsin Conservation Department Pittman-Robertson Deer Research Project materials; Bud Kuhrasch, pers. comm., 1980.

Woods Creek Wolf Range

DENNING GROUNDS. Between Wheeler Lake, Cody Creek, and the headwaters of Morgan Creek.

PHENOLOGY OF DECLINE

Year	Number of wolves	Locale, comments
1930–32	5	in the Goodman timber tract west of Fence
1933	7	Two were shot from the pack.
1934	15	Anderson Marsh–Morgan Lake country
1942	8	Popple River and Riley Creek area
1945	3	Tracks of two adults and a single pup were found by deer biologists near Robago Lake.
1946	4	tracks in snow on the Pine River north of Grubhoe Lake
	pack	Morgan Lake area
1952–53	3	two miles south of Savage Lake

LAST NOTABLE SIGN. Bounty records list single wolves taken from Florence County in 1952–53 and 1955–56. The latter wolf was probably the one Milwaukee deer hunter David Christie shot southeast of Long Lake near the Popple River in November of 1955. During the 1958 deer season, game manager LeRoy Linteruer recorded that a subadult female timber wolf was shot near the Woods Creek Flowage of Florence County.

PHOTO. 6.3

SOURCE. Wisconsin Conservation Department, miscellaneous materials, in author's possession; Wisconsin Conservation Department Pittman-Robertson Deer Research Project materials; David Christie, pers. comm., 1980; LeRoy Linteruer, pers. comm., 1973, 1984; Mr. Milcheski, pers. comm., 1981; Bo Popov, pers. comm., 1975; Ray Smith, pers. comm., 1976; *Florence Mining News*, "145 Coyote Bounties in County in 1945," January 12, 1946; *Forest Republican*, December 1, 1955; *Rhinelander Daily News*, "Milwaukee Man Kills Timber Wolf in Forest County," November 30, 1955.

Upper Michigan's Western Wolf Ranges

Cisco Lake Wolf Range

Note. This was the northern area of the range that extended from Wisconsin Highway B to U.S. Highway 2 in Michigan.

DENNING GROUNDS. In the early 1950s a pup was caught between Pomeroy and Langford lakes. The homesite and denning area were presumably nearby.

PHENOLOGY OF DECLINE

Year	Number of wolves	Locale, comments
before 1935	6	A pack of six wolves frightened an ice fisherman who claimed they chased him up a tree. He actually voluntarily climbed the tree while the wolves exited the lake.
1954–56	—	Seven timber wolves were bountied from this area in a two-year period.

LAST NOTABLE SIGN. Clarence Allen trapped a wolf pup in the summer of 1956. This was the last sign noted from the area.

SOURCES. Clarence Allen, pers. comm., 1979; Arnold and Schofield, "Status of Michigan Timber Wolves, 1954–56."

Porcupine Mountains

Wolves were found in this rugged range when Clarence Allen was hired to cruise the timber stands on General Motors property there in 1930. He trapped 10, "because they had been killing deer." In 1948 Detroit socialites proposed using this area as a release site to replenish wolves. No wolves were thought to remain there by that time, and no release ever materialized.

SOURCES. Clarence Allen, pers. comm., 1979; *Milwaukee Journal*, "Sanctuary for Wolves Suggested in Michigan, January 25, 1948, part 3, p. 8.

Sandstone Rapids

A big pack of wolves roamed the upper stretches of the Ontonagon River in the 1930s. Its range lay between Sandstone Rapids and the little community of Ewen. The pack was wiped out sometime in the 1940s.

SOURCE. Clarence Allen, pers. comm., 1979.

Kenton–Perch Lake

PHENOLOGY OF DECLINE

Year	Number of wolves	Locale, comments
1914	pack	howling commonly heard near Lake Mitigwaki
1920s and 1930s	4–5	tracks commonly found in the Bond Falls Flowage area
1950	—	den raided along Deadman Creek
1955	no wolf activity reported	Michigan Conservation Department report

SOURCES. Don Lappala, pers. comm., 1976; *Florence Mining News*, "Unarmed Man Chased by Wolves, Resorts to 'Trick' and Escapes," January 27, 1939; Arnold and Schofield, "Status of Michigan Timber Wolves, 1954–56"; A. Cahn, "Notes on the Vertebrate Fauna of Houghton and Iron Counties, Michigan," *Trans. Wis. Acad. Sci., Arts and Lett.* 19(1918):483–510.

Huron Mountains

PHENOLOGY OF DECLINE

Year	Number of wolves	Locale, comments
1907	pack	A den was raided with five pups near Mountain Lake.
1952 or 1953	pack	A den was raided near Big Bay.
mid-1950s	2–5	Two wolves were bountied between 1954–56.

SOURCES. Don Lappala, pers. comm., 1976; Arnold and Schofield, "Status of Michigan Timber Wolves, 1954–56"; Bailey, *Destruction of Wolves and Coyotes.*

Floodwood

This range of wild land stretched north from the Wisconsin line for about 30 miles between Iron River and Iron Mountain. Two dens, containing a total of nine pups, were dug up in 1907 near Floodwood. A wolf was bountied there in the mid-1950s.

SOURCES. Arnold and Schofield, "Status of Michigan Timber Wolves, 1954–56"; Bailey, *Destruction of Wolves and Coyotes.*

Upper Escanaba

This range reached south from Marquette to the Wisconsin line east of Iron Mountain and north of Escanaba. One to three wolves were still reported in the area in the early to mid-1950s. Three were bountied there between 1954–1956.

SOURCE. Source. Arnold and Schofield, "Status of Michigan Timber Wolves, 1954–56."

Eastern Upper Michigan's Wolf Ranges

Trout Plains

Located southwest of Munising, this range held only one or two wolves in the mid-1950s. Five wolves were known to have been bountied between 1954 and 1956.

SOURCE. Arnold and Schofield, "Status of Michigan Timber Wolves, 1954–56."

Cusino Wolf Range

PHENOLOGY OF DECLINE

Year	Number of wolves	Locale, comments
1936	3	Adolf Stebler described their range as 260 square miles.
1937	4	(nothing specific among A. Stebler's observations)
mid-1950s	1–3	Ten wolves were bountied in two years between 1954–1956.

SOURCES. Michigan Conservation Department, miscellaneous materials, in author's possession; Arnold and Schofield, "Status of Michigan Timber Wolves, 1954–56"; Stebler, "The Ecology of Michigan Coyotes and Wolves."

Hulbert Wolf Range

PHENOLOGY OF DECLINE

Year	Number of wolves	Locale, comments
1940	pack	The 100-pound timber wolf "Clubfoot" was trapped near Newberry.
1941	pack	A den raid yielded one adult and seven pups.
1949–50	6	(nothing specific among A. Stebler's observations)
1950	—	A den was raided and one adult female and eight pups were taken.
mid-1950s	1–3	six wolves bountied between 1954–1956

SOURCES. *Milwaukee Journal*, "Clubfoot, a Timber Wolf, Is Trapped by Neophyte," November 10, 1940; Arnold and Schofield, "Status of Michigan Timber Wolves, 1954–56"; Stebler, "The Ecology of Michigan Coyotes and Wolves".

Appendix E. Calculating the Wisconsin Timber Wolf Population Decline

On the basis of testimonies and notes left by trappers, woods-men, and biologists, estimates of the number of wolves were made for each of the 18 packs that existed until 1960. Estimates were tallied for nine five-year periods from around 1915 to 1959. Within each period a notation was made indicating whether each formerly censused pack was now active or extinct. In a period for which there were no estimates for some of the active packs, the reported estimates of the remaining pack populations were used to establish an average pack size; this average was then used to calculate the total *pack* population for that period. For example, in 1925 there were 18 packs, but population estimates were lacking for 8 of them. Seventy wolves were reported in the 10 remaining packs, for an average pack size of seven wolves. This information can be used to compute the total pack population by either of two methods: 18 packs multiplied by an average of 7 wolves per pack equals 126 pack wolves; or the average of 7 wolves per pack multiplied by the 8 unaccounted packs equals 56 wolves plus the 70 wolves in the 10 accounted packs equals 126 wolves (see table E.1).

Table E.1. Estimated Wisconsin timber wolf population, 1920–64

Period[a]	Average pack size	Number of packs	Number of timber wolves		
			Pack (75%)	Lone (25%)	Total
Before 1920	8.7	18	157	52	209
1920–24	8.5	18	153	51	204
1925–29	7.0	18	126	42	168
1930–34	6.9	17	117	39	156
1935–39	5.2	17	88	29	117
1940–44	4.3	17	73	24	97
1945–49	3.7	17	63	21	84
1950–54	2.8	13	36	12	48
1955–59	2.0	9	18	6	24
1960–64	0	0	0	<5	<5

Source: The data in this table have been estimated using information from over 60 woodsmen, trappers, and Wisconsin Conservation Department personnel.

[a]All entries for each period represent five-year averages.

Within each wolf population is a certain proportion of lone wolves. Owing to the difficulty in estimating the percentage of lone wolves that occurred at any one time within the original Wisconsin population (probably a greater percentage when packs disintegrated in later years), I selected 25 percent of the total population, which is an average of the percentages that have been reported in various wolf studies in recent decades. To calculate the total population (pack wolves + lone wolves), again using the 1925–29 period in table E.1, the number of pack wolves (126) is divided by 75 percent, which equals 168 wolves. Lone wolves are calculated by multiplying the total population by 25 percent, which equals 42 lone wolves.

Estimating Bounty Mortality

Wisconsin bounty records differentiated between coyotes and wolves only during the 10-year period from 1947 to 1956. Some of the "wolves" listed were taken in counties outside known wolf ranges (e.g., Juneau County); these were deleted from computation. Within counties known to have harbored wolves, 153 were taken (table E.2).

A yearly surviving population estimate was calculated by extrapolating the mean decrease in wolves between periods from table E.1, on a yearly basis. For example, between 1950 and 1955 the population decreased from 48 to 24 wolves, or an average decline of 4.8 wolves per year. If there were 48 wolves present in 1950, then

Table E.2.   Timber wolf bounty records adjusted for take within the counties in which wolves are known to have ranged

Fiscal year	"Take" Year[a]	Total take	Take outside wolf range	Take inside wolf range
1947–48	1947	46	6	40
1948–49	1948	27	3	24
1949–50[b]				
1950–51[b]				
1951–52	1951	34	0	34
1952–53	1952	26	3	23
1953–54	1953	7	2	5
1954–55	1954	22	6	16
1955–56	1955	13	3	10
1956–57	1956	1	0	1
		—	—	—
Total	8 yrs	176	23	153
Percent of total take				87

Source: Data are taken from the Wisconsin Conservation Department, miscellaneous file records, in author's possession.

[a]The state fiscal year ran from July 1 to June 30, Hence the bounty take began in July of any given year and affected that year's reproductive output.

[b]No data available for these years.

there were 48 minus 4.8, or 43 wolves, present in 1951. These computations were made for most of the years between 1945 and 1960 (see Table E.3).

The adjusted bounty figures were used to determine the summer wolf population size, which differed from the surviving population size because of recruitment of pups (an unknown value). As an example, in 1951 the surviving population size was 43 wolves. The 1952 surviving population was 38 (43 [from 1951] − 4.8 wolves = 38). The 1951 bounty take was 34 wolves. Therefore, 34 bountied wolves plus 38 wolves surviving into 1952 equals the summer, or prebounty, 1951 population of 72 wolves. The bounty mortality rate can then be calculated:

$$\frac{34 \text{ bountied wolves}}{72 \text{ wolves in summer population}}$$

or 47 percent mortality caused by bounty in 1951.

The overall mortality rate caused by the bounty averaged 37 percent during the final 10 years, 1947–56 (table E.3). Today's biologists recognize that this is above the level of mortality that will precipitate declines in wolf populations.[1]

Table E.3.   The calculated yearly mortality rate caused by the bounty, using extrapolated yearly midwinter wolf population figures in table E.1 and bounty figures in table E.2.

Year	Surviving population	Net reproduction	Summer population	Bounty take	Mortality rate (%)	End of year population
1947	70	33	103	40	39	63
1948	63	17	80	24	30	56
1949	56	—	—	—	—	48
1950	48	—	—	—	—	43
1951	43	29	72	34	47	38
1952	38	18	56	23	41	33
1953	33	0	33	5	15	28
1954	28	12	40	16	40	24
1955	24	5	29	10	35	19
1956	19	—	—	1	—	14
1957	14	—	—	0	—	9
1958	9	—	—	0	—	—
			—	—		
			—	—		
Total			413	153		
Average mortality[a]					37	

[a]Calculated from the summer population and bounty take totals.

Notes

Preface

1. *Lake Mills Leader,* April 26, 1945.

Chapter 1. The Wolf: A Biological Review

1. S. Young and E. Goldman, *The Wolves of North America,* part 1 and part 2 (New York: Dover Publications, 1964), p. 389.

2. L. N. Carbyn, "Management of Non-Endangered Wolf Populations in Canada," *Acta Zoologica Fennica* 174(1983):239–243; D. I. Bibikov, N. G. Ovsyannikov, and A. N. Filimonov, "The Status and Management of the Wolf Population in the USSR," *Acta Zoologica Fennica* 174(1983):269–271; J. Voskar, "Present Problems of Wolf Preservation in Czechoslovakia," *Acta Zoologica Fennica* 174(1983):287–288; H. Mendelssohn "Status of the Wolf in the Middle East," *Acta Zoologica Fennica* 174(1983):279–280; S. P. Sahki, "Status of the Grey Wolf (*Canis lupus pallipes,* Sykes) in India," *Acta Zoologica Fennica* 174(1983):283–286; L. Boitani, "Wolf and Dog Competition in Italy," *Acta Zoologica Fennica* 174(1983):259–264; A. Bjarvall, "Scandinavia's Response to a Natural Repopulation of Wolves," *Acta Zoologica Fennica* 174(1983):173–175.

3. Young and Goldman, *The Wolves of North America.*

4. Young and Goldman, *The Wolves of North America;* D. E. Brown, *The Wolf in the Southwest* (Tucson: University of Arizona Press, 1983).

5. Young and Goldman, *The Wolves of North America.*

6. L. D. Mech and L. D. Frenzel, Jr., "The Possible Occurrence of the Great Plains Wolf in Northeastern Minnesota," in *Ecological Studies of the Timber Wolf in Northeastern Minnesota,* ed. L. D. Mech and L. D. Frenzel, Jr., pp. 60–62, U.S. Dep. Agric., For. Serv. Res. Pap. NC-52, North Cent. For. Exp. Stn., St. Paul, Minn., 1971.

7. C. Butterfield, Ed., *History of Green County, Wisconsin* (Springfield, Ill.: Union Publishing Co., 1884), p. 244.

8. L. D. Mech, *The Wolf: Ecology and Behavior of an Endangered Species* (Garden City, N.Y.: Natural History Press, 1970); M. Stenlund, *A Field of the Timber Wolf* (Canis lupus) *on the Superior Antional Forest in Minnesota,* Minn. D-124 Dep. Conserv. Tech. Bull. No. 4, 1955; V. Van Ballenberghe, A. Erickson, and D. Byman, *Ecology of the Timber Wolf in Northeastern Minnesota,* Wildl. Monogr. No. 43, 1975.

9. Young and Goldman, *The Wolves of North America.*

10. Mech, *The Wolf.*

11. Mech, *The Wolf.*

12. Young and Goldman, *The Wolves of North America;* D. Thompson, "A Preliminary Study of the Timber Wolf in Wisconsin," M.S. thesis, University of Wisconsin, Madison, 1950; G. Kolenosky, "Wolf Predation on Wintering Deer in East-Central Ontario," *J. Wildl. Manage.* 36(1972):357–368; L. D. Mech and L. Frenzel, Jr., "An Analysis of the Age, Sex, and Condition of Deer Killed by Wolves in Northeastern Minnesota," in *Ecological Studies of the Timber Wolf,* pp. 35–51; Stenlund, *A Field Study of the Timber Wolf;* T. Fuller, *Dynamics of a Declining White-tailed Deer Population in North-central Minnesota,* Wildl. Monogr. No. 110, 1990.

13. Bjarvall, "Scandanavia's Response"; Fuller, *Dynamics of a Declining White-tailed Deer Population;* R. O. Peterson, *Wolf Ecology and Prey Relationships on Isle Royale,* Natl. Park Serv. Sci. Monogr. Ser. 11, 1977; W. C. Gasaway et al., *Interrelationships of Wolves, Prey and Man in Interior Alaska.* Wildl. Monogr. No. 84, 1983; F. Messier, "Social Organization, Spacial Distribution, and Population Density of Wolves in Relation to Moose Density," *Can. J. Zool.* 63(1985):1068–1077; Mech, *The Wolf.*

14. Kolenosky, "Wolf Predation"; Mech and Frenzel, "An Analysis of the Age, Sex, and Condition of Deer"; D. Pimlott, J. Shannon, and G. Kolenosky, *The Ecology of the Timber Wolf in Algonquin Provincial Park,* Ont. Dep. Lands and For., 1969; A. Stebler, "The Status of the Wolf in Michigan," *J. Mammal.* 35(1944):37–43; Stenlund, *A Field Study of the Timber Wold;* Thompson, "A Preliminary Study of the Timber Wolf."

15. Kolenosky, "Wolf Predation"; Mech and Frenzel, "An Analysis of the Age, Sex, and Condition of Deer."

16. L. Rogers et al., "Deer Distribution in Relation to Wolf Pack Territory Edges," *J Wildl. Manage.* 44(1980):253–258.

17. Gasaway et al., *Interrelationships of Wolves, Prey and Man;* L. D. Mech and P. Karns, *Role of the Wolf in a Deer Decline in the Superior National Forest,* U.S. Dep. Agric., For. Serv. Res. Pap. NC-148, North Cent. For. Exp. Stn., St. Paul, Minn., 1977.

18. Fuller, *Dynamics of a Declining White-tailed Deer Population;* Fuller, *Population Dynamics of Wolves in North-central Minnesota.* Wildl. Monogr. No. 105, 1989.

19. Wisconsin Conservation Department Pittman-Robertson Deer Research Project materials, Department of Natural Resources Ranger Station, Bureau of Research, Rhinelander; Young and Goldman, *The Wolves of North America;* A. Murie, *The Wolves of Mt. McKinley,* Natl. Park Serv. Fauna Ser. 5, 1944; Peterson, *Wolf Ecology and Prey Relationships.*

20. Bailey, *Destruction of Wolves and Coyotes.* U.S. Dep. Agric. Bur. Biol. Surv. Circ. No. 63, 1908; Perry Petts, pers. comm., 1974; A. Stebler, "The Ecology of Michigan Coyotes and Wolves," Ph.D. dissertation, University of Michigan, Ann Arbor, 1951.

21. Wisconsin Conservation Department Pittman-Robertson Deer Research Project materials; Bob Biller, Sr., pers. comm., 1976; Bo Popov, pers. comm., 1975;

Perry Petts, pers. comm., 1974; *Forest Republican*, "Houston Stamper Gets $90 Bounty on Eight Wolves," May 18, 1933; D. Thompson, "Travel, Range, and Food Habits of Timber Wolves in Wisconsin," *J. Mammal.* 33(1952):429–442; V. Bailey, *Destruction of Wolves and Coyotes*, U.S. Dep. Agric. Bur. Biol. Surv. Circ. No. 63, 1908; Don Lappala, pers. comm., 1975, 1976; Orvid Donner, pers. comm., 1979; Stebler, "The Ecology of Michigan Coyotes and Wolves."

22. Wisconsin Conservation Department, "Timber Wolf," *Wis. Conserv. Bull.* 9, no. 1(1944):24; L. D. Mech, "Longevity in Wild Wolves," *J. Mammal.* 69(1988):197–198.

23. Stebler, "The Ecology of Michigan Coyotes and Wolves"; Van Ballenberghe, Erickson, and Byman, *Ecology of the Timber Wolf*; S. Fritts and L. D. Mech, *Dynamics, Movements and Feeding Ecology of a Newly Protected Wolf Population in Northwestern Minnesota*, Wildl. Monogr. No. 80, 1981.

24. Young and Goldman, *The Wolves of North America*, p. 109.

25. Bernie Ernest, pers. comm., 1983; Walter Rosenlaf, pers. comm., 1980.

26. F. Harrington et al., "Monogamy in Wolves: A Review of the Evidence," in *Wolves of the World*, ed. F. Harrington and P. Paquet, pp. 209–222 (Park Ridge, N.J.: Noyes Publishing, 1982).

27. R. Peters and L. D. Mech, "Scent-Marking in Wolves," *Am. Sci.* 63, no. 6(1975):628–637.

28. F. Harrington and L. D. Mech, "Wolf Pack Spacing: Howling as a Territory-Independent Spacing Mechanism in a Territorial Population," *Behav. Ecol. Sociobiol.* 12(1983):161–168.

29. Mech, *The Wolf.*

30. Mech and Karns, *Role of the Wolf in a Deer Decline.*

31. Mech, *The Wolf;* J. Packard and L. D. Mech, "Population Regulation in Wolves," in *Biosocial Mechanisms of Population Regulation*, ed. M. Cohen, R. Malpass, and H. Klein, pp. 135–148 (New Haven, Conn.: Yale University Press, 1980).

32. Packard and Mech, "Population Regulation in Wolves"; T. Fuller, *Population Dynamics of Wolves in North-central Minnesota*, Wildl. Monogr. No. 105, 1989; L. D. Mech, "Age, Season, Distance, Direction, and Social Aspects of Wolf Dispersal from a Minnesota Wolf Pack," in *Mammalian Dispersal Patterns*, ed. B. D. Chepko-Sade and Z. Halpin, pp. 55–74 (Chicago: University of Chicago Press, 1987).

33. R. Rothman and L. D. Mech, "Scent-Marking in Lone Wolves and Newly Formed Pairs," *Anim. Behav.* 27(1979):750–760; Mech, *The Wolf.*

34. Fritts and Mech, *Dynamics, Movements and Feedings Ecology;* Van Ballenberghe, Erickson, and Byman, *Ecology of the Timber Wolf;* Gasaway et al., *Interrelationships of Wolves, Prey and Man.*

35. Fuller, *Population Dynamics of Wolves;* L. Keith, "Population Dynamics of Wolves," in *Wolves of Canada and Alaska*, ed. L. Carbyn, pp. 66–77, Can. Wildl. Serv. Rep. Ser. No. 45, 1983.

36. Murie, *The Wolves of Mt. McKinley;* Stenlund, *A Field Study of the Timber Wolf;* Peterson, *Wolf Ecology and Prey Relationships;* Pimlott, Shannon and Kolenosky, *The Ecology of the Timber Wolf.*

37. R. Nowak, *North American Quaternary Canis*, Museum of Natural History, University of Kansas, Monogr. No. 6, 1979; M. Stevenson, "Dire Wolf Systematics and Behavior," in *Wolf and Man: Evolution in Parallel*, ed. R. Hall and H. Sharp, pp. 179–196 (New York: Academic Press, 1978); O. Hay, *The Pleistocene of North America and Its Vertebrate Animals from the States East of the Mississippi River and from the Canadian Provinces East of Longitude 95°*, Carnegie Institute Publ. No. 322, Washington, D.C., 1923.

38. Nowak, *North American Quaternary Canis*.

Chapter 2. From Wilderness to Civilization

1. L. Martin, *The Physical Geography of Wisconsin* (Madison: University of Wisconsin Press, 1965); R. Paull and R. Paull, *Geology of Wisconsin and Upper Michigan* (Dubuque, Iowa: Kendall/Hunt Publishing Co., 1977).

2. Wisconsin Statistical Reporting Service, *Snow and Frost in Wisconsin*, Madison, 1970; J. Curtis, *The Vegetation of Wisconsin* (Madison: University of Wisconsin Press, 1959).

3. V. Mitchell, "Drought in Wisconsin," *Trans. Wis. Acad. Sci., Arts and Lett.* 67(1979):131–134.

4. F. Lyman, *A History of Kenosha County* (Chicago: J. S. Clarke Publishing Co., 1916), p. 41.

5. O. Guernsey and J. Willard, Eds., *History of Rock County and Transactions of the Rock County Agricultural Society and Mechanics Institute* (Janesville, Wis.: Wm. M. Doty and Bros. Printers, 1856), p. 96.

6. Curtis, *The Vegetation of Wisconsin*.

7. J. Kay, "Wisconsin Indian Hunting Patterns 1634–1836," *Ann. Assoc. Am. Geogr.* 69, no. 3(1979):402–418.

8. J. Parker, Ed., *The Journals of Jonathan Carver and Related Documents, 1766–1770* (St. Paul: Minnesota Historical Society, 1976), p. 126.

9. *History of Vernon County, Wisconsin* (Springfield, Ill.: Union Publishing Co., 1884); L. Kane, J. Holmquist, and C. Gilman, Eds., *The Northern Expeditions of Stephan H. Long* (St. Paul: Minnesota Historical Society, 1978); A. Schorger, 1978); A. Schorger, "Extinct and Endangered Mammals and Birds of the Upper Great Lakes Region," *Trans. Wis. Acad. Sci, Arts and Lett.* 34(1942):23–44; W. Scott, "Rare and Extinct Mammals of Wisconsin," *Wis. Conserv. Bull.* 4, no. 10(1939):21–28.

10. C. Gates, Ed., *Five Fur Traders of the Northwest* (St. Paul: Minnesota Historical Society, 1965), p. 56.

11. Thwaites. Ed. *Wisconsin Historical Collections*, Vol. 20. (Madison, Wis: Democrat Publishing Co., State Printer, 1911), p. 421.

12. C. Butterfield, Ed., *History of Crawford County, Wisconsin* (Springfield, Ill.: Union Publishing Co., 1884), p. 450.

13. Butterfield, Ed., *History of Crawford County.*

14. Butterfield, Ed., *History of Crawford County.*

15. T. Rodolf, "Pioneering in the Wisconsin Lead Region," in *Wisconsin Historical Collections*, vol. 15, ed. R. G. Thwaites (Madison: Democrat Publishing Co., 1900), pp. 353–354.

16. *History of Northern Wisconsin* (Chicago: Western Historical Co., 1881), p. 228.

17. C. Butterfield, Ed., *History of Dane County, Wisconsin* (Chicago: Western Historical Co., 1880), p. 698.

18. *A Merry Briton in Pioneer Wisconsin* (Madison: State Historical Society of Wisconsin, 1950).

19. Guernsey and Willard, *History of Rock County*, p. 119.

20. A. Schorger, "The Black Bear in Early Wisconsin," *Trans. Wis. Acad. Sci., Arts and Lett.* 39(1949):151–194.

21. *Janesville Daily Gazette*, March 7, 1866.

22. *Janesville Daily Gazette*, December 17, 1853; W. Bartlett, *History, Tradition, and Adventure in the Chippewa Valley* (Chippewa Falls, Wis., 1929).

23. A. Schorger, "The Elk in Early Wisconsin," *Trans. Wis. Acad. Sci., Arts and Lett.* 43(1954):5–23.

24. *Janesville Daily Gazette*, June 21, 1866, and May 18, 1867.

25. *Edgerton Independent*, February 1, 1878.

26. *Janesville Weekly Review*, February 2, 1878.

27. *Wisconsin Tobacco Reporter*, December 27, 1878.

28. L. Marchetti, *History of Marathon County, Wisconsin and Representative Citizens* (Chicago: Richmund-Arnold Publishing Co., 1913); B. Dahlberg and R. Guettinger, *The White-tailed Deer in Wisconsin*, Wis. Conserv. Dep. Tech. Bull. No. 14, 1956; Schorger, "Extinct and Endangered Mammals."

29. E. Swift, *A History of Wisconsin Deer*, Wis. Conserv. Dep. Publ. No. 323, 1946.

30. G. Corrigan, *Caulked Boots and Cant Hooks* (Park Falls, Wis.: MacGregor Litho, 1976); G. Corrigan, "Tanneries and the Hemlock Bark Industry in Wisconsin," in *Proceedings of the Third Annual Meeting of the Forest History Association of Wisconsin*, pp. 23–29 (Wausau, Wis., 1978); Dahlberg and Guettinger, *The White-tailed Deer*; R. Current, *Wisconsin: A Bicentennial History* (New York: W. W. Norton and Co., 1977).

31. H. Jackson, *Mammals of Wisconsin* (Madison: University of Wisconsin Press, 1961); C. Pils, "Furbearer Profiles—No. 1: Beaver," Wis. Dep. Nat. Resour., mimeo, 1981; Schorger, "Extinct and Endangered Mammals"; Scott, "Rare and Extinct Mammals."

Chapter 3. Wolves and Humans

1. P. Radin, *The Winnebago Tribe* (Lincoln: University of Nebraska Press, 1973).

2. P. Parmalee, "Vertebrate Remains from the Bell Site, Winnebago County, Wisconsin," *Wis. Archeology* 44, no. 1(1963):58–69.

3. Loren Fishel, pers. comm., 1973.

4. *History of Vernon County, Wisconsin,* p. 445.

5. Gates, Ed., *Five Fur Traders,* p. 273.

6. Draper, Ed., *Wisconsin Historical Collections,* vol. 7, p. 353.

7. R. Thwaites, Ed., *Wisconsin Historical Collections,* vol. 20 (Madison, Wis.: Democrat Publishing Co., State Printer, 1911), p. 160.

8. Clarence Searles, pers. comm., 1977.

9. Thwaites, Ed., *Wisconsin Historical Collections,* vol. 20.

10. *Forest Republican.* "Wolves Get Buck," November 24, 1949.

11. Butterfield, Ed., *History of Crawford County,* p. 453.

12. Perry Petts, pers. comm., 1974.

13. Perry Petts, pers. comm., 1974.

14. R. Schraufnagal, *History of the Glidden Four-Town Area* (Park Falls, Wis.: McGregor Litho, 1976).

15. *History of Grant County, Wisconsin* (Chicago: Western Historical Co., 1881), p. 484.

16. *Florence Mining News,* "Conservation Notes," March 14, 1936.

17. Wisconsin Conservation Department, "Wolf Drive," *Wis. Convers. Bull.* 1, no. 4(1936):9.

18. *Forest Republican,* "Stage Second Wold Hunt in Argonne Refuge Sunday," January 20, 1938.

19. *Rhinelander Daily News,* "Youth's Curiosity Nets Timber Wolf," October 4, 1944.

20. B. Biller, "Biller Bros. Hunt Savage Wolves," *Florence Mining News,* January 9, 1953.

21. *Lakeland Times,* "Single Shot Ends Wolf-Dog Affair Two Months Old," January 24, 1947.

22. Emma Witt, pers. comm., 1979; Wisconsin Conservation Department Pittman-Robertson Deer Research Project materials.

23. Reino Herlevi, pers. comm., 1971; Clarence Schmidt, pers. comm., 1974; Wisconsin Conservation Department Pittman-Robertson Deer Research Project materials.

24. Walter Rosenlaf, pers. comm., 1980.

25. Walter Rosenlaf, pers. comm., 1980.

26. Ray Sensenbrenner, pers. comm., 1979.

27. James Hale, pers. comm., 1981.

28. *Janesville Daily Gazette,* February 5, 1862.

29. *Northern Wisconsin Alma Bleatter,* February 18, 1897.

30. V. Bailey, *Destruction of Deer by the Northern Timber Wolf,* U.S. Dep. Agric., Bur. Biol. Surv. Circ. No. 58, 1907, p. 1.

31. *Minocqua Times,* "Post Season Discussion," December 2, 1938.

32. *Lakeland Times,* "Going Like the Bison," January 20, 1940.

33. *Lakeland Times,* "Many Queer Accidents, Hwy. Report Shows," December 1, 1939.

34. F. Harrington and L. D. Mech, "Wolf Howling and Its Role in Territory Maintenance," *Behaviour* 68, nos. 3–4(1979):207–249.

35. L. D. Draper, Ed., *Wisconsin Historical Collections,* vol. 6 (Madison, Wis.: Atwood and Culver, 1872), p. 349.

36. Butterfield, Ed., *History of Green County,* p. 230.

37. L. Barland, *Sawdust City* (Stevens Point, Wis., 1960).

38. *History of Northern Wisconsin,* p. 1194.

39. J. Grenning, "A Mazomanie Pioneer of 1847," *Wis. Mag. Hist.* 26, no. 2(1942):211.

40. Lyman, *A History of Kenosha County,* p. 17.

41. *Evansville Review,* February 19, 1873.

42. Gordon Sorenson, pers. comm., 1973.

43. *The History of Waukesha County, Wisconsin* (Chicago: Western Historical Co., 1880), p. 482.

44. W. Gustafson, *Glen Flora Pioneers* (Chicago: Adams Press, 1971), p. 124.

45. Warren Holger, pers. comm., 1979.

46. Mech, *The Wolf;* A. Wolter, "The Boy Who Cried Wolf," *Outdoor Life* (July 1982):68–69, 100–101.

47. *The History of Waukesha County,* p. 357.

48. *History of Grant County,* p. 800.

49. *History of Grant County,* pp. 843–844.

50. L. C. Draper, Ed., *Wisconsin Historical Collections,* vol. 1, reprint ed. (Madison, Wis.: Democrat Printing Co., 1903 [1853]), pp. 141–142.

51. J. H. Ott, *History of Jefferson County Wisconsin, and Its People: A Record of Settlement, Organization, Progress and Achievement* (Chicago: J. S. Clarke Publishing Co., 1917).

52. Ott, *History of Jefferson County.*

53. C. Zillier, Ed., *History of Sheboygan County Past and Present* (Chicago: J. S. Clarke Publishing Co., 1912), p. 87.

54. Stenlund, *A Field Study of the Timber Wolf,* p. 12.

55. Ott, *History of Jefferson County.*

56. *The History of Waukesha County,* p. 357.

57. *Janesville Daily Gazette,* December 17, 1853.

58. *Janesville Daily Gazette,* February 9, 1866.

59. *Wisconsin Magazine of History,* "Snow and the Winter Wolves," *Wis. Mag. Hist.* 41, no. 2(1958):101.

60. Bartlett, *History, Tradition, and Adventure; Centennial Phillips, Wisconsin 1876–1976* (n.p., 1976).

61. *Florence Mining News,* "Unarmed Man, Chased by Wolves, Resorts to 'Trick' and Escapes," January 27, 1939.

62. E. Epler, *80 Years in God's Country* (Arlington Heights, Ill.: Ink Spot, 1973), pp. 111–112.

63. *Wisconsin Historical Collections,* vol. 9, (Madison, Wis.: David Atwood, 1882), pp. 296–297.

64. *Morning Chronicle,* "Farmer Torn by Wolves," January 18, 1902.

65. *Morning Chronicle,* "Wolves Kill Hunting Dog," January 21, 1902; *Morning Chronicle,* "To Purchase Wolf Hounds," January 28, 1902; *Wisconsin Blue Book* (Madison: Wisconsin Legislative Reference Bureau, 1909), p. 866.

66. *Lakeland Times*, "Attacked by Wolf," December 1, 1939.

67. *Florence Mining News*, "Find No Proof of Story Man Killed by Timber Wolf," *February 8, 1936.*

68. Stenlund, *A Field Study of the Timber Wolf*, p. 12.

69. Ray Sensenbrenner, pers. comm., 1979.

70. Russell Olson, pers. comm, 1979.

71. Epler, *80 Years in God's Country*, p. 105.

72. A. Latton, *Reminiscences and Anecdotes of Early Taylor County* (n.p., 1947).

73. Russell Olson, pers. comm., 1979.

74. Clarence Allen, pers. comm., 1979.

75. Walter Rosenlaf, pers. comm., 1980.

76. Walter Rosenlaf, pers. comm., 1970.

77. Russell Olson, pers. comm., 1979.

78. Walter Rosenlaf, pers. comm., 1970.

79. Frank Tomaier, pers. comm., 1979.

80. Russell Olson, pers. comm., 1979.

81. Walter Rosenlaf, pers. comm., 1980.

82. Wisconsin Conservation Department Pittman-Robertson Deer Research Project materials.

83. Thompson, "A Preliminary Study of the Timber Wolf," p. 10.

84. Stebler, "The Ecology of Michigan Coyotes and Wolves," pp. 91–92.

85. Thompson, "A Preliminary Study of the Timber Wolf."

86. Stebler, "The Ecology of Michigan Coyotes and Wolves," p. 90.

87. Wisconsin Conservation Department Pittman-Robertson Deer Research Project materials.

88. Stebler, "The Ecology of Michigan Coyotes and Wolves," p. 91.

89. Ray Smith, pers. comm., 1976.

90. Ray Smith, pers. comm., 1976.

Chapter 4. Tales from the Trapline

1. Butterfield, Ed., *History of Green County*, p. 676.

2. Butterfield, Ed., *History of Green County*.

3. Butterfield, Ed., *History of Green County*, pp. 484–485.

4. Butterfield, Ed., *History of Green County*, p. 849.

5. H. T. Ames, "Wolves and Foxes Plentiful," *Wis. Conservationist* 3, no. 1(1921):16.

6. Russell Olson, pers. comm., 1979.

7. Walter Rosenlaf, pers. comm., 1970.

8. Walter Rosenlaf, pers. comm., 1980.

9. Walter Rosenlaf, pers. comm., 1980.

10. E. Swift, "The Biography of a Self-made Naturalist," part 1, *Wis. Conserv. Bull.* 5, no. 12(1940):9.

11. Swift, "The Biography of a Self-made Naturalist," part 1, p. 6.

12. Swift, "The Biography of a Self-made Naturalist," part 2, *Wis. Conserv. Bull.* 6, no. 1(1941):41–52; E. Swift, "The Biography of a Self-made Naturalist," part 4, *Wis. Conserv. Bull.* 6, no. 4(1941):3–8; Swift, *A History of Wisconsin Deer.*

13. SHSW, Game Management Division materials.

14. SHSW, Game Management Division materials.

15. Swift, "The Biography of a Self-made Naturalist," part 2, p. 46.

16. SHSW, Game Management Division materials.

17. SHSW, Game Management Division materials.

18. SHSW, Game Management Division materials.

19. SHSW, Game Management Division materials.

20. SHSW, Game Management Division materials.

21. SHSW, Game Management Division materials.

22. SHSW, Game Management Division materials.

23. *Park Falls Herald,* "Live Wolf Hunt Finally Succeeds," February 19, 1937.

24. Swift, "The Biography of a Self-made Naturalist," part 2, p. 46.

25. Swift, "The Biography of a Self-made Naturalist," part 2, p. 46.

26. Swift, "The Biography of a Self-made Naturalist," part 2, pp. 46–47.

27. George Fleming, pers. comm., 1980.

28. Swift, "The Biography of a Self-made Naturalist," part 2, p. 47.

29. SHSW, Game Management Division materials; *Florence Mining News,* "Conservation Notes. Wolves," June 12, 1937.

30. SHSW, ser. 1901, box 1, folder 1.

31. SHSW, ser. 1901, box 1, folder 1; SHSW, ser. 271, box 30, folder 1; SHSW, Game Management Division materials.

32. *Glidden Enterprise,* "Sells Live Wolf to the State," October 25, 1946; see also, *Mellen Weekly Record,* "Conversation Department Purchases Live Wolf," September 19, 1946.

33. Joe Heizler, pers. comm., 1984; Stanley Kolnik, pers. comm., 1984.

34. The following account was constructed from personal communication with Clarence Allen, 1979.

Chapter 5. The Bounty in Wisconsin and Michigan

1. Although the people involved in the following account really existed, the tale was fabricated to illustrate how bounty claims were processed in the 1930s.

2. The wording of the bounty affidavits varied from year to year, but the intent was always the same: leave no predator alive. SHSW, Game Management Division materials.

3. Young and Goldman, *The Wolves of North America,* p. 337.

4. *The History of Waukesha County,* p. 787.

5. Michigan Department of Natural Resources, Wolf and Predator Bounty files, 1945–1955, Lansing.

6. *The History of Waukesha County,* p. 624.

7. M. Johnson, "Wolves in Early Waukesha County," *Landmark*, Summer-Autumn(1975):6–10.

8. Butterfield, Ed., *History of Dane County*, p. 698.

9. Wisconsin Conservation Department, miscellaneous materials, in author's possession; Walter Scott Collections.

10. Wisconsin Conservation Department, miscellaneous materials, in author's possession; Walter Scott Collections.

11. SHSW, Game Management Division materials.

12. Stebler, "The Status of the Wolf in Michigan."

13. Michigan Department of Natural Resources, Wolf and Predator Bounty files.

14. Michigan Department of Natural Resources, Wolf and Predator Bounty files.

15. *The History of Waukesha County*, p. 624.

16. *The History of Waukesha County*, p. 687.

17. L. G. Nagler, "A Price on His Head," *LaFollette's Weekly*, March 22, 1913.

18. *Wisconsin Tobacco Reporter*, May 3, 1878.

19. *Janesville Daily Gazette*, February 9, 1866.

20. Walter Scott Collections; SHSW, Game Management Division materials.

21. Nagler, "A Price on His Head."

22. Nagler, "A Price on His Head."

23. Nagler, "A Price on His Head."

24. Nagler, "A Price on His Head."

25. George Fleming, pers. comm., 1980.

26. B. Stollberg, "Differentiation of Police Dog, Coyote, and Timber Wolf. Hairs. Wisconsin Wildlife Research." *Pittman-Robertson Q. Reps.* 7, no. 1(1948):31–32.

27. *Florence Mining News*, "Hard to Distinguish Wolf Pups from Dogs," October 7, 1944.

28. Wisconsin Conservation Department, miscellaneous materials, in author's possession.

29. *Florence Mining News*, "Chapman Gets $70 Bounty on Wolf," May 29, 1937.

30. Young and Goldman, *The Wolves of North America*.

31. Butterfield, Ed., *History of Dane County*, p. 698.

32. *Janesville Daily Gazette*, March 16, 1861.

33. Bartlett, *History, Tradition, and Adventure*, p. 219–220.

34. Stan Plis, pers. comm., 1979.

35. Young and Goldman, *The Wolves of North America*.

36. Michigan Department of Natural Resources, Wolf and Predator Bounty files.

37. *Milwaukee Journal*, "Sanctuary for Wolves Suggested in Michigan," January 25, 1948, part 3, p. 6.

38. Michigan Department of Natural Resources, Wolf and Predator Bounty files.

39. Michigan Department of Natural Resources, Wolf and Predator Bounty files.

40. Clarence Allen, pers. comm., 1979.

41. Michigan Department of Natural Resources, Wolf and Predator Bounty files.

42. Michigan Department of Natural Resources, Wolf and Predator Bounty files.

43. Michigan Department of Natural Resources, Wolf and Predator Bounty files.

44. Michigan Department of Natural Resources, Wolf and Predator Bounty files.
45. Michigan Department of Natural Resources, Wolf and Predator Bounty files.
46. Michigan Department of Natural Resources, Wolf and Predator Bounty files.

Chapter 6. Deer, Wolves, and Politics

1. SHSW, Game Management Division materials.
2. A. Schorger, "The White-tailed Deer in Early Wisconsin," *Trans. Wis. Acad. Sci., Arts and Lett.* 42(1953).
3. Schorger, "The White-tailed Deer," p. 287.
4. L. Klessig and J. Hale, *A Profile of Wisconsin Hunters*, Wis. Dep. Nat. Resour. Tech. Bull. No. 60, 1972.
5. Schorger, "The White-tailed Deer."
6. O. Bersing, *A Century of Wisconsin Deer*, 2d ed., Wis. Conserv. Dep. Publ. 353–66, 1966; Stan Plis, pers. comm., 1979; *Forest Republican*, "Gets Another Wolf and Bobcat Thursday," January 31, 1929.
7. SHSW, Game Management Division materials; Stan Plis, pers. comm., 1979; *Mellen Weekly Record*, "State Trapper Located Here; Trapping Predatory Animals," April 3, 1930.
8. SHSW, Game Management Division materials.
9. Stan Plis, pers. comm., 1979.
10. W. J. Kraemer, "Notice to Trappers," *Mellen Weekly Record*, October 16, 1930.
11. SHSW, Game Management Division materials.
12. SHSW, Game Management Division materials.
13. *The Bee*, "Bill Introduced to Abolish Trappers Appropriation," March 5, 1931.
14. SHSW, Game Management Division materials.
15. K. Elliott, *History of the Nicolet National Forest 1928–1976*, U.S. For. Serv., U.S. Dep. Agric. and For. Hist. Assoc. Wis., Inc., 1977.
16. Bersing, *A Century of Wisconsin Deer.*
17. SHSW, Game Management Division materials.
18. Nicolet National Forest historical materials, Nicolet National Forest Headquarters, Rhinelander.
19. Swift, *A History of Wisconsin Deer;* Bersing, *A Century of Wisconsin Deer.*
20. S. Flader, *Thinking Like a Mountain* (Columbia: University of Missouri Press, 1974), p. 145.
21. Dahlberg and Guettinger, *The White-tailed Deer*, pp. 152–153.
22. Nicolet National Forest historical materials; Royce Dallman, pers. comm., 1976.
23. SHSW, Game Management Division materials.
24. SHSW, Game Management Division materials.
25. Swift, *A History of Wisconsin Deer.*
26. V. E. Cole, "Why Protect the Wolf?" *Florence Mining News*, May 1, 1937.

27. SHSW, Game Management Division materials; Wisconsin Conservation Department, "Open Season for Wolves," *Wis. Conserv. Bull.* 2, 3, nos. 12, 1(1937–38):47.

28. *Forest Republican,* "Stage Second Wolf Hunt in Argonne Refuge Sunday," January 20, 1938; see also: *Forest Republican,* "Argonne Refuge to Open Sunday for Wolf Hunters," January 6, 1938; *Forest Republican,* "Bad Weather Slows Down Wolf Hunt," January 13, 1938.

29. SHSW, Game Management Division materials.

30. SHSW, Game Management Division materials.

31. George Becker materials, wolf files, now in author's possession; SHSW, ser. 271, box 25, folder 6.

32. SHSW, Game Management Division materials.

33. SHSW, Game Management Division materials.

34. SHSW, Game Management Division materials.

35. SHSW, Game Management Division materials.

36. Wisconsin Conservation Department, "Wolf Diet," *Wis. Conserv. Bull.* 1, no. 5(1936):13.

37. SHSW, Game Management Division materials.

38. SHSW, Game Management Division materials.

39. SHSW, Game Management Division materials.

40. SHSW, Game Management Division materials; Swift, "The Biography of a Self-made Naturalist," part 2.

41. SHSW, Game Management Division materials.

42. SHSW, Game Management Division materials.

43. SHSW, Game Management Division materials.

44. SHSW, Game Management Division materials; Walter Rosenlaf, pers. comm., 1980.

45. SHSW, Game Management Division materials.

46. SHSW, Game Management Division materials.

47. SHSW, Game Management Division materials.

48. SHSW, Game Management Division materials.

49. SHSW, Game Management Division materials.

50. Walter Scott Collections; Flader, *Thinking Like a Mountain;* Dahlberg and Guettinger, *The White-tailed Deer.*

51. SHSW, Game Management Division materials.

52. Flader, *Thinking Like a Mountain,* p. 182.

53. Flader, *Thinking Like a Mountain,* p. 182.

54. Dahlberg and Guettinger, *The White-tailed Deer;* Flader, *Thinking Like a Mountain;* Swift, *A History of Wisconsin Deer.*

55. Flader, *Thinking Like a Mountain.*

56. A. Leopold et al., "Majority Report of the Citizens' Deer Committee to Wisconsin Conservation Commission," *Wis. Conserv. Bull.* 8, no. 8(1943):20.

57. AL, ser. 9/25/10 4, box 4.

58. SHSW, Game Management Division materials.

59. *Florence Mining News.* Conservation News, "Bounties," January 15, 1944.

60. *Florence Mining News*, "Wisconsin Passes Wolf Bounty Law," January 29, 1944.

61. *Florence Mining News*, "North Indignant Over Wolf Bill," March 4, 1944.

62. Bersing, *A Century of Wisconsin Deer*; Flader, *Thinking Like a Mountain*.

63. SHSW, Game Management Division materials.

64. SHSW, Game Management Division materials.

65. AL, ser. 9/25/20, box 10; Swift, "The Biography of a Self-Made Naturalist," part 1.

66. SHSW, Game Management Division materials.

67. Bernie Bradle, pers. comm., 1980.

68. SHSW, ser. 271, box 25, folder 6.

69. SHSW, ser. 271, box 26, folder 1.

70. Thompson, "Travel, Range, and Food Habits of Timber Wolves," p. 440.

71. Wisconsin Conservation Department Pittman-Robertson Deer Research Project materials.

72. A. Leopold, "Deer Irruptions," *Wis. Conserv. Bull.* 8, no. 8(1943):3–11.

73. *Lakeland Times*, "Protest against Slaughter of Deer," May 26, 1944; see also Wisconsin Conservation Department Pittman-Robertson Deer Research Project materials.

74. *Rhinelander Daily News*, "Deer Hair Found in Wolf's Innards," October 30, 1944.

75. *Rhinelander Daily News*, "Deer Hair Found in Wolf's Innards," October 30, 1944.

76. Wisconsin Conservation Department Pittman-Robertson Deer Research Project materials.

77. H. Witt, "The Public Pulse," *Lakeland Times*, April 6, 1945.

78. Walter Scott, pers. comm., 1982.

79. AL, ser. 9/25/10 4, box 1.

80. AL, ser. 9/25/10 4, box 1.

81. SHSW, Game Management Division materials.

82. Flader, *Thinking Like a Mountain*, pp. 211–212; see also SHSW, Game Management Division materials.

83. Flader, *Thinking Like a Mountain*, p. 217.

84. *Lakeland Times*, "Bounty Report Blasts Leopold Wolf Statements," December 7, 1945.

85. *Glidden Enterprize*, "Funds Asked for Liberal Wolf Bounties," December 8, 1944.

86. Flader, *Thinking Like a Mountain*, p. 213.

87. Flader, *Thinking Like a Mountain*, p. 214.

88. A. Leopold, "Deer, Wolves, Foxes and Pheasants," *Wis. Conserv. Bull.* 10, no. 4(1945):3–4.

89. AL, ser. 9.15.10 4, box 1.

90. SHSW, ser. 271, box 26, folder 1.

91. *Lakeland Times*, "Refuses to Sign Bounty Bill; Becomes Law," March 16, 1945.

92. *Florence Mining News*, "New Bounty Law Now in Effect," March 17, 1945.

93. AL, ser. 9.25.10 4, box 4.

94. Miscellaneous materials from the Wisconsin Conservation Department, in author's possession.

95. Bernie Bradle, pers. comm., 1980.

96. L. Woerpel, "Wolf Protection, Duck Stamp Questions," *Wis. Conservationist* 1, no. 6(1952):8.

97. J. Keener, "The Case for the Timber Wolf," *Wis. Conserv. Bull.* 20, no. 11(1955):24.

98. Woerpel, "Wolf Protection," p. 8.

99. L. Peterson, M. Martin, and C. Pils, *Status of Fishers in Wisconsin*, Wis. Dep. Nat. Resour. Rep. No. 92, 1977.

100. Wisconsin Conservation Department, miscellaneous materials, in author's possession.

101. Thompson, "A Preliminary Study of the Timber Wolf," p. 43.

102. Neil LeMay, pers. comm., 1981.

103. Thompson, "Travel, Range, and Food Habits of Timber Wolves," p. 439.

104. Neil LaMay, pers. comm., 1981.

105. Thompson, "Travel, Range, and Food Habits of Timbers Wolves," p. 439.

106. Thompson, "Travel, Range, and Food Habits of Timber Wolves."

107. *Passenger Pigeon*, "Report of the Bird Conservation Committee," *Passenger Pigeon* 12(1950):86–88; Thompson, pers. comm., 1970.

108 Keener, "The Case for the Timber Wolf," p. 22.

109. H. Jordahl, "Canada Lynx," *Wis. Conserv. Bull.* 2, no. 11(1956):25.

110. SHSW, Game Management Division materials.

111. N. C. Anderson, pers. comm., 1980.

112. SHSW, ser. 160/797.

113. N. C. Anderson, pers. comm., 1980.

114. SHSW, Game Management Division materials.

115. SHSW, Game Management Division materials; *Badger Sportsman*, "No More Wolves in Wisconsin," August 1967.

116. R. Thiel, "The Status of the Timber Wolf in Wisconsin—1975." *Trans. Wis. Acad. Sci., Arts and Lett.* 66(1978):186–194.

Chapter 7. Wisconsin's Secret Wolf Study

1. SHSW, Game Management Division materials; Bill Feeney, pers. comm., 1979.

2. Clarence Searles, pers. comm., 1977.

3. Wisconsin Conservation Department Pittman-Robertson Deer Research Project materials.

4. Clarence Searles, pers. comm., 1977.

5. Bernie Bradle, pers. comm., 1980.

6. Wisconsin Conservation Department Pittman-Robertson Deer Research Project materials.

7. AL, ser. 9/25/10 2, box 10.

8. AL, ser. 9/25/10 2, box 10.

9. Bernie Bradle, pers. comm., 1980.

10. AL, ser. 9/25/3 1; SHSW, ser. 1901, box 12, folder 13.

11. Dahlberg and Guettinger, "The White-tailed Deer."

12. Bernie Bradle, pers. comm., 1980.

13. Wisconsin Conservation Department, miscellaneous materials, in author's possession.

14. Bernie Bradle, pers. comm., 1980.

15. Clarence Searles, pers. comm., 1977.

16. This account was constructed from the Wisconsin Conservation Department Pittman-Robertson Deer Research Project materials; and from personal communication with Clarence Searles, 1977.

17. This account also was constructed from the Wisconsin Conservation Department Pittman-Robertson Deer Research Project materials; and from personal communication with Clarence Searles, 1977.

18. Bernie Bradle, pers. comm., 1980; see also, Wisconsin Conservation Department Pittman-Robertson Deer Research Project materials.

19. Wisconsin Conservation Department Pittman-Robertson Deer Research Project materials.

20. Wisconsin Conservation Department Pittman-Robertson Deer Research Project materials.

21. Bill Feeney, pers. comm., 1979.

22. Wisconsin Conservation Department Pittman-Robertson Deer Research Project materials.

23. Wisconsin Conservation Department Pittman-Robertson Deer Research Project materials.

24. Wisconsin Conservation Department Pittman-Robertson Deer Research Project materials.

25. Wisconsin Conservation Department Pittman-Robertson Deer Research Project materials.

26. Wisconsin Conservation Department Pittman-Robertson Deer Research Project materials.

27. Wisconsin Conservation Department Pittman-Robertson Deer Research Project materials.

28. Wisconsin Conservation Department Pittman-Robertson Deer Research Project materials.

29. SHSW, Game Management Division materials; Wisconsin Conservation Department Pittman-Robertson Deer Research Project materials; Thompson, "Travel, Range, and Food Habits of Timber Wolves."

30. Stenlund, A Field Study of the Timber Wolf.

31. Thompson, "A Preliminary Study of the Timber Wolf," p. 12.

32. Stenlund, A Field Study of the Timber Wolf.

33. Wisconsin Conservation Department Pittman-Robertson Deer Research Project materials.

34. "Pete" Tyler, pers. comm., 1975.

35. Wisconsin Conservation Department Pittman-Robertson Deer Research Project materials.

36. Wisconsin Conservation Department Pittman-Robertson Deer Research Project materials.

37. Wisconsin Conservation Department Pittman-Robertson Deer Research Project materials.

38. Bill Feeney, pers. comm., 1979; Clarence Searles, pers. comm., 1977.

39. W. Feeney, "Deer Management Research. Wisconsin Wildlife Research." *Pittman-Robertson Q. Reps.* 4, no. 4(1943):3.

40. Wisconsin Conservation Department Pittman-Robertson Deer Research Project materials.

41. Bill Feeney, pers. comm., 1979.

42. Bill Feeney, pers. comm., 1979.

43. Wisconsin Conservation Department Pittman-Robertson Deer Research Project materials.

44. Wisconsin Conservation Department Pittman-Robertson Deer Research Project materials.

45. Wisconsin Conservation Department Pittman-Robertson Deer Research Project materials.

46. Wisconsin Conservation Department Pittman-Robertson Deer Research Project materials.

47. C. Severinghaus, "Tooth Development and Wear as Criteria of Age in White-tailed Deer," *J. Wildl. Manage.* 13(1949):195–216.

48. Bill Feeney, pers. comm., 1979.

49. Thompson, "A Preliminary Study of the Timber Wolf."

50. Bill Feeney, pers. comm., 1979.

51. Clarence Searles, pers. comm., 1977; Wisconsin Conservation Department Pittman-Robertson Deer Research Project materials.

52. Thompson, "A Preliminary Study of the Timber Wolf," p. 2.

53. Thompson, "A Preliminary Study of the Timber Wolf"; Thompson, "Travel, Range, and Food Habits of Timber Wolves."

54. T. Floyd, L. D. Mech, and P. Jordan, "Relating Wolf Scat Content to Prey Consumed," *J. Wildl. Manage.* 36, no. 3(1978):528–532.

55. Thompson, "A Preliminary Study of the Timber Wolf"; Thompson, "Travel, Range, and Food Habits of Timber Wolves."

56. SHSW, Game Management Division materials.

57. SHSW, Game Management Division materials.

58. Thompson, "A Preliminary Study of the Timber Wolf"; Thompson, "Travel, Range, and Food Habits of Timber Wolves."

59. Reino Herlevi, pers. comm., 1970.

60. Stenlund, *A Field Study of the Timber Wolf.*

61. Wisconsin Conservation Department Pittman-Robertson Deer Research Project materials.

62. Stenlund, *A Field Study of the Timber Wolf.*

63. Wisconsin Conservation Department Pittman-Robertson Deer Research Project materials.

64. Wisconsin Conservation Department Pittman-Robertson Deer Research Project materials.

65. Bill Feeney, pers. comm., 1979.

66. Wisconsin Conservation Department Pittman-Robertson Deer Research Project materials.

67. Wisconsin Conservation Department Pittman-Robertson Deer Research Project materials.

68. Wisconsin Conservation Department Pittman-Robertson Deer Research Project materials.

69. *Lake Mills Leader*, "Passing of the Wolf," April 26, 1945.

70. Wisconsin Conservation Department Pittman-Robertson Deer Research Project materials.

71. Wisconsin Conservation Department Pittman-Robertson Deer Research Project materials.

72. Wisconsin Conservation Department Pittman-Robertson Deer Research Project materials.

73. Thompson, "A Preliminary Study of the Timber Wolf," p. 12; also Dan Thompson, pers. comm., 1984.

74. Bill Feeney, pers. comm., 1979; Bernie Bradle, pers. comm., 1980.

75. Bernie Bradle, pers. comm., 1980.

76. Bill Feeney, pers. comm., 1979.

77. Wisconsin Conservation Department Pittman-Robertson Deer Research Project materials.

78. Clarence Searles, pers. comm., 1977.

79. D. Q. Thompson, "Daniel Q. Thompson. 1940," in *Aldo Leopold: Mentor. Proceedings of an Aldo Leopold Symposium*, ed. R. McCabe, p. 106, Department of Wildlife Ecology, University of Wisconsin, Madison, 1988.

80. Walter Scott, pers. comm., 1982; SHSW, ser. 1901, box 12, folder 13.

Chapter 8. The Annihilation of the Wolf South of Lake Superior

1. Jackson, *Mammals of Wisconsin.*

2. Jackson, *Mammals of Wisconsin;* Stebler, "The Status of the Wolf in Michigan."

3. Henry Schrader, pers. comm., 1982.

4. Schorger, "Extinct and Endangered Mammals," p. 31.

5. Schorger, "Extinct and Endangered Mammals," p. 31.

6. Thompson, "Travel, Range, and Food Habits of Timber Wolves," p. 2.

7. Michigan Department of Natural Resources, Wolf and Predator Bounty files.

8. Stebler, "The Ecology of Michigan Coyotes and Wolves"; Walter Rosenlaf, pers. comm., 1970; Frank Tomaier, pers. comm., 1979 and 1980.

9. Russell Olson, pers. comm., 1979.

10. Orvid Donner, pers. comm., 1979; Frank Tomaier, pers. comm., 1979.

11. Wisconsin Conservation Department, "Giant Wolf Dies," *Wis. Conserv.*

Bull. 2, no. 11(1937):36; *Wisconsin Conservationist,* "Wolf Drags Trap in Chase of Four Dogs," *Wis. Conservationist* 1, no. 6(1952):38.

12. Wisconsin Conservation Department Pittman-Robertson Deer Research Project materials; Walter Rosenlaf, pers. comm., 1980.

13. Wisconsin Conservation Department Pittman-Robertson Deer Research Project materials.

14. Thompson, "Travel, Range and Food Habits of Timber Wolves."

15. Wisconsin Conservation Department Pittman-Robertson Deer Research Project materials.

16. Bert Dahlberg, pers. comm., 1969; *Milwaukee Journal,* "Clubfoot, a Timber Wolf, Is Trapped by Neophyte," November 10, 1940, part 3, p. 5.

17. Ray Smith, pers. comm., 1976; *Milwaukee Journal,* "Clubfoot, a Timber Wolf"; Clarence Allen, pers. comm., 1979.

18. Orvid Donner, pers. comm., 1979; *Florence Mining News,* "Sore-jawed Coyote Killed in County," November 12, 1954.

19. AL, ser. 9/25/10 4, box 4; E. Swift, "The Biography of a Self-made Naturalist," part 3, *Wis. Conserv. Bull.* 6, no. 3(1941):3–17.

20. Russell Olson, pers. comm., 1979.

21. Bob Biller, Sr., pers. comm., 1976.

22. *Florence Mining News,* "Millie and Bert Biller Picking Gensing Run into Wolf Pack," January 23, 1953.

23. Don Lappala, pers. comm., 1975; Perry Petts, pers. comm., 1974.

24. Keith Jesse, pers. comm., 1979; M. Ellis, "Old Lobo, the Timber Wolf, Makes a Comeback in Northern Wisconsin," *Milwaukee Journal,* March 6, 1952, part 3, p. 8; Thompson "Travel, Range, and Food Habits of Timber Wolves."

25. SHSW, Game Management Division materials.

26. Bernie Bradle, pers. comm., 1980; John Keener, pers. comm., 1973.

27. Fritts and Mech, *Dynamics, Movements and Feeding Ecology;* Kolenosky, "Wolf Predation."

28. Thompson, "A Preliminary Study of the Timber Wolf"; Thompson, "Travel Range, and Food Habits of Timber Wolves."

29. Walter Rosenlaf, pers. comm., 1970; *Rhinelander Daily News,* "Deer Hair Found in Wolf's Innards"; Wisconsin Conservation Department Pittman-Robertson Deer Research Project materials; Emma Witt, pers. comm., 1979.

30. Thompson, "A Preliminary Study of the Time Wolf," p. 13.

31. Thompson, "A Preliminary Study of the Timber Wolf," p. 13.

32. Alfred Denzine, pers. comm., 1971; Thompson, "A Preliminary Study of the Timber Wolf," p. 13.

33. Thompson, "A Preliminary Study of the Timber Wolf," p. 14.

34. Bernie Bradle, pers. comm., 1980; Ellis, "Old Lobo, the Timber Wolf."

35. Carl Heizler, pers. comm., 1984; Russell Olson, pers. comm., 1979; *Merrill Daily Herald,* "He Captured a Prize," November 25, 1950.

36. L. Krak, "Proper Number of Wolves in County Is Zero," *Star News,* April 16, 1981; *Wisconsin Conservationist,* "Wolf Drags Trap in Chase of Four Dogs."

37. Willard Ogren, pers. comm., 1985.

Chapter 9. Epilogue: A Future for the Wolf?

1. LeRoy Linteruer, pers. comm., 1973; Gerald Wick, pers. comm., 1970.
2. Bernie Bradle, pers. comm., 1980.
3. Frank Vanacek, pers. comm., 1970; Bert Dahlberg, pers. comm., 1969.
4. R. P. Thiel and J. H. Hammill, "Wolf Specimen Records in Upper Michigan, 1960–1988," *Jack-pine Warbler* 66(1988):149–153.
5. Wisconsin Department of Natural Resources, Bureau of Endangered Resources, Madison, Endangered Species List.
6. Wisconsin Department of Natural Resources, Bureau of Endangered Resources records; L. D. Mech and R. M. Nowak, "Return of the Gray Wolf to Wisconsin," *Am. Midland Naturalist* 105(1981):408–409.
7. Wisconsin Department of Natural Resources, Bureau of Endangered Resources records; Mech and Nowak, "Return of the Gray Wolf."
8. R. P. Thiel, "Status of the Timber Wolf in Wisconsin (Study 101), October 1, 1981–September 30, 1982," Wis. Dep. Nat. Resour. Performance Rep., 1983, 18 pp; R. P. Thiel, "Status of the Timber Wolf in Wisconsin, October 1, 1982–September 30, 1983," Wis. Dep. Nat. Resour. Performance Rep., 1984, 16 pp.
9. Keith, "Population Dynamics of Wolves"; Fuller, "Population Dynamics of Wolves."
10. R. P. Thiel, "Status of the Timber Wolf in Wisconsin, October 1, 1987–September 30, 1988," Wis. Dep. Nat. Resour. Performance Rep., 1989; Wisconsin Department of Natural Resources, *Wisconsin Timber Wolf Recovery Plan*, Wis. Endangered Resour. Rep. 50, 1989, p. 2; Adrian Wydeven, pers. comm., 1991.
11. Jim Hammill (Michigan Department of Natural Resources), pers. comm., 1992.
12. R. P. Thiel, "Relationship between Road Densities and Wolf Habitat Suitability in Wisconsin," *Am. Midland Naturalist* 113, no. 2(1985):404–407.
13. T. K. Fuller et al., "A History and Current Estimate of Wolf Distribution and Numbers in Minnesota," *Wildlife Society Bulletin* 20(1992):42–55; Adrian Wydeven, pers. comm., 1992; J. Hammill, "Wolf Reproduction Confirmed on Mainland Michigan!" *Internatl. Wolf* 2, no. 1(1992):14–15; Rolf Peterson, pers. comm., 1992.

Appendix B. The Wolf and Its Relatives

1. *A Merry Briton in Pioneer Wisconsin*, p. 78.
2. Young and Goldman, *The Wolves of North America.*
3. "Symposium of predator animal control," *J. Mammal.* 11(1930):335.
4. H. Ryden, *God's Dog* (New York: Penguin Books, 1979); R. Gard and L. Sorden, *The Romance of Wisconsin Place Names* (New York: October House, Inc., 1968).
5. P. Parmalee, "Animal Remains from the Durst Rockshelter, Sauk County, Wisconsin," *Wis. Archeology* 41, no. 1(1960):11–17.

6. J. Kinzie, *Wau-bun. The Early Day in the Northwest*, National Society of Colonial Dames in Wisconsin, Portage, Wis. 1975.

7. *History of Grant County*, p. 108.

8. Draper, Ed., *Wisconsin Historical Collections*, vol. 6.

9. *Janesville Daily Gazette*, January 4, 1866; see also *Wisconsin Magazine of History*, "Documents: Letters of Joseph V. Quarles," *Wis. Mag. Hist.* 16(1933): 297–320; Butterfield, Ed., *History of Dane County*.

10. I. Lapham, *Fauna and Flora of Wisconsin. A Systematic Catalogue of the Animals of Wisconsin*. Vol. 2 of *Transactions of the Wisconsin State Agricultural Society*, ed. A. Ingham, pp. 337–340 (Beriah Brown, State Printer, 1853).

11. J. Chapple, "In the Days when Wolves Abounded," *Ashland Daily Press*, August 4, 1981.

12. Reino Herlevi, pers. comm., 1971.

Appendix C. Biographies of Wisconsin Biologists Influential in Wolf Conservation

1. Bernie Bradle, pers. comm., 1980.

2. Bill Feeney, pers. comm., 1979; Wisconsin Department of Natural Resources, Bureau of Research records, Madison; Flader, *Thinking Like a Mountain*.

3. Wisconsin Department of Natural Resources, Bureau of Research records; Walter Scott, pers. comm., 1982; Bill Feeney, pers. comm., 1979.

4. S. Flader and C. Meine, *Aldo Leopold: His Life and His Work* (Madison: University of Wisconsin Press, 1988).

5. Clarence Searles, pers. comm., 1977.

6. Daniel Q. Thompson, pers. comm., 1984, 1986; Thompson, "Travel, Range, and Food Habits of Timber Wolves."

7. Bernie Bradle pers. comm., 1980.

8. Daniel Q. Thompson, pers. comm., 1984.

Appendix E. Calculating the Wisconsin Timber Wolf Population Decline

1. Keith, "Population Dynamics of Wolves"; Fuller, *Population Dynamics of Wolves*.

References

Archival Sources

AL: Aldo Leopold Papers, University of Wisconsin–Madison Archives

These sources consist of letters and memos.
Series 9/25/3 1
Series 9/25/10 2, box 10
Series 9/25/10 4, box 1
Series 9/25/10 4, box 4

SWSH: State Historical Society of Wisconsin Archives, Madison

These sources are composed of the records of the Wisconsin Conservation Department, and they provided a wealth of material. The majority of the documents are, however, unprocessed.

Series 160, box 797
Series 271, box 25, folder 6
Series 271, box 26, folder 1
Series 271, box 30, folder 1
Series 1901, box 1, folder 1
Series 1901, box 12, folder 13
Game Management Division materials, unprocessed

Other Collections

George Becker materials.
 Wolf files of G. Becker, professor emeritus of the University of Wisconsin–Stevens Point, now in the author's possession.
Michigan Department of Natural Resources, Wolf and Predator Bounty files, ca. 1945–1955, Lansing.
Nicolet National Forest historical materials, Nicolet National Forest Headquarters, Rhinelander.
 Nicolet National Forest White-tailed Deer Atlas and related materials, in the care of the staff wildlife biologist at the headquarters.
Walter Scott Collections.
 Miscellaneous items from the private collections of Walter (deceased) and Trudy Scott, Madison. Copies of items now in author's collections.
Wisconsin Conservation Department, miscellaneous materials.
 Now in the author's possession.

Wisconsin Conservation Department Pittman-Robertson Deer Research Project
   materials, Department of Natural Resources Ranger Station, Bureau of Re-
   search, Rhinelander.
   Biologist field notes, 1942–47 (boxed notebooks); Deer Yard notes, 1945–59
   (filed data forms).
   Additional notes from this project, provided by Bernie Bradle and Clarence
   Searles, are now in the author's possession.
Wisconsin Department of Natural Resources, Bureau of Endangered Resources,
   Endangered Species List and other records, Madison.
Wisconsin Department of Natural Resources, Bureau of Research
   records, Madison.

Personal Communication: Interviews and Correspondence

Letters, tapes, and transcripts of interviews are in the author's possession.

Allen, Clarence. May 16, 1979.
Anderson, N. C. October 29, 1980.
Beghin, Kenneth. July 2, 1979.
Biller, Bob, Sr. March 6, 1976.
Bradle, Bernie. March 25 and November 10, 1980.
Burhans, Pat. October 31, 1978.
Christie, David. June 20, 1980.
Corrigan, George. May 17, 1979.
Dahlberg, Bert. May 27 and November 20, 1969.
Dallman, Royce. December 1976.
Denzine, Aflred. December 24, 1971.
Donner, Orvid. May 18, 1979.
Ellerman, Lawrence. February 4 and November 4, 1973.
Elliott, Kennell. February 25, 1979.
Epler, Ed. August 16, 1974.
Ernest, Bernie. July 28, 1983.
Feeney, Bill. Summer, 1979.
Fishel, Loren. August 19, 1973.
Fleming, George. February 20, 1980.
Gerry, Bert. October 30, 1970.
Hale, James. February 10, 1981.
Hammill, Jim. 1992.
Heizler, Carl. May 18, 1979; January 13, 1984.
Heizler, Joe. July 11, 1984.
Herlevi, Reino. November 2, 1970; January 28, 1971.
Holger, Warren. October 29, 1969; August 17, 1971; May 16, 1979.
Huff, James. November 8, 1971.
Jesse, Keith. May 16, 1979.
Keener, John. August 13, 1973.

Knudtson, Bud. March 19, 1975.

Kolnik, Stanley. July 11, 1984.

Kuhrasch, Bud. March 4, 1980.

Lappala, Don. May 16, 1975; February 19 and March 17, 1976.

LeMay, Neil. May 2 and June 26, 1979; October 13, 1981.

Linteruer, LeRoy. March 27, 1973; June 27, 1984.

Milcheski, Mr. September 19, 1981.

Minor, Fred. July 23, 1970.

Morehouse, Max. October 6, 1971.

Novak, Joe. July 10, 1984.

Ogren, Willard. July 8, 1985.

Olson, Russell. May 17, 1979.

Peltonen, Walter. November 2, 1970.

Peterson, Rolf. 1992.

Petts, Perry. March 8, 1974.

Plis, Stan. October 9, 1979.

Popov, Bo. April 28, 1975.

Rosenlaf, Walter. March 14, 1970; July 3, 1972; March 1, 1973; March 24,
    1980.

Ruegger, Sam. August 11, 1974.

Rugg, Leslie. January 14, 1980.

Schmidt, Clarence. June 2, 1974.

Schrader, Henry. October 26, 1982.

Scott, Walter. November 15, 1982.

Searles, Clarence. December 20, 1977.

Sensenbrenner, Ray. May 16, 1979.

Smith, Ray. March 6, 1976.

Sorenson, Gordon. November 13, 1973.

Spurgeon, Tom, Sr. November 22, 1974.

Stover, David. February 24, 1971.

Thompson, Daniel Q. December 26, 1969; July 10, 1970; April 9, 1984; Octo-
    ber 16, 1986.

Tomaier, Frank. May 17, 1979; February 21, 1980.

Tyler, "Pete." April 28, 1975.

Vanacek, Frank. March 31, 1970.

Wendt, Ellis. February 28, 1980.

Wick, Gerald. November 5, 1970.

Wilsie, Pat, Sr. March 7, 1976.

Witt, Emma. October 29, 1979.

Wydeven, Adrian. 1991, 1992.

Unattributed Periodical and Newspaper Articles

The following editions of newspapers and newsletters contain written pieces for
which no author was identified. For pieces that carried a title, that title has been

included here. Signed newspaper and newsletter articles can be found in the final subsection, "Other Secondary Sources."

Badger Sportsman. "No More Wolves in Wisconsin." August 1967.
The Bee. "Bill Introduced to Abolish Trappers Appropriation." March 5, 1931.
Beloit Free Press. "Wolf Culture." February 13, 1879.
Eau Claire Free Press. March 22, 1860.
Edgerton Independent. February 1, 1878.
Elroy Leader Tribune. "Gets Wolf Instead of Deer." November 25, 1955.
Evansville Review. March 12, 1873; February 19, 1879.
Evansville Weekly Review. February 19, 1879.
Florence Mining News. "Assembly Votes $20 Wolf Bounty." February 17, 1945.
Florence Mining News. "Chapman Gets $70 Bounty on Wolf." May 29, 1937.
Florence Mining News. "Conservation Notes. March 14, 1936.
Florence Mining News. "Conservation Notes. Bounties." January 15, 1944.
Florence Mining News. "Conservation Notes. Wolves." June 12, 1937.
Florence Mining News. "Deer Kill Reported Small; Bad Weather Blamed." December 2, 1939.
Florence Mining News. "Find No Proof of Story Man Killed by Timber Wolf." February 8, 1936.
Florence Mining News. "Hard to Distinguish Wolf Pups from Dogs." October 7, 1944.
Florence Mining News. "Kills Two Big Timber Wolves." November 28, 1936.
Florence Mining News. "Millie and Bert Biller Picking Gensing run into Wolf Pack." January 23, 1953.
Florence Mining News. "New Bounty Law Now in Effect." March 17, 1945.
Florence Mining News. "North Indignant over Wolf Bill." March 4, 1944.
Florence Mining News. "145 Coyote Bounties in County in 1945." January 12, 1946.
Florence Mining News. "Pays Bounty on Wolf and Coyote." August 12, 1939.
Florence Mining News. "Sore-jawed Coyote Killed in County." November 12, 1954.
Florence Mining News. "State Permits Wolf Hunting on Nicolet." January 27, 1940.
Florence Mining News. "Unarmed Man, Chased by Wolves, Resorts to 'Tricks' and Escapes." January 27, 1939.
Florence Mining News. "Wisconsin Passes Wolf Bounty Law." January 29, 1944.
Florence Mining News. "Woodsmen Capture Mature Coyote, Wolf." December 7, 1949.
Forest Republican. October 20, 1938; December 1, 1955.
Forest Republican. "Argonne Refuge to Open Sunday for Wolf Hunters." January 6, 1938.
Forest Republican. "Bad Weather Slows Down Wolf Hunt." January 13, 1938.
Forest Republican. "Gets Another Wolf and Bobcat Thursday." January 31, 1929.

Forest Republican. "Houston Stamper Gets $90 Bounty on Eight Wolves." May 18, 1933.

Forest Republican. "Shot Two Big Timber Wolves." September 7, 1933.

Forest Republican. "Stage Second Wolf Hunt in Argonne Refuge Sunday." January 20, 1938.

Forest Republican. "Wolves Get Buck." November 24, 1949.

Glidden Enterprise. "Funds Asked for Liberal Wolf Bounties." December 8, 1944.

Glidden Enterprise. "Sells Live Wolf to the State." October 24, 1946.

Janesville Daily Free Press. December 17, 1853; February 9, 1857.

Janesville Daily Gazette. December 17, 1853; March 16, 1861; February 5, 1862; January 4, 1866; February 9, 1866; March 7, 1866; June 21, 1866; May 18, 1867.

Janesville Weekly Review. February 2, 1878.

Lakeland Times. "Attacked by Wolf." December 1, 1939.

Lakeland Times. "Bounty Report Blasts Leopold Wolf Statements." December 7, 1945.

Lakeland Times. "Many Queer Accidents, Hwy. Report Shows." December 1, 1939.

Lakeland Times. "Going Like the Bison." January 20, 1940.

Lakeland Times. "Protest against Slaughter of Deer." May 26, 1944.

Lakeland Times. "Refuses to Sign Bounty Bill; Becomes Law." March 16, 1945.

Lakeland Times. "Single Shot Ends Wolf-Dog Affair Two Months Old." January 24, 1947.

Lake Mills Leader. "Passing of the Wolf." April 26, 1945.

Mellen Weekly Record. "Conservation Department Purchases Live Wolf." September 19, 1946.

Mellen Weekly Record. "State Trapper Located Here; Trapping Predatory Animals." April 3, 1930.

Merrill Daily Herald. "He Captured a Prize." November 25, 1950.

Milwaukee Journal. "Clubfoot, a Timber Wolf, Is Trapped by Neophyte." November 10, 1940. Part 3, p. 5.

Milwaukee Journal. "Few Timber Wolves Left." January 31, 1954. Part 4, p. 4.

Milwaukee Journal. "Old Three Legs." January 11, 1948. Part 3, p. 6.

Milwaukee Journal. "Sanctuary for Wolves Suggested in Michigan." January 25, 1948. Part 3, p. 6.

Milwaukee Sentinel. April 18, 1954.

Minocqua Times. "Post Season Discussion." December 2, 1938.

Morning Chronicle. "Farmer Torn by Wolves." January 18, 1902.

Morning Chronicle. "To Purchase Wolf Hounds." January 28, 1902.

Morning Chronicle. "Wolves Kill Hunting Dog." January 21, 1902.

Northern Wisconsin Alma Bleatter. February 18, 1897.

Park Falls Herald. "Live Wolf Hunt Finally Succeeds." February 19, 1937.

Rhinelander Daily News. "Deer Hair Found in Wolf's Innards." October 30, 1944.

Rhinelander Daily News. "Milwaukee Man Kills Timber Wolf in Forest County." November 30, 1955.

Rhinelander Daily News. "Youth's Curiosity Nets Timber Wolf." October 4, 1944.

Superior Evening Telegram. "Wolf Problem Investigation to Be Launched." March 31, 1944. p. 2.

Superior Evening Telegram. "Wolves Not Serious Problem, Aberg Says." March 31, 1944. p. 8.

Wisconsin Tobacco Reporter. May 3, 1878; December 27, 1878.

Other Secondary Sources

Allen, J. A. "Description of Some Remains of an Extinct Species of Wolf, and an Extinct Species of Deer from the Lead Region of the Upper Mississippi." *Am. J. Sci.*, ser. 3, no. 11(1876):47–51.

Ames, H. T. "Wolves and Foxes Plentiful." *Wis. Conservationist* 3, no. 1(1921):15–16.

Arnold, D., and R. Schofield. "Status of Michigan Timber Wolves, 1954–56." Mich. Dep. Conserv., Game Div. Rep. No. 2097, mimeo, 1956. 2 pp.

Bailey, V. *Destruction of Deer by the Northern Timber Wolf.* U.S. Dep. Agric., Bur. Biol. Surv. Circ. No. 58, 1907. 2 pp.

Bailey, V. *Destruction of Wolves and Coyotes.* U.S. Dep. Agric., Bur. Biol. Surv. Circ. No. 63, 1908. 11 pp.

Barland, L. *Sawdust City.* Stevens Point, Wis., 1960. 155 pp.

Bartlett, W. *History, Tradition, and Adventure in the Chippewa Valley.* Chippewa Falls, Wis., 1929. 244 pp.

Berg, W., and D. Kuehn. "Ecology of Wolves in North-central Minnesota." In *Wolves of the World*, ed. F. H. Harrington and P. C. Paquet, pp. 4–11. Park Ridge, N.J.: Noyes Publishing, 1982. 474 pp.

Bersing, O. *A Century of Wisconsin Deer*, 2d ed. Wis. Conserv. Dep. Publ. No. 353–66, 1966. 272 pp.

Bibikov, D. I., N. G. Ovsyannikov, and A. N. Filimonov. "The Status and Management of the Wolf Population in the USSR." *Acta Zoologica Fennica* 174(1983):269–271.

Biller, B. "Biller Bros. Hunt Savage Wolves." *Florence Mining News*, January 9, 1953.

Bjarvall, A. "Scandinavia's Response to a Natural Repopulation of Wolves." *Acta Zoologica Fennica* 174(1983):273–275.

Boitani, L. "Wolf and Dog Competition in Italy." *Acta Zoologica Fennica* 174(1983):259–264.

Brown, D. E. *The Wolf in the Southwest.* Tuscon: University of Arizona Press, 1983. 195 pp.

Burkholder, B. "Movements and Behavior of a Wolf Pack in Alaska." *J. Wildl. Manage.* 23(1959):1–11.

Butterfield, C., Ed. *History of Crawford County, Wisconsin.* Springfield, Ill.: Union Publ. Co., 1884. 1308 pp.

Butterfield, C., Ed. *History of Dane County, Wisconsin*. Chicago: Western Historical Co., 1880. 1289 pp.

Butterfield, C., Ed. *History of Green County, Wisconsin*. Springfield, Ill.: Union Publ. Co., 1884. 1158 pp.

Cahn, A. "Notes on the Vertebrate Fauna of Houghton and Iron Counties, Michigan." *Trans. Wis. Acad. Sci., Arts and Lett.* 19(1918);483–510.

Carbyn, L. N. "Management of Non-Endangered Wolf Populations in Canada. *Acta Zoologica Fennica* 174(1983):239–243.

Centennial Phillips, Wisconsin 1876–1976. N.p., 1976. 201 pp.

Chapple, J. "In the Days when Wolves Abounded." *Ashland Daily Press*, August 4, 1981.

Cole, V. E. "Why Protect the Wolf?" *Florence Mining News*, May 1, 1937.

Corrigan, G. *Caulked Boots and Cant Hooks*. Park Falls, Wis.: MacGregor Litho, 1976. 247 pp.

Corrigan, G. "Tanneries and the Hemlock Bark Industry in Wisconsin." In *Proceedings of the Third Annual Meeting of the Forest History Association of Wisconsin, Inc.*, pp. 23–29. Wausau, Wis., 1978. 48 pp.

Current, R. *Wisconsin: A Bicentennial History*. New York: W. W. Norton and Co., 1977. 226 pp.

Curtis, J. *The Vegetation of Wisconsin*. Madison: University of Wisconsin Press, 1959. 657 pp.

Dahlberg, B., and R. Guettinger. *The White-tailed Deer in Wisconsin*. Wis. Conserv. Dep. Tech. Bull. No. 14, 1956. 282 pp.

Draper, L. C., Ed. *Wisconsin Historical Collections*. Vol. 1, reprint ed. Madison, Wis.: Democrat Printing Co., 1903 [1853]. 164 pp.

Draper, L. C., Ed. *Wisconsin Historical Collections*. Vol. 6. Madison, Wis.: Atwood and Culver, 1872. 504 pp.

Draper, L. C., Ed. *Wisconsin Historical Collections*. Vol. 7. Madison, Wis.: E. B. Bolens, 1876. 495 pp.

Draper, L. C., Ed. *Wisconsin Historical Collections*. Vol. 9. Madison, Wis.: David Atwood, 1882. 498 pp.

Elliott, K. *History of the Nicolet National Forest 1928–1976*. U.S. For. Serv., U.S. Dep. Agric. and the For. Hist. Assoc. Wis., 1977. 71 pp.

Ellis, M. "Old Lobo, the Timber Wolf, Makes a Comeback in Northern Wisconsin." *Milwaukee Journal*, March 16, 1952, part 3, p. 8.

Epler, E. *80 Years in God's Country*. Arlington Heights, Ill.: Ink Spot, 1973. 116 pp.

Feeney, W. "Deer Management Research. Wisconsin Wildlife Research." *Pittman-Robertson Q. Reps.* 4, no. 4(1943):1–19.

Flader, S. *Thinking Like a Mountain: Aldo Leopold and the Evolution of an Ecological Attitude toward Deer, Wolves, and Forests*. Columbia: University of Missouri Press, 1974. 284 pp.

Floyd, T., L. D. Mech, and P. Jordan. "Relating Wolf Scat Content to Prey Consumed." *J. Wildl. Manage.* 36, no. 3(1978):528–532.

Fox, M. *Behaviour of Wolves, Dogs, and Related Canids*. New York: Harper and Row Publishers, 1971. 220 pp.

Fritts, S., and L. D. Mech. *Dynamics, Movements and Feeding Ecology of a Newly Protected Wolf Population in Northwestern Minnesota.* Wildl. Monogr. No. 80, 1981. 79 pp.

Fuller, T. *Dynamics of a Declining White-tailed Deer Population in North-central Minnesota.* Wildl. Monogr. No. 110, 1990. 37 pp.

Fuller, T. *Population Dynamics of Wolves in North-central Minnesota.* Wildl. Monogr. No. 105, 1989. 41 pp.

Fuller, T. K., et al. "A History and Current Estimate of Wolf Distribution and Numbers in Minnesota." *Wildlife Society Bulletin* 20(1992):42–55.

Fuller, W., and N. Novakowski. *Wolf Control Operations, Wood Buffalo National Park, 1951–52.* Wildl. Mange. Bull., ser. no. 2, Can. Wildl. Serv., 1955. 19 pp.

Gard, R., and L. Sorden. *The Romance of Wisconsin Place Names.* New York: October House, 1968. 201 pp.

Gasaway, W. C., R. O. Stephenson, J. L. Davis, P. Shepard, and O. Burris. *Interrelationships of Wolves, Prey and Man in Interior Alaska.* Wildl. Monogr. No. 84, 1983. 50 pp.

Gates, C., Ed. *Five Fur Traders of the Northwest.* St. Paul: Minnesota Historical Society, 1965. 296 pp.

Greening, J. "A Mazomanie Pioneer of 1847." *Wis. Mag. Hist.* 26, no. 2(1942):208–218.

Guernsey, O., and J. Willard, Eds. *History of Rock County and Transactions of the Rock Country Agricultural Society and Mechanics Institute.* Janesville, Wis.: William M. Doty and Bros. Printers, 1856. 350 pp.

Gustafson, W. *Glen Flora Pioneers.* Chicago: Adams Press, 1971. 292 pp.

Hammill, J. "Wolf Reproduction Confirmed on Mainland Michigan!" *Internatl. Wolf* 2, no. 1(1992):14–15.

Harrington, F., and L. D. Mech. "Wolf Howling and Its Role in Territory Maintenance." *Behaviour* 68, no. 304(1979):207–249.

Harrington, F., and L. D. Mech. "Wolf Pack Spacing: Howling as a Territory-independent Spacing Mechanism in a Territorial Population." *Behav. Ecol. Sociobiol.* 12(1983):161–168.

Harrington, F., P. Paquet, J. Ryon, and J. Fentress. "Monogamy in Wolves: A Review of the Evidence. In *Wolves of the World*, ed. F. Harrington and P. Paquet, pp. 209–222. Park Ridge, N.J.: Noyes Publishing, 1982. 474 pp.

Hay, O. *The Pleistocene of North America and Its Vertebrated Animals from the States East of the Mississippi River and from the Canadian Provinces East of Longitude 95°.* Carnegie Institute Publ. No. 322, Washington, D.C., 1923. 499 pp.

History of Grant County, Wisconsin. Chicago: Western Historical Co., 1881. 1046 pp.

History of Northern Wisconsin. Chicago: Western Historical Co.,1881. 1218 pp.

History of Vernon County, Wisconsin. Springfield, Ill.: Union Publishing Co., 1884. 826 pp.

The History of Waukesha County, Wisconsin. Chicago: Western Historical Co., 1880. 1008 pp.

Jackson, H. *Mammals of Wisconsin*. Madison: University of Wisconsin Press, 1961. 504 pp.

Johnson, C. "A Note of the Habits of the Timber Wolf." *J. Mammal.* 2(1921):11–15.

Johnson, M. "Wolves in Early Waukesha County." *Landmark*, Summer-Autumn(1975):6–10.

Jordahl, H. "Canada Lynx." *Wis. Conserv. Bull.* 2, no. 11(1956):22–26.

Jordan, P., P. Shelton, and D. Allen. "Numbers, Turnover, and Social Structure of the Isle Royale Wolf Population." *Am. Zool.* 7(1967):233–252.

Journal of Mammalogy. "Symposium of Predatory Animal Control." *J. Mammal.* 11, no. 3(1930);335.

Kane, L., J. Holmquist, and C. Gilman, Eds. *The Northern Expeditions of Stephan H. Long*. St. Paul: Minnesota Historical Society, 1978. 407 pp.

Kay, J. "Wisconsin Indian Hunting Patterns 1634–1836." *Ann. Assoc. Am. Geogr.* 69, no. 3(1979):402–418.

Keener, J. "The Case for the Timber Wolf." *Wis. Conserv. Bull.* 20, no. 11(1955):22–24.

Keith, L. ""Population Dynamics of Wolves." In *Wolves of Canada and Alaska*, ed. L. Carbyn, pp. 66–77. Can. Wildl. Serv. Rep., Ser. No. 45, 1983. 134 pp.

Kinzie, J. *Wau-bun. The Early Day in the Northwest*. National Society of Colonial Dames in Wisconsin, Portage, Wis., 1975. 390 pp.

Klessig, L., and J. Hale. *A Profile of Wisconsin Hunters*. Wis. Dep. Nat. Resour. Tech. Bull. No. 60, 1972. 24 pp.

Kohn, B. *Status and Management of Black Bears in Wisconsin*. Wis. Dep. Nat. Rep. Bull. No. 129, 1982. 33 pp.

Kolenosky, G. "Wolf Predation on Wintering Deer in East-central Ontario. *J. Wildl. Manage.* 36(1972):357–368.

Kraemer, W. J. "Notice to Trappers." *Mellen Weekly Record*, October 16, 1930.

Krak, L. "Proper Number of Wolves in County Is Zero." *Star News*, April 16, 1981.

Lapham, I. *Fauna and Flora of Wisconsin. A Systematic Catalogue of the Animals of Wisconsin*. Vol. 2 of *Transactions of the Wisconsin State Agricultural Society*, ed. A. Ingham, pp. 337–340. Beriah Brown, State Printer, 1853.

Latton, A. *Reminiscences and Anecdotes of Early Taylor County*. N.p., 1947. 224 pp.

Leopold, A. "Deer Irruptions." *Wis. Conserv. Bull.* 8, no. 8(1943):3–11.

Leopold, A. "Deer, Wolves, Foxes and Pheasants." *Wis. Conserv. Bull.* 10, no. 4(1945):3–5.

Leopold, A., et al. "Minority Report of the Citizen's Deer Committee to the Wisconsin Conservation Commission." *Wis. Conserv. Bull.* 8, no. 8(1943):19–22.

Lofgren, F. *Historical Album. Stone Lake, Wisconsin*. Park Falls, Wis.: F. A. Weber and Sons, 1977. 124 pp.

Lyman, F. *A History of Kenosha County.* Chicago: J. S. Clarke Publishing Co., 1916. 392 pp.

McCabe, R. "The Mammals of the Pine and Popple River Area." *Trans. Wis. Acad. Sci., Arts and Lett.* 60(1972):275–289.

McCarley, H., and C. Carley. *Recent Changes in Distribution and Status of Red Wolves* (Canis rufus). U.S. Fish and Wildl. Serv. Endangered Species Rep. No. 4, Albuquerque, N.M., 1979. 38 pp.

Marchetti, L. *History of Marathon County, Wisconsin, and Representative Citizens.* Chicago: Richmund-Arnold Publishing Co., 1913. 982 pp.

Martin, L. *The Physical Geography of Wisconsin.* Madison: University of Wisconsin Press, 1965. 608 pp.

Mech, L. D. "Age, Season, Distance, Direction, and Social Aspects of Wolf Dispersal from a Minnesota Wolf Pack." In *Mammalian Dispersal Patterns,* ed. B. D. Chepko-Sade and Z. Halpin, pp. 55–74. Chicago: University of Chicago Press, 1987. 342 pp.

Mech, L. D. "Longevity in Wild Wolves." *J. Mammal.* 69(1988):197–198.

Mech, L. D. *The Wolf: The Ecology and Behavior of an Endangered Species.* Garden City, N.Y.: Natural History Press, 1970. 384 pp.

Mech, L. D., and L. Frenzel, Jr. "An Analysis of the Age, Sex, and Condition of Deer Killed by Wolves in Northeastern Minnesota." In *Ecological Studies of the Timber Wolf in Northeastern Minnesota,* ed. L. D. Mech and L. Frenzel, Jr., pp. 35–51. U.S. Dep. Agric., For. Serv. Res. Pap. NC-52, North Cent. For. Exp. Sta., St. Paul, Minn., 1971. 62 pp.

Mech, L. D., and L. Frenzel, Jr. "The Possible Occurrence of the Great Plains Wolf in Northeastern Minnesota." In *Ecological Studies of the Timber Wolf in Northeastern Minnesota,* ed. L. D. Mech and L. Frenzel, Jr., pp. 60–62. U.S. Dep. Agric., For. Serv. Res. Pap. NC-52, North Cent. For. Exp. Sta., St. Paul, Minn., 1971. 62 pp.

Mech, L. D., and P. Karns. *Role of the Wolf in a Deer Decline in the Superior National Forest.* U.S. Dep. Agric., For. Serv. Res. Pap. NC-148, North Cent. For. Exp. Sta., St. Paul, Minn., 1977. 23 pp.

Mech, L. D., and R. M. Nowak. "Return of the Gray Wolf to Wisconsin." *Am. Midland Naturalist* 105(1981):408–409.

Medjo, D., and L. D. Mech. "Reproductive Activity in Nine and Ten Month-old Wolves. *J. Mammal.* 57(1976):406–408.

Meine, C. *Aldo Leopold: His Life and His Work.* Madison: University of Wisconsin Press, 1988. 638 pp.

Mendelssohn, H. "Status of the Wolf in the Middle East." *Acta Zoologica Fennica* 174(1983):279–280.

A Merry Briton in Pioneer Wisconsin. State Historical Society of Wisconsin, Madison, 1950. 108 pp.

Messier, F. "Social Organization, Spatial Distribution, and Population Density of Wolves in Relation to Moose Density." *Can. J. Zool.* 63(1985): 1068–1077.

Mitchell, V. "Drought in Wisconsin." *Trans. Wis. Acad. Sci., Arts and Lett.* 67(1979):131–134.

Murie, A. *The Wolves of Mt. McKinley.* Natl. Park Serv. Fauna Ser. 5, 1944. 238 pp.

Nagler, L. G. "A Price on His Head." *LaFollette's Weekly,* March 22, 1913.

Nowak, R. *North American Quarternary Canis.* Museum of Natural History, University of Kansas, Monogr. No. 6, 1979. 154 pp.

Ott, J. H. *History of Jefferson County, Wisconsin, and Its People: A Record of Settlement, Organization, Progress and Achievement.* Chicago: J. S. Clarke Publishing Co., 1917. 304 pp.

Packard, J., and L. D. Mech. "Population Regulation in Wolves." In *Biosocial Mechanisms of Population Regulation,* ed. M. Cohen, R. Malpass, and H. Klein, pp. 135–148. New Haven, Conn.: Yale University Press, 1980.

Packard, J., L. D. Mech, and U. S. Seal. "Social Influences on Reproduction in Wolves." In *Wolves in Canada and Alaska,* ed. L. Carbyn, pp. 78–85. Can. Wildl. Serv. Rep., ser. no. 45, 1983. 135 pp.

Parker, J., Ed. *The Journals of Jonathan Carver and Related Documents, 1766–1770.* St. Paul: Minnesota Historical Society, 1976. 244 pp.

Parmalee, P. "Animal Remains from the Durst Rockshelter, Sauk County, Wisconsin." *Wis. Archeology* 41, no. 1(1960):11–17.

Parmalee, P. "Animal Remains from the Radatz Rockshelter Sk5, Wisconsin." *Wis. Archeology* 40, no. 2(1959):83–90.

Parmalee, P. "Vertebrate Remains from the Bell Site, Winnebago County, Wisconsin. *Wis. Archeology* 44, no. 1(1963):58–69.

Passenger Pigeon. "Report of the Bird Conservation Committee." *Passenger Pigeon* 12(1950):86–88.

Paull, R., and R. Paull. *Geology of Wisconsin and Upper Michigan.* Dubuque, Iowa: Kendall/Hunt Publishing Co., 1977. 232 pp.

Peters, R., and L. D. Mech. "Scent-Marking in Wolves." *Am. Scientist* 63, no. 6(1975):628–637.

Petersen, L., M. Martin, and C. Pils. *Status of Fishers in Wisconsin.* Wis. Dep. Nat. Resour. Res. Rep. No. 92, 1977. 15 pp.

Peterson, R. O. *Wolf Ecology and Prey Relationships on Isle Royale.* Natl. Park Serv. Sci. Monogr. Ser. 11, 1977. 210 pp.

Pils, C. "Furbearer Profiles—No. 1: Beaver." Wis. Dep. Nat. Resour., 1981, mimeo. 19 pp.

Pimlott, D. H., Ed. *Wolves.* IUCN Publ., n.s., Suppl. Pap. No. 43, 1975. 145 pp.

Pimlott, D., J. Shannon, and G. Kolenosky. *The Ecology of the Timber Wolf in Algonquin Provincial Park.* Ont. Dep. Lands and For., 1969. 92 pp.

Radin, P. *The Winnebago Tribe.* Lincoln: University of Nebraska Press, 1973. 511 pp.

Rodolf, T. "Pioneering in the Wisconsin Lead Region." In *Wisconsin Historical Collections,* vol. 15, ed. R. G. Thwaites, pp. 353–354. Democrat Printing Co., 1900. 491 pp.

Rogers, L., L. D. Mech, D. Dawson, J. Peek, and M. Korb. "Deer Distribution in Relation to Wolf Pack Territory Edges." *J. Wildl. Manage.* 44(1980):253–258.

Rothman, R., and L. D. Mech. "Scent-Marking in Lone Wolves and Newly Formed Pairs." *Anim. Behav.* 27(1979):750–760.

Ryden, H. *God's Dog.* New York: Penguin Books, 1979. 201 pp.

Sands, M., R. Coppinger, and C. Phillips. "Comparisons of Thermal Sweating and Histology of Sweat Glands of Selected Canids." *J. Mammal.* 58(1977):74–78.

Schorger, A. "The Black Bear in Early Wisconsin." *Trans. Wis. Acad. Sci., Arts, and Lett.* 39(1949):151–194.

Schorger, A. "The Elk in Early Wisconsin." *Trans. Wis. Acad. Sci., Arts and Lett.* 43(1953):5–23.

Schorger, A. "Extinct and Endangered Mammals and Birds of the Upper Great Lakes Region." *Trans. Wis. Acad. Sci., Arts and Lett.* 34(1942):23–44.

Schorger, A. "The Moose in Early Wisconsin." *Trans. Wis. Acad. Sci., Arts and Lett.* 45(1957):1–10.

Schraufnagal, R. *History of the Glidden Four-Town Area.* Park Falls, Wis.: McGregor Litho, 1976. 128 pp.

Scott, W. "Rare and Extinct Mammals of Wisconsin." *Wis. Conserv. Bull.* 4, no. 10(1939):21–28.

Seal, U., E. Plotka, J. Packard, and L. D. Mech. "Endocrine Correlates of Reproduction in the Wolf. 1. Serum Progesterone, Estradiol, and LH during the Estrus Cycle." *Biol. Reprod.* 21(1979):1057–1066.

Severinghaus, C. "Tooth Development and Wear as Criteria of Age in White-tailed Deer." *J. Wildl. Manage.* 13(1949):195–216.

Shaki, S. P. "Status of the Grey Wolf (*Canis lupus pallipes*, Sykes) in India." *Acta Zoologica Fennica* 174(1983):283–286.

Stebler, A. "The Ecology of Michigan Coyotes and Wolves." Ph.D. dissertation, University of Michigan, Ann Arbor, 1951. 198 pp.

Stebler, A. "The Status of the Wolf in Michigan." *J. Mammal.* 35(1944):37–43.

Stenlund, M. *A Field Study of the Timber Wolf* (Canis lupus) *in the Superior National Forest in Minnesota.* Minn. D-124 Dep. Conserv. Tech. Bull. No. 4, 1955. 55 pp.

Stevenson, M. "Dire Wolf Systematics and Behavior." In *Wolf and Man: Evolution in Parallel,* ed. R. Hall and H. Sharp, pp. 179–196. New York: Academic Press, 1978. 210 pp.

Stollberg, B. "Differentiation of Police Dog, Coyote, and Timber Wolf Hairs. Wisconsin Wildlife Research." *Pittman-Robertson Q. Reps.* 7, no. 1(1948):31–32.

Strand, J. *Diamond Jubilee Edition—Iron County, Wisconsin.* Taylor Publishing Co., 1968.

Swift, E. "The Biography of a Self-made Naturalist." Part 1. *Wis. Conserv. Bull.* 5, no. 12(1940):3–12.

Swift, E. "The Biography of a Self-made Naturalist." Part 2. *Wis. Conserv. Bull.* 6, no. 1(1941):41–52.

Swift, E. "The Biography of a Self-made Naturalist." Part 3. *Wis. Conserv. Bull.* 6, no. 3(1941):3–17.

Swift, E. "The Biography of a Self-made Naturalist." Part 4 *Wis. Conserv. Bull.* 6, no. 4(1941):3–8.

Swift, E. *A History of Wisconsin Deer.* Wis. Conserv. Dep. Publ. No. 323, 1946. 96 pp.

Taylor, L. " 'Wolves Don't Hurt the Deer,' Says Leopold." *St. Paul Pioneer Press*, December 4, 1945.

Thiel, R. P. "Relationship between Road Densities and Wolf Habitat Suitability in Wisconsin." *Am Midland Naturalist* 113, no. 2(1985):404–407.

Thiel, R. "The Status of the Timber Wolf in Wisconsin—1975." *Trans. Wis. Acad. Sci., Arts and Lett.* 66(1978):186–194.

Thiel, R. P. "Status of the Timber Wolf in Wisconsin (Study 101), October 1, 1981—September 30, 1982." Wis. Dep. Nat. Resour. Performance Rep. 1983. 18 pp.

Thiel, R. P. "Status of the Timber Wolf in Wisconsin, October 1, 1982—September 30, 1983." Wis. Dep. Nat. Resour. Performance Rep. 1984. 16 pp.

Thiel R. P. "Status of the Timber Wolf in Wisconsin, October 1, 1987—September 30, 1988." Wis. Dep. Nat. Resour. Performance Rep. 1989.

Thiel, R. P., and J. Hammill. "Wolf Specimen Records in Upper Michigan, 1960–1988." *Jack-pine Warbler* 66(1988):149–153.

Thompson, D. Q. "Daniel Q. Thompson, 1940." In *Aldo Leopold: Mentor. Proceedings of an Aldo Leopold Symposium*, ed. R. McCabe, pp. 102–108. Department of Wildlife Ecology, University of Wisconsin–Madison, 1988. 126 pp.

Thompson, D. "A Preliminary Study of the Timber Wolf in Wisconsin." M.S. thesis, University of Wisconsin–Madison, 1950. 61 pp.

Thompson, D. "Travel, Range, and Food Habits of Timber Wolves in Wisconsin." *J. Mammal.* 33(1952):429–442.

Thwaites, R., Ed. *Wisconsin Historical Collections.* Vol. 14. Madison: Democrat Printing Co., State Printer, 1898. 553 pp.

Thwaites, R., Ed. *Wisconsin Historical Collections.* Vol. 20. Madison: Democrat Publishing Co., State Printer, 1911. 497 pp.

Van Ballenberghe, V., A. Erickson, and D. Byman. *Ecology of the Timber Wolf in Northeastern Minnesota.* Wildl. Monogr. No. 43, 1975. 43 pp.

Voskar, J. "Present Problems of Wolf Preservation in Czechoslovakia." *Acta Zoologica Fennica* 174(1983):287–288.

Wisconsin Blue Book. Vol. 35. Wisconsin Legislative Reference Bureau, Madison, 1909. 1191 pp.

Wisconsin Conservation Department. "Giant Wolf Dies." *Wis. Conserv. Bull.* 2, no. 11(1937):36.

Wisconsin Conservation Department. "Praise Hunters." *Wis. Conserv. Bull.* 1, no. 5(1936):10.

Wisconsin Conservation Department. "Open Season for Wolves." *Wis. Conserv. Bull.* 2, 3, nos. 12 and 1(1937–38):47.

Wisconsin Conservation Department. "Taylor County Legends of Wild Animal Raids." *Wis. Conserv. Bull.* 18, no. 9(1953):27–28.

Wisconsin Conservation Department. "Timber Wolf." *Wis. Conserv. Bull.* 9, no. 1(1944):24.

Wisconsin Conservation Department. "Timber Wolf." *Wis. Conserv. Bull.* 11, no. 1(1946):10.

Wisconsin Conservation Department. "What's Going On?" *Wis. Conserv. Bull.* 24, no. 1(1959):40.

Wisconsin Conservation Department. "Wolf Diet." *Wis. Conserv. Bull.* 1, no. 5(1936):13.

Wisconsin Conservation Department. "Wolf Drive." *Wis. Conserv. Bull.* 1, no. 4(1936):9–10.

Wisconsin Conservationist. 1952. "Wolf Drags Trap in Chase of Four Dogs." *Wis. Conservationist* 1, no. 6(1952):38.

Wisconsin Department of Natural Resources. *Wisconsin Timber Wolf Recovery Plan.* Wisconsin Endangered Resources Report 50. 1989. 37 pp.

Wisconsin Magazine of History. "Documents: Letters of Joseph V. Quarles." *Wis. Mag. Hist.* 16(1933):297–320.

Wisconsin Magazine of History. "Snow and the Winter Wolves." *Wis. Mag. Hist.* 41, no. 2(1958):101.

Wisconsin Statistical Reporting Service. *Snow and Frost in Wisconsin.* Madison, 1970. 28 pp.

Witt, H. "The Public Pulse." *Lakeland Times,* April 6, 1945.

Woerpel, L. "Wolf Protection, Duck Stamp Questions." Wis. Conservationist 1, no. 6(1952):8.

Wolter, A. "The Boy Who Cried Wolf." *Outdoor Life* (July 1982):68–69, 100–101.

Young, S., and E. Goldman. *The Wolves of North America.* Parts 1 and 2. New York: Dover Publications, 1964. 636 pp.

Zillier, C., Ed. *History of Sheboygan County Past and Present.* Chicago: S. J. Clarke Publishing Co., 1912. 346 pp.

Zimen, E. "Social Dynamics of the Wolf Pack." In *The Wild Canids,* ed. M. Fox, pp. 336–362. New York: Van Nostrand Reinhold, 1975. 508 pp.

Zimen, E. *The Wolf: A Species in Danger.* New York: Delacorte Press, 1980. 373 pp.

Index

247